ISRAEL
YESTERDAY, TODAY AND TOMORROW

A fully documented, dramatic history of the tur-
bulent events which shaped the crisis of the Middle
East.

Every key problem, conflict and decision is carefully analyzed, from the questionable policies of
Britain in 1948—to the explosive issues of today.
Issues such as: the Arab refugees in occupied
land, the return of territory won in the war of
1967, the terrorist war of attrition that has become
worldwide—and issues that will determine the
fate of a nation.

**BATTLEGROUND**
**Fact and Fantasy in Palestine**
**by Samuel Katz**

# BATTLEGROUND

## Fact and Fantasy
## in Palestine

## Samuel Katz

BANTAM BOOKS · TORONTO · LONDON · NEW YORK

A NATIONAL GENERAL COMPANY

BATTLEGROUND: FACT AND FANTASY IN PALESTINE
*A Bantam Book / published January 1973*

Library of Congress Cataloging in Publication Data

Katz, Samuel, 1914—
  Battleground; fact and fantasy in Palestine.

  Bibliography: p.
  1. Jewish-Arab relations. I. Title.
DS119.7.K33           327.5694'017'4927           72-10941

*Published simultaneously in the United States and Canada*

PRINTED IN THE UNITED STATES OF AMERICA

To the Memory of
YOSEF YOEL RIVLIN
One-time Professor of Arabic
at the Hebrew University, Jerusalem.

# Contents

# Maps

# Introduction

The British newspaper *Sunday Times* in the spring of 1972 published a series of articles entitled the "Unofficial History of the Twentieth Century." The purpose of the series, written by a team of distinguished historians and journalists, was to tell "the true stories of events that have been ignored by history books or have been misrepresented by conventional and officially inspired narratives.

"On some occasions," the newspaper wrote, "deliberate lies have been devised to bury a truth that powerful people wanted hidden ... Many realities have been concealed by a more subtle censorship, the creation of myths in which historians, official or otherwise, publicists, pressure groups, and sometimes entire nations have conspired to present the past not as it really was but as they would have liked it to be."

This grim but sober judgment is relevant not only to the completed and probably irreversible wrongs of the century but it also has a continuing and growing application in an age which gave birth to a special word for the idea of brainwashing, and to the frighteningly plausible vision of "1984." There has probably been no area, however, in which myths, knavery, and dissimulation have been so widely applied, by so many powerful interests and for so long, as in the dispute over Palestine.

In a British television interview on December 12, 1971, Mr. Richard Crossman, one of Britain's famous left-wing intellectuals, a member of the Labor Government between 1964 and 1970 and subsequently editor of the prestigious Socialist weekly *The New Statesman*, lifted the curtain on one important example. Mr. Crossman bluntly accused the former Labor Prime Minister Clement Attlee and Foreign

Minister Ernest Bevin, who presided over the destinies of Britain after World War II, of having "tried to destroy the Jews of Palestine." Mr. Crossman recalled that he was intended by Mr. Bevin in 1945 to be one of the instruments of his policy. He thus discovered first hand what that policy was.

His accusation, with its implication of a violent British passion against the Jews of Mandated Palestine, must have startled many well-meaning people who innocently believed that the conflict over Palestine was a straightforward clash "between Jews and Arabs." If they knew of Britain's role in the Mandate period it was as merely an honest broker caught in the middle. In fact, Mr. Crossman added authoritative support to those who have long known and insisted that Britain was an active participant in the dispute, and was indeed the prime driving force in the resistance to Jewish restoration in Palestine.

In the immediate context of this book Mr. Crossman's charge will lend piquancy and color to the contents of Chapter Three which tells of the motives and the vital part of successive British governments and their agents in the creation and perpetuation of the conflict between Jews and Arabs.

In the larger perspective, Mr. Crossman's revelation about a single period and a single aspect of the conflict illustrates sharply how remote from reality are some popular conceptions about all the periods and aspects of that conflict. It demonstrates how easily even simple, obvious, well-known, or at least readily ascertainable truths can be smothered or disguised by a well-directed fog of fantasy and dissimulation as they have been in the case of Palestine. I hope *Battleground* will help dissipate the fog.

Most of the facts about Palestine revealed and dealt with here have of course been published before in places varying from dust-covered history books to the news columns of contemporary newspapers. This is the first time, to the best of my knowledge, that they have been gathered together, and presented in the context of the ongoing clash between the State of Israel and the Arab States. Some of the facts are recent discoveries made by diligent researchers in history. Many others have been known to scholars or, vaguely, to some laymen. What is certain is that many people throughout the world who are prepared at the slightest provocation to pontificate on the Israel-Arab conflict have never troubled to check the veracity of the information by which they are presumably influenced. What is more relevant: they have accepted the myths and fantasies which have been disseminated over the years. Historians and students of the problem, who know the truth and have themselves published relevant facts about it, are no doubt appalled at some of the grotesque notions that have gained a hold on the public mind as the result of British, Arab, and Soviet propaganda. For one legitimate reason or another, however, they usually refrain from advertising even the plainest implications of their own discoveries which could demolish the myths and could place the fantasies in their proper perspective.

From the various sources quoted in this book, it is enough to refer, for example, to the "debunking" of Lawrence of Arabia by Richard Aldington, to the Diaries of Colonel Richard Meinertzhagen, to the researches of Professor Eli Kedourie, or to Professor Philip K. Hitti's monumental work on Arab history, in order to see the very foundations of some of the widely accepted assumptions about the Palestine dispute crumble in ruins. Except for a portion of Eli Kedourie's *Chatham House Version and Other Middle Eastern Studies,* all this material has been in print for years.

Arab and other propaganda are not alone responsible for the degree of success of the deception that has been practiced about the respective Jewish and Arab relationships in Palestine. Dr. James Parkes, the British historian and Christian theologian, specified one astonishing area of Jewish neglect in his recent book *Whose Land?*

[The Zionists'] real title deeds were written by the . . . heroic endurance of those who had maintained a Jewish presence in the land all through the centuries, and in spite of every discouragement. This page of history found no place in the constant flow of Zionist propaganda

. . . . The omission allowed the anti-Zionist . . . to paint an entirely false picture of the wickedness of Jewry trying to establish a two-thousand-year-old claim to the country.

Even otherwise knowledgeable people who have read the manuscript of *Battleground* were startled at the realization, in Chapters Four and Five, of the gap between what is generally known and the facts of the continuity of Jewish life in Palestine since the destruction of the Second Temple.

Some of the ignorance that governs the assertions of many of the pundits on the Palestine problem is of course nurtured by prejudice or by vested interests. Nobody will expect a Washington lobbyist of the American oil companies, dedicated to the purveyance of the fantasies of their Arab clients, to be interested in learning from the facts gathered in this book, nor an official in the British Foreign Office, nourished on the Laurentian pan-Arab vision; nor a hard-core Vatican doctrinaire to whom a Jewish State is by definition an impossibility; nor a New Left writer (especially if he happens to have been born Jewish) who has achieved fame by the very arrogance and self-righteousness of his ignorance.

There is, I believe however, a great body of people whose lack of knowledge of basic facts is the cause of a bewilderment, honest and free of prejudice. It is these people who I hope will be able to benefit from the factual narrative in *Battleground,* and weigh the conclusions I have drawn and the outlook to which I have given expression.

I would urge all those who find the book's contents new and perhaps, as I realize, in part even startling, not to content themselves with reading it. I have provided many references to sources from which may be gleaned fuller and deeper knowledge of the panorama of fact and fancy, of truth and mystification which envelop the history of modern, reawakened Palestine and of the many-pronged attacks on the Jewish restoration.

I hope moreover that the Hebrew sources on the historic period between the Second and the Nineteenth centuries reflecting the researches, to mention a few, of Yitshak Ben Zvi, Avraham Yaari, Michael Assaf and Michael Ish Shalom will find their way into English and other languages. I dare to hope too that this book may encourage young scholars to dig deeper and wider into the extensive area of history, ancient and recent, which provides the essential illumination for the present-day problem.

I am grateful to the many friends who read the manuscript of the book, or parts of it, and who offered their comments. They all helped me gain a better perspective of the text. I was glad to be able to avail myself of at least some of their advice. My special thanks to Elly Gross, Joshua Bension, Dr. Reuben Hecht, Pessach Mor, Moshe Shamir, and Dr. Haim Yahil.

To Joshua Bension, moreover, and to Sam Givelber of Cleveland, Ohio, I owe a debt of gratitude for their spontaneous encouragement and help in ensuring the popular distribution of the book.

SAMUEL KATZ

*Tel Aviv, July 1972*

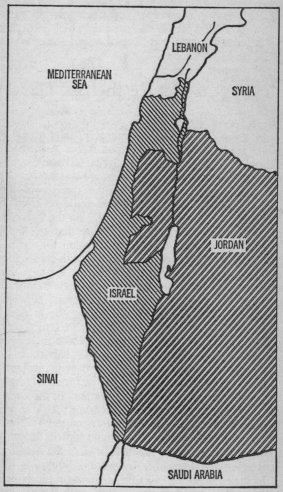

MAP No. 1: Israel in the armistice lines
(1949–June 5, 1967)

# 1

# The War Before the Six Day War

On May 14, 1967, the territorial limits of the State of Israel were the lines agreed upon in her Armistice Agreements of 1949 with Jordan, Syria, Lebanon, and Egypt. Israel held none of the territories which she was to gain as a result of the still undreamed-of-war three weeks away.

No more vulnerable boundaries could be imagined (see Map No.1). Along its middle strip, on the Mediterranean coast, the country was nowhere more than ten miles wide. Within this narrow waist were crowded the main centers of the Israeli population: Tel Aviv, with its smaller sister towns Ramat Gan and Petah Tiqva to the east, Bat Yam and Holon to the south, Herzliya and Natanya in the north. These formed its main commercial concentrations and most of its industry. Overlooking the strip from the east was the central range of Palestine's mountains: the mountains of Ephraim; and holding these mountains were the Arabs of the Kingdom of Jordan. This central area of the State of Israel could be raked with shellfire, clear through from border to border, without a single gun's having to be moved across the frontier. In the early morning of June 6, 1967, a shell fired from the Arab village of Kalkilieh, beyond the northeastern corner of the coastal strip, sailed southwestward through half its length and all its width and exploded half a mile from the Mediterranean beach, in an apartment near Masaryk Square in Tel Aviv.

In the northeastern section of the state the Huleh plain, reclaimed from the swamp, dotted with Israel's green villages, lay flat as a billiard table under the stark overhang of the Golan Heights—and the heights were held by the Arabs of Syria.

In the southwestern sector the Sinai desert, though almost empty of population, was nevertheless well provided with Egyptian military airfields, within three to ten minutes' flying time from Israel's densely populated coastal strip.

It was from these frontiers that on June 5, 1967, Israel launched her Air Force and her Army against the Egyptian armed forces, subsequently resisted the invading forces from Jordan and Syria, defeated them all, and gained control of the remainder of Western Palestine clear to the Jordan River, of the Golan Heights, and of the Sinai Peninsula down to the Suez Canal and the Red Sea.

It is to those frontiers of June 5, 1967—to be precise, the armistice lines of 1949—"with minor insubstantial modifications," that Israel has since then been called on to return, even by some of her friends. The pressures suggest that such a withdrawal—from Sinai and the Gaza district to the gates of Ashkelon, from Samaria and Judea back to the ten-mile-wide coastal strip—and the restoration to Syria of the Golan Heights above the Huleh Valley—will bring peace between Israel and the Arab States. The way to peace, it is implied, lies in restoring the conditions that existed before June 5, 1967.

The central fact in the life of Israel in the period before June 5 was that in those restricted and confined and frighteningly fragile frontiers the Arab states threatened, planned, and tried to destroy her. It was against Israel in *those* borders that on May 14, 1967, the neighboring Arab states—Egypt, and after her Syria and Jordan, with some support from Iraq—began massing their forces and their resources to prepare for an imminent onslaught on Israel from three sides. In simultaneous action they set in motion all the available means of communication with the world at large to make known Israel's forthcoming annihilation. Israel saved herself from that threat and that purpose by the only strategy feasible in her topographical circumstances: a preventive attack on the forces of Egypt, the main enemy. The battles that followed on three fronts for all their startling, spectacular, even historic success,

cost Israel in six days twice as many dead in proportion to
her total population as the United States lost in eight years
of fighting in Vietnam.

The offensive that took shape in Arab minds and began
to emerge in May 1967 was the climax—indeed, the
grand finale—of eighteen years of hostilities against Israel
on every front except the direct confrontation of the military battlefield. During these eighteen years the various
hostile acts of the Arab states broke every relevant paragraph in the Armistice Agreements of 1949, which all
the states had negotiated and signed and which theoretically governed their relations with Israel.

Who today remembers a ship called *Rimfrost?* Or *Fran-
ca Maria*, or *Capetan Manolis?* Who remembers *Inge Toft*
and *Astypalea?* The sailors who manned them, no doubt,
and the merchants whose cargoes they carried. In the
1950s they, and many others like them, were actors in
the drama of the continuing and all-embracing Arab
attack on Israel. The *Inge Toft,* a Danish ship carrying an
Israeli cargo of phosphates and cement, was arrested in
the Suez Canal in May 1959. She was detained for 262
days, until her owners, despairing of their legal rights,
ordered the captain to submit to the demands of the
Egyptian authorities. The captain released the cargo; and
the Egyptians confiscated it. The *Inge Toft* sailed back to
Haifa with emptied holds. In those 262 days many protests were made in direct communications to Cairo and in
debates in the United Nations Assembly against Egypt's
flagrant violation of international rights and decisions.
None had any effect.

By sending a Danish ship through the Suez Canal, the
Israeli government was in fact retreating from a defense of
Israel's absolute right to send her own ships freely through
the Canal. For eight years Egypt had forcibly prevented
Israeli ships from doing so. International advice—in fact,
the urgings of the Secretary General of the UN—had
prompted Israel's government to try the compromise of
sending an Israeli cargo on a non-Israeli ship. While the
imprisoned *Inge Toft* continued to demonstrate daily that
the Egyptian government would not allow an Israeli cargo

through even when carried on a non-Israeli vessel, new advice was forthcoming. The Secretary General of the United Nations, Dag Hammarskjöld, informed the Israeli government that he had reason to believe that if, now, on a non-Israeli ship they were to send a *non-Israeli cargo*—that is an FOB cargo already the property of the non-Israeli buyer—Egyptian President Nasser would show what was described as moderation and allow the ships through the Canal. This proposal was accepted by the Israeli government, which even agreed to keeping the transaction secret. The *Inge Toft* was thus still in detention when, on December 17, 1959, the Greek vessel *Astypalea*, carrying an FOB cargo, sailed into the Suez Canal. She was promptly arrested and detained. After four months of international protests, her owners also submitted to the Egyptians' demands and allowed the cargo to be confiscated.

In the tense months of diplomatic and undiplomatic struggle over these ships, most of the world's maritime powers protested volubly and often. Their own ships, however, continued to sail freely through the Canal. Egypt was thus given daily, even hourly, assurance that, except for name calling, she need fear no reprisals, no punitive or even admonitory action for violating the famous, hitherto sacrosanct and unequivocal Constantinople Convention of 1888. That international compact laid down that:

> The Suez Maritime Canal shall always be free and open, in time of war as in time of peace, to every vessel of commerce or war, without distinction of flags. . . . The Canal shall never be subjected to the exercise of the right of blockade.

The daily unblushing procession past the imprisoned *Inge Toft* by ships of members of the United Nations made it plain, moreover, that the resolutions they had themselves passed in the Security Council against such a breach of international law need not be taken too seriously. The Council had passed such a resolution in 1951, when the Egyptians first blockaded the Canal against Israel. It had reaffirmed it in 1954. The resolution called on Egypt "to terminate the restrictions on the passage of international commercial shipping and goods through the Suez Canal wherever found, and to cease all interference with such shipping."

The closing of the Suez Canal to Israel was one detail of the economic war which the Arab states pursued with unrelenting ferocity ever since the State of Israel was established. After signing the 1949 Armistice Agreements, in which they forswore "any warlike or hostile acts," they progressively broadened the scope and deepened the intensity of an all-embracing range of economic hostilities.

The Arab states tried to starve Israel of water. First they refused to cooperate in an American-sponsored scheme for regional exploitation of the sources of the Jordan. Next they tried by force—employing artillery—to interfere with Israel's own efforts to realize her meager water resources (by diverting that part of the Jordan River that ran within her territory). Indeed, because the water shortage was a built-in weakness of Israel's economic structure, throughout those years the Arabs saw Israel's water supply as a prime target for their offensive.

The Arab boycott of Israeli goods and services had been launched against the Palestine Jewish community even before the State of Israel was created, and it developed from year to year. In the Arab countries themselves all commercial relationships with Israel were forbidden on pain of heavy penalties. In fact, any contact whatever with Israel was prohibited. The governments enforced the suspension of all postal, telephone, and telegraph facilities for communications with Israel and prohibited all communication by sea, air, and rail. Any traveler whose passport showed that he had at any time been in Israel, or intended going to Israel, was refused admission to any Arab state.

The boycott was extended to every corner of the world. A vast machine saw to its organization and operation. Over the years the central boycott office in Damascus compiled a long blacklist of firms the world over who traded with or in Israel, of ships that called at Israeli ports, even of actors or musicians who visited Israel or expressed friendship for Israel. From Damascus a campaign of pressure, threatening blackmail or coercion, was directed at all of them. Questionnaires and admonitory letters were sent to large numbers of firms in many countries to impress upon them that they would not be allowed to do business with the states of the Arab League if they tried to do business with Israel. In Damascus a worldwide network of inspection was also developed to detect breaches of the boycott.

This campaign met with substantial success. The Arab states, with their 100 million potential customers, exercised considerable appeal to manufacturers and merchants hungry for markets. In some of them, soaring oil production had brought about a steep increase in the citizens' spending power. Many firms throughout the world consequently succumbed to the demands, or threats, of the Arab states and quietly joined in the boycott of Israel.

The tactics of economic warfare were early extended into every phase of international intercourse and activity, and to the utmost extremity. Planes touching at an Israeli airport were forbidden to fly over Arab territory; they would ask in vain for flight information or even rescue services from an Arab airport. The Arab states refused to cooperate with Israel in any international agency or operation whatsoever—regional health operations, the war against locusts, the war against narcotics.

Economic warfare carried on day in-day out was the unchanging accompaniment to the military and paramilitary siege warfare which Egypt, Jordan, and Syria waged almost incessantly against Iraael. Only for two of the eighteen years governed by the Armistice Agreements did Israel enjoy comparative peace with her neighbors. Between 1949, the year of the armistice, and 1956 attacks from Sinai and the Gaza area, from across the Jordan and down from the Golan Heights, became more frequent and more intense; they were directed mainly at civilians and civilian targets. In that seven-year period the Arabs carried out 11,873 acts of sabotage and murder. Israel suffered 1,335 casualties; of these, over 1,000 were civilians.

In the year 1956 the campaign reached a climax. Suddenly the Egyptian government blockaded the Straits of Tiran, the only approach to Israel's southern port of Eilat. On Sanafir and Tiran—two tiny, otherwise unused islands in the straits—they installed gun emplacements. From these, Egypt could straddle and control the southern gateway to Israel, which was thus cut off from direct contact with the southern hemisphere, with the east coast of Africa, and with the Far East.

Now, too, armed Egyptian raids into Israel became a daily occurrence. The infiltrators grew ever bolder. From short penetrations across the border they developed a longer reach, into the heart of the country. Individual acts of terror were carried out at the very gates of Tel Aviv.

Then, in the early autumn, convoys of Egyptian tanks began to cross the Suez Canal into the Sinai Peninsula. A front line took shape in the desert along the demarcation lines with Israel and in the Gaza Strip; and behind the front line there was a mass of new armor.

The tanks gave concrete expression to the purposeful entry of a new element into the arena: the Soviet Union. In 1955 Moscow had begun sending into Egypt tanks and guns and planes in quantities unknown in the area since the major battles in the Western Desert during the Second World War.

With these preliminaries in train, the Egyptian government now reached agreement with Jordan, Syria, and Iraq for setting up a joint command. In an atmosphere of high expectation they prepared for the invasion of Israel. The Israeli Army forestalled them. At the end of October, in a swift campaign, it forced the Egyptian Army back across the Suez Canal into Egypt, eliminated the offensive bases of the infiltrators, and reopened the Straits of Tiran to Israeli shipping. But the United States government, displaying—not for the first time—considerable misapprehension of Arab purposes and the Arab character and a less understandable failure to grasp the elements of Soviet imperialistic strategy, bore down on Israel with heavy diplomatic pressure and the veiled threat of punitive economic action.[1] Israel's government succumbed, and its Army drew back from Sinai and the Gaza plain. United States pressure was accompanied at the United Nations by undertakings, seconded by France and Britain and other maritime powers, that they would assure Israel's freedom of navigation in the Straits. There were even promises, though more nebulous, from Washington to assure Israel's right of navigation in the Suez Canal. (When the time of trial came in May 1967, none of these promises was kept.)

Yet the swift defeat in battle had battered and demoralized the Egyptian Army. A large part of its armor and equipment were destroyed or captured. Then came two years of comparative tranquillity.

It was not long before the Soviet Union invited Egypt to submit specifications of the arms and equipment needed to replenish her armed strength. The flow of tanks and planes and guns from the Black Sea ports to Egypt was renewed. Later the Soviet Union began to supply arms in even more pronounced exclusivity to Syria as well. Thenceforward Egypt's and Syria's relations with the Soviet Union grew increasingly close. The flow of arms grew ever greater.

The Arab campaign of violence was resumed in 1959 and never relaxed thereafter. Across the various armistice lines (except that with Lebanon), Israel was under constant attack: from Jordan-held territory in the heart of western Palestine, from the Gaza plain and Sinai, and from the Golan Heights to the northeast. Tension and harassment were Israel's daily bread. Especially popular with the Arabs were the artillery bombardments from the sheer bluffs of the Golan Heights on the Israeli villages

---

[1] The attitude of the United States was perhaps determined by its anger at the parallel attack on Egypt launched by Britain and France on their own in reprisal for Egypt's nationalization of the Suez Canal Company. Both countries had collaborated with Israel. This broad subject does not, however, affect the realities of the Egyptian designs on Israel.

below. There are hundreds of young people in Israel today, born in proximity to the armistice lines of 1949, who spent most of the nights of their childhood, and many of their daylight hours, in underground shelters.

From time to time the Israeli Army carried out retaliatory raids, on the principle of accumulative retribution. It usually succeeded in halting the Arab belligerence temporarily, but it could not stop it altogether.

The full significance of Israel's vulnerability was made manifest, suddenly and to almost universal surprise, in May 1967. Ostensibly everybody knew that Egypt was capable of turning Sinai into a vast offensive base threatening the very heart of the Jewish state. Ostensibly it was common knowledge that the United Nations Observer Force, set up in 1957 after the Sinai campaign, would evaporate if Egypt decided to attack. Ostensibly it was common knowledge that at a moment of destructive exhilaration the Arab states might be capable of united action, forcing a war on three fronts against an Israel outmanned, outgunned, and outnumbered in planes by nearly three to one and in tanks by more than three to one. These elementary facts were largely ignored even by many people in Israel itself—just as, since the war, Israel has been pressed to forget them again.

The facts became clear in quick succession. On May 14 President Nasser started moving his troops and tanks into Sinai. Three days later the Syrians announced that their forces on the Golan Heights were also ready for action. On the same day Nasser demanded the immediate withdrawal of the United Nations force from Sinai. The UN Secretary General, U Thant, promptly complied; the United Nations force disappeared. Simultaneously the Commander of the Egyptian forces in Sinai, General Murtagi, issued an Order of the Day. For greater effect it was broadcast on Cairo Radio on May 18, 1967:

The Egyptian forces have taken up positions in accordance with our predetermined plans. The morale of our armed forces is very high, for this is the day they have so long been waiting for, for this holy war.

Four days later Nasser announced the renewed blockade of the Tiran Straits. Then on May 30, King Hussein
of Jordan hastened to Cairo and there signed a mutual-
defense pact with Nasser. All now seemed ready. In two
weeks a noose had been drawn around Israel's neck.

Believing in the power of their numbers, in their unity,
and in their ability to exploit Israel's glaring strategic
weakness, the Arabic leaders and spokesmen now articulated the simple objective of their policy and their labors:
annihilation of the Jewish state.

The Arab leaders, as it turned out, had miscalculated.
They were, it is true, united; they did outnumber the
Israelis heavily, in men, planes, tanks, guns, and ships; if
they had been able to exploit these conditions, Israel's
topographical weakness could have been fatal to her. Israel is now being asked (or told, or cajoled) to resume that
topographical weakness, or that topographical weakness
with, in the words of the United States government, "insubstantial modifications."

The Arabs' war against Israel in the years between
1949 and 1967 was accompanied and dramatized by an
incessant diplomatic offensive and a campaign of propaganda that grew progressively in volume and scope. Its
purpose was not kept secret. It was repeated again and
again. "Our aim," it was epitomized by Nasser on November 18, 1965, "is the full restoration of the rights of the
Palestinian people. In other words, we aim at the destruction of the State of Israel. The immediate aim: perfection
of Arab military might. The national aim: the eradication
of Israel."

Year after year, the autumn sessions of the United
Nations in New York were converted into a sounding
board for the combined verbal onslaught on Israel of the
delegates of the ever-growing number of Arab states.

The war against Israel on its many fronts was pursued
against an Israel which did not embrace the "occupied
territories" of today. At that time, too, Israel was pressed
and urged from many sides to make concessions. What
could these concessions have been? In those years, too,
Israel was pressed to offer concessions of "territory." But

it was the Arab refugee problem which was named as the prime cause of Arab intransigence, as the *fons et origo* of all the trouble in the Middle East. That was then proclaimed the major obstacle to peace.

# 2

# Arab Refugees

Only a George Orwell or a Franz Kafka could have done justice to the story of the Arab refugee problem. For twenty years the world has been indoctrinated with a vision of its origins, its scope, the responsibilities for its solution. The intent of this picture is, roughly, that in 1948 the Jewish people launched an attack on the Arab inhabitants of Palestine, drove them out, and thus established the State of Israel. The number of innocent peace-loving Arabs thus turned refugee was—here you may insert any figure that occurs to you, such as a million, one and a half million, two million. Justice demands that the refugees be restored to their homes, and until that day the world (everyone, that is, except the Arab people) must care for their upkeep.

The Arabs are the only declared refugees who became refugees not by the action of their enemies or because of well-grounded fear of their enemies, but by the initiative of their own leaders. For nearly a generation those leaders have willfully kept as many people as they possibly could in degenerating squalor, preventing their rehabilitation, and holding out to all of them the hope of return and of "vengeance" on the Jews of Israel, to whom they have transferred the blame for their plight.

The fabrication can probably most easily be seen in the simple circumstance that at the time the alleged cruel expulsion of Arabs by Zionists was in progress, it passed unnoticed. Foreign newspapermen who covered the war of 1948 on both sides did, indeed, write about the flight of the Arabs, but even those most hostile to the Jews saw nothing to suggest that it was not voluntary. In the three months during which the major part of the flight took place—April, May, and June, 1948—the London *Times,* at that time [openly] hostile to Zionism, published eleven leading articles on the situation in Palestine in addition to extensive news reports and articles. In none was there even a hint of the charge that the Zionists were driving the Arabs from their homes.

More interesting still, no Arab spokesman mentioned the subject. At the height of the flight, on April 27, Jamal Husseini, the Palestine Arab's chief representative at the United Nations, made a long political statement, which was not lacking in hostility toward the Zionists; he did not mention refugees. Three weeks later (while the flight was still in progress) the Secretary General of the Arab League, Azzam Pasha, made a fiercely worded political statement on Palestine; it contained not a word about refugees.

The Arab refugees were not driven from Palestine by anyone. The vast majority left, whether of their own free will or at the orders or exhortations of their leaders, always with the same reassurance—that their departure would help in the war against Israel. Attacks by Palestinian Arabs on the Jews had begun two days after the United Nations adopted its decision of November 29, 1947, to divide Western Palestine into an Arab and a Jewish state. The seven neighboring Arab states—Syria, Lebanon, Transjordan, Iraq, Saudi Arabia, Yemen, and Egypt—then prepared to invade the country as soon as the birth of the infant State of Israel was announced. Their victory was certain, they claimed, but it would be speeded and made easier if the local Arab population got out of the way. The refugees would come back in the wake of the victorious Arab armies and not only recover their own property but also inherit the houses and farms of the vanquished and annihilated Jews. Between December 1, 1947, and May 15, 1948, the clash was largely between bands of local Arabs, aided in diverse ways by the disintegrating British authority, and the Jewish fighting organizations.

The earliest voluntary refugees were understandably the

wealthier Arabs of the towns, who made a comparatively leisurely departure in December 1947 and in early 1948. At that stage, departure had not yet been proclaimed as a policy or recognized as a potential propaganda weapon. The Jaffa newspaper *Ash Sha'ab* thus wrote on January 30, 1948:

> The first group of our fifth column consists of those who abandon their houses and businesses and go to live elsewhere. . . . At the first sign of trouble they take to their heels to escape sharing the burden of struggle.

The weekly *As Sarih* of Jaffa used even more scathing terms on March 30, 1948, to accuse the inhabitants of Sheikh Munis and other villages in the neighborhood of Tel Aviv of "bringing down disgrace on us all" by "abandoning their villages." On May 5 the Jerusalem correspondent of the London *Times* was reporting: "The Arab streets are curiously deserted and, evidently following the poor example of the more moneyed class there has been an exodus from Jerusalem too, though not to the same extent as in Jaffa and Haifa."

As the local Arab offensive spread during the late winter and early spring of 1948, the Palestinian Arabs were urged to take to the hills, so as to leave the invading Arab armies unencumbered by a civilian population. Before the State of Israel had been formally declared—and while the British still ruled the country—over 200,000 Arabs left their homes in the coastal plain of Palestine.

These exhortations came primarily from their own local leaders. Monsignor George Hakim, then Greek Catholic Bishop of Galilee, the leading Christian personality in Palestine for many years, told a Beirut newspaper in the summer of 1948, before the flight of Arabs had ended:

> The refugees were confident that their absence would not last long, and that they would return within a week or two. Their leaders had promised them that the Arab Armies would crush the "Zionist gangs" very quickly and that there was no need for panic or fear of a long exile. [*Sada al Janub*, August 16, 1948]

The exodus was indeed common knowledge. The London weekly *Economist* reported on October 2, 1948:

Of the 62,000 Arabs who formerly lived in Haifa not more than 5,000 or 6,000 remained. Various factors influenced their decision to seek safety in flight. There is but little doubt that the most potent of the factors were the announcements made over the air by the Higher Arab Executive, urging the Arabs to quit. . . . It was clearly intimated that those Arabs who remained in Haifa and accepted Jewish protection would be regarded as renegades.

And the Near East Arabic Broadcasting Station from Cyprus stated on April 3, 1949:

It must not be forgotten that the Arab Higher Committee encouraged the refugees' flight from their homes in Jaffa, Haifa, and Jerusalem.

Even in retrospect, in an effort to describe the deliberateness of the flight, the leading Arab propagandist of the day, Edward Atiyah (then Secretary of the Arab League Office in London) reaffirmed the facts:

This wholesale exodus was due partly to the belief of the Arabs, encouraged by the boasting of an unrealistic Arab press and the irresponsible utterances of some of the Arab leaders that it could be only a matter of some weeks before the Jews were defeated by the armies of the Arab States and the Palestinian Arabs enabled to re-enter and retake possession of their country. [*The Arabs,* London, 1955, p. 183]

Kenneth Bilby, one of the American correspondents who covered Palestine for several years before and during the war of 1948, soon afterward wrote a book on his experience and observations. In it he reported:

The Arab exodus, initially at least, was encouraged by many Arab leaders, such as Haj Amin el Husseini, the exiled pro-Nazi Mufti of Jerusalem, and by the Arab Higher Committee for Palestine. They viewed the first

wave of Arab setbacks as merely transitory. Let the
Palestine Arabs flee into neighboring countries. It would
serve to arouse the other Arab peoples to greater effort,
and when the Arab invasion struck, the Palestinians could
return to their homes and be compensated with the property of Jews driven into the sea. [*New Star in the Near
East,* New York, 1950, pp. 30-31]

After the war the Palestine Arab leaders did try to help
people—including their own—to forget that it was they
who had called for the exodus in the early spring of 1948.
They now blamed the leaders of the invading Arab states
themselves. These had added their voices to the exodus
call, though not until some weeks after the Palestine Arab
Higher Committee had taken a stand.

The war was not yet over when Emil Ghoury, Secretary
of the Arab High Committee, the official leadership of the
Palestinian Arabs, stated in an interview with a Beirut
newspaper:

> I do not want to impugn anybody but only to help the
> refugees. The fact that there are these refugees is the
> direct consequence of the action of the Arab States in
> opposing partition and the Jewish State. The Arab
> States agreed upon this policy unanimously and they
> must share in the solution of the problem. [*Daily Tele-
> graph,* September 6, 1948]

In retrospect, the Jordanian newspaper *Falastin* wrote
on February 19, 1949:

> The Arab States encouraged the Palestine Arabs to leave
> their homes temporarily in order to be out of the way
> of the Arab invasion armies.

Nimr el Hawari, the Commander of the Palestine Arab
Youth Organization, in his book *Sir Am Nakbah* ("The
Secret Behind the Disaster", published in Nazareth in
1952), more specifically quoted the Iraqi Prime Minister
Nuri Said. Nuri, he wrote, had thundered: "We will smash
the country with our guns and obliterate every place the
Jews seek shelter in. The Arabs should conduct their

wives and children to safe areas until the fighting has died down."

Equally specifically brought to public notice was the part played by the chief spokesman for the combined Arab states, the Secretary General of the Arab League himself. Habib Issa, in the New York Lebanese daily newspaper *Al Hoda* wrote on June 8, 1951,

> The Secretary General of the Arab League, Azzam Pasha, assured the Arab peoples that the occupation of Palestine and of Tel Aviv would be as simple as a military promenade. . . . He pointed out that they were already on the frontiers and that all the millions the Jews had spent on land and economic development would be easy booty, for it would be a simple matter to throw Jews into the Mediterranean. . . . Brotherly advice was given to the Arabs of Palestine to leave their land, homes, and property and to stay temporarily in neighboring fraternal states, lest the guns of the invading Arab armies mow them down.

As late as 1952 the charge had the official stamp of the Arab Higher Committee. In a memorandum to the Arab League states, the Committee wrote:

> Some of the Arab leaders and their ministers in Arab capitals . . . declared that they welcomed the immigration of Palestinian Arabs into the Arab countries until they saved Palestine. Many of the Palestinian Arabs were misled by their declarations. . . . It was natural for those Palestinian Arabs who felt impelled to leave their country to take refuge in Arab lands . . . and to stay in such adjacent places in order to maintain contact with their country so that to return to it would be easy when, according to the promises of many of those responsible in the Arab countries (promises which were given wastefully), the time was ripe. Many were of the opinion that such an opportunity would come in the hours between sunset and sunrise.[1]

---

[1] Published in Cairo. Quoted by Joseph B. Schechtman, *The Refugee in the World* (New York, 1963), pp. 197–198.

Most pointed of all was the comment of one of the refugees themselves, "The Arab governments told us: Get out so that we can get in. So we got out, but they did not get in."[2]

When the onslaught of the local Arabs had been in progress for over four months, and a month before the planned invasion by the seven Arab states, about half the population still remained in the area mapped out by the United Nations as the Jewish state. Now began the fantastic phase of the exodus. A large part of the population panicked. Suddenly the countryside was filled with rumors and alleged reports of Jewish "atrocities." A highly colored report of a battle near Jerusalem became the driving theme. At the village of Dir Yassin, one of the bases of the Arab forces maintaining pressure on the Jerusalem-Tel Aviv road, an assault by the "dissident" Irgun Zvai Leumi and the FFI (Stern Group) had continued for eight hours before the village was finally captured, and then only with the help of a Palmach[3] armored car which arrived on the scene unexpectedly. The element of surprise having been lost, the Arab soldiers could turn every house in the village into a fortress. Jewish casualties amounted to one-third of the attacking force (40 out of 120). The Arabs, barricading themselves in the houses, had omitted to evacuate women and children, many of whom were thus killed during the attack.

The Arab leaders seized on the opportunity to tell an utterly fantastic story of a "massacre," which was disseminated throughout the world by all the arms of British propaganda. The accepted "orthodox" version to this day, it has served enemies of Israel and anti-Semites faithfully.[4]

---

[2] Jordan daily *Ad Difaa*, September 6, 1954.

[3] Palmach—the striking force of the Haganah.

[4] I have dealt in depth with the Dir Yassin libel in *Days of Fire* (New York, 1968). The Zionist establishment of 1948, in its eagerness to blacken the dissident underground, helped the libel along. Only years later did the Israeli Foreign Office correct the record (in *Israel's Struggle for Peace*, Israel Office of Information, New

The effect of the story was immediate and electric. The British officer who had done most in the years before 1948 to build up the Transjordanian Army, General Glubb Pasha, wrote in the London *Daily Mail* on August 12, 1948: "The Arab civilians panicked and fled ignominiously. Villages were frequently abandoned before they were threatened by the progress of war." And the refugee from Dir Yassin, Yunes Ahmed Assad, has soberly recorded that "The Arab exodus from other villages was not caused by the actual battle, but by the exaggerated description spread by Arab leaders to incite them to fight the Jews" (*Al Urdun,* April 9, 1953).

Another quarter of a million Arabs thus left the area of the State of Israel in the late spring and early summer of 1948.

Where they had the opportunity, the Jews tried to prevent the Arabs flight. Bishop Hakim of Galilee confirmed to the Rev. Karl Baehr, Executive Secretary of the American Christian Palestine Committee that the Arabs of Haifa "fled in spite of the fact that the Jewish authorities guaranteed their safety and rights as citizens of Israel."[5] This episode is described in a report by the Haifa District HQ of the British Palestine Police sent on April 26, 1948 to Police HQ in Jerusalem.

"Every effort is being made by the Jews to persuade the Arab populace to stay and carry on with their normal lives, to get their shops and businesses open and to be assured that their lives and interests will be safe." The Jewish effort was in vain. The police report continues: "A large road convoy, escorted by [British] military . . . left Haifa for Beirut yesterday. . . Evacuation by sea goes on

---

York, 1960) and in an extensive statement entitled "Dir Yassin," published on March 16, 1969. An earlier Arab eye-witness account is a stunning refutation of the libel. On the fifth anniversary of the battle, Yunes Ahmed Assad of Dir Yassin wrote in the Jordan daily *Al Urdun* (April 9, 1953): "The Jews never intended to hurt the population of the village but were forced to do so after they met hostile fire from the population which killed the Irgun commander."

[5] *New York Herald Tribune,* June 30, 1949.

steadily." Two days later the Haifa police continued to report. The Jews were "still making every effort to persuade the Arab populace to remain and to settle back into their normal lives in the towns;" as for the Arabs, "another convoy left Tireh for Transjordan, and the evacuation by sea continues. The quays and harbor are still crowded with refugees and their household effects, all omitting no opportunity to get a place on one of the boats leaving Haifa."[6]

This orderly evacuation took place as the outcome of truce negotiations after the Jewish forces had broken the Arab offensive and taken control of the city. The Arab military delegates, refusing the truce, asked for British help in transferring the Arab population to the neighboring Arab countries. The British provided facilities, including trucks.

The voluntary nature of the evacuation was proclaimed a virtue by the leader and chief spokesman of the Palestinian Arabs. While it was in progress, Jamal Husseini, Acting Chairman of the Palestine Arab Higher Committee, told the United Nations Security Council:

> The Arabs did not want to submit to a truce . . . they rather preferred to abandon their homes, their belongings and everything they possessed in the world and leave the town. This is in fact what they did.[7]

Most of the Arab evacuees did not go so far as the neighboring Arab states. Many went to towns in Judea and Samaria and remained there under Transjordanian rule. Others stopped at Acre, where they could look across the bay at their home town and wait patiently for the day a month later when they would make their triumphant way back in the wake of the victorious Arab armies. The victorious Arab armies never arrived; instead, Acre was

---

[6] These documents were in the British police files taken over by the Haganah on the evacuation of Haifa by the British a fortnight later.

[7] UN Security Council Official Records Third Year N. 62, April 23, 1948, p. 14.

won by the Jewish forces; and the evacuees moved on again. Only now they were to be called "refugees."

The Arab National Committee of Haifa, in a memorandum two years later to the governments of the Arab League, recalled frankly that "the military and civil authorities and the Jewish representative expressed their profound regret at this grave decision [to evacuate]. The [Jewish] Mayor of Haifa made a passionate appeal to the delegation to reconsider its decision."[8]

When the Arab onslaught on Israel failed and the Arab leaders' promise of an early return and a take-over of Jewish property was revealed as an irresponsible, malicious miscalculation, the theme of Israel's responsibility for the flight and the plight of the Arab refugees developed.

The transfer of blame to the Jews was first of all a natural act of self-exculpation by the Arab leaders. It soon became a powerful propaganda weapon in the general war against Israel. Even sophisticated Arab apologists, pressed at times by the courtesies of debate to meet the challenge of the facts, parry the question. Thus, Albert Hourani, in an article in the London *Observer* on September 3, 1967, talks of the "myth that the Arabs left willingly under orders from their leaders." "No more than the most tenuous evidence was produced for this," writes Mr. Hourani. How many of his readers would know the facts, would know that Mr. Hourani's own words represented an act of collaboration in a monstrous fraud perpetuated by the Arab leaders responsible for the refugee problem?

The fraud developed. Its next feature was the inflation of the numbers of the refugees. Mr. Emil Ghoury, Secretary of the Arab Higher Committee during the was, is a typical purveyor. In his 1960 speech at the United Nations he set the number of "expelled" Arabs at two million. The Arab spokesmen who succeeded him in the debate presumably considered this figure too high. On November 25 the Lebanese representative, Nadim Dimechkie, declared that "more than one million Arabs have been expelled." Four days later, the spokesman for Sudan

---

[8] Quoted by Schechtmann, p. 192.

struck an average, speaking of the "expulsion of one and a half million Arabs." These speeches are characteristic; ever since the policy of falsification was adopted, the figure used by Arab spokesmen has never fallen below a million. The misrepresentation may be epitomized in a comparison of two of Emil Ghoury's statements.

| Emil Ghoury to the Beirut *Daily Telegraph*, September 6, 1948 | Emil Ghoury in a speech at the United Nations Special Political Committee, November 17, 1960[9] |
|---|---|
| I do not want to impugn anybody, but only to help the refugees. The fact that there are these refugees is the direct consequence of the action of the Arab States in opposing partition and the Jewish State. The Arab States agreed upon this policy unanimously and they must share in the solution of the problem. | It has been those [Zionist] acts of terror, accompanied by wholesale depredations, which caused the exodus of the Palestine Arabs. |

In 1947 there were approximately one million Arabs in the whole of western Palestine. (British figures, certainly inflated, put the number at 1,200,000; independent calculations claim 800–900,000). Of these, the total number actually living in that part of Palestine which became Israel was, *according to the British figure,* 561,000.[10] Not all of them left. After the end of hostilities in 1949, there were 140,000 Arabs in Israel. The total number of Arabs who left could not mathematically have been more than some 420,000.

At the time, before the policy of inflation had been conceived, these were the commonly stated proportions of the problem. At the end of May 1948 Faris el Khoury,

---

[9] UN Document A/SPC/SR 209, p. 9.

[10] This figure was compiled by Dr. Oscar K. Rabinowicz on the basis of the statistics in the British *Survey of Palestine,* Vol. I, and published in *Jewish Social Studies,* October 1959, pp. 240–242 (quoted by Schechtman, p. 195).

the Syrian representative on the UN Security Council, estimated their number at 250,000. The even more authoritative Emil Ghoury (who twelve years later talked of two million) announced on September 6, 1948, that by the middle of June, at the time of the first truce, the number of Arabs who had fled was 200,000. "By the time the second truce began (on July 17)," he said, "their number had risen to 300,000."[11] Count Bernadotte, the UN Special Representative in Palestine, reporting on September 16, 1948 informed the United Nations that he estimated the number of Arab refugees at 360,000, including 50,000 in Israel territory (UN Document A1648). After July 1948 there was a fourth exodus of some 50,000 Arabs from Galilee and from the Negev.

The inflation may at first have been accidental. The United Nations at once provided the refugees with food, clothes, shelter, and medical attention. There was no system of identification; any Arab could register as a refugee and receive free aid. Immediately a large number of needy Arabs from various Arab countries flocked to the refugee camps, were registered, and thenceforth received their rations. Already by December 1948, when their total could not yet have reached the maximum of 425,000, the Director of the United Nations Disaster Relief Organization, Sir Rafael Cilento, reported that he was feeding 750,000 refugees. Seven months later the official figure had increased to a round million in the report of W. de St. Aubin, the United Nations Director of Field Operations.

The inflation of the numbers was helped not only by the understandable readiness of needy and greedy people to take advantage of free upkeep. The International Committee of the Red Cross pressed the United Nations Relief headquarters to recognize as refugees *any* destitute Arab in Palestine and to let him have refugee facilities in his own home. The Red Cross Committee made no effort to conceal its purpose; it claimed that it was becoming increasingly difficult to differentiate levels of need "between

---

[11] Beirut *Telegraph*, September 6, 1948.

the refugees and the residents, as the Arab-occupied areas do not produce sufficient food or salable goods to nourish more than a small percentage of the resident population." If this fraudulent addition of 100,000 to the rolls for food and medical care was feasible, it would indeed be "senseless," as the Red Cross communication noted, also to force them "to abandon their homes to be able to get food as refugees." At least 100,000 ordinary Arab citizens in this category thus became refugees *de luxe*.

To round out the picture, both the Jordanian authorities and the Egyptian administration in the Gaza Strip insisted that the refugee rolls include any Arab who could be described as needing support as a result of the war of 1948. Though the United Nations Relief and Works Administration made gestures of protest, it finally accepted this situation, thus becoming a major partner in the deception. Moreover, it submitted to the decision of the host governments to deny it any opportunity to investigate the bona fides of claimant refugees. It was never possible to establish even whether the names on the relief rolls were those of living people or of persons long since dead.

Nor were the relief organizations permitted by the host governments to investigate or to take steps to combat the large-scale forging of and trading in ration cards, which had become a major well-known "racket" throughout the Middle East.

"There is reason to believe," reported the UNRWA Director as early as 1950, "that births are always registered for ration purposes, but deaths are often, if not usually, concealed so that the family may continue to collect rations for the deceased" (UN Document A-1451 pp. 9-10).

Nine years later, the UNRWA Director's report for 1959-1960 equally laconically records that its figures of Arabs receiving relief—1,120,000—do not necessarily reflect the actual refugee population owing to factors such as the high scale of unreported deaths, undetected false registration, etc." (UN Document A/4478 p. 13). In October, 1959 the Director had admitted that ration lists *in Jordan alone* "are believed to include 150,000 ineligibles and many persons who have died."

The result has been the creation of a large, amorphous mass of names, some of them relating to real people, some of them purely fictitious or relating to persons long since dead, a minority relating to people without a home as a result of their or their parents' leaving Palestine in 1948, the majority relating to people who, whatever their origins, are now living and working as ordinary citizens but continuing to draw rations and obtaining medical attention at the expense of the world's taxpayers—all of them comfortably lumped together in official United Nations lists as Arab refugees and vehemently described as "victims of Jewish aggression."

The economic interest of the individual Arab in the perpetuation of the refugee problem and of his free keep is backed by the accumulating vested interest of UNRWA itself to keep itself in being and to expand. The United Nations Relief and Works Agency is thought of as some Olympian, philanthropic body directed and operated by a band of dedicated humanitarians, devoted exclusively to the task of helping suffering refugees. The fact is that the organization consists of some 11,000 officials, of whom all but a handful are Arabs who are themselves inscribed on the rolls as "refugees." They perform the field work; they, that is, hand out the relief. The remaining handful consist of some 120 Americans and Europeans, who man the organization's central offices. Since UNRWA itself is thus a source of livelihood for some 50,000 people, no one connected with it has the slightest interest in seeing its task end or in protesting the fraud and deception it has perpetuated for over twenty years. The myth continues to live and to thrive, feeding on itself.

A strict examination of the reports of UNRWA itself will show that the facts of the fraud are essentially not concealed, rendering the misrepresentation in definitions and figures all the more deliberate. It is a misrepresentation which has been publicly exposed by diligent independent investigators. The American writer Martha Gellhorn publicly made these charges. Somewhat earlier, a detailed analysis of every aspect of the problem, the fruit of study year after year, had been published by Dr. Walter Pinner, who was able consequently to confront the international authorities with the facts and to publish them in two books.[12]

The UNRWA—disregarding its own reports in 1966 set the number of refugees at 1,317,749. In fact, the number of real refugees, as calculated by Dr. Pinner, was 367,000.

The difference of over 950,000 is roughly made up as follows:

| | |
|---|---:|
| Unrecorded deaths | 117,000 |
| Ex-refugees resettled in 1948 | 109,000 |
| Ex-refugees who became self-supporting between 1948 and 1966 (85,000 in Syria, 60,000 in Lebanon, and 80,000 in Jordan) | 225,000 |
| Frontier villagers in Jordan (nonrefugees) | 15,000 |
| Self-appointed nonrefugees (pre-1948 residents of "West Jordan" and the Gaza Strip registered as refugees) | 484,000 |

Of the real refugees, nearly half were in the Gaza Strip—155,000 out of 367,000. The reason is simple. Control of the Gaza Strip was in the hands of Egypt. While Jordan, Lebanon, and even Syria did not restrict the movement of refugees or obstruct the efforts of the refugees themselves to rehabilitate themselves (provided they did not give up their status as "refugees"),[13] the Egyptian authorities maintained a strict separation between "refugees" and the ordinary population of the area. The Gaza Strip, wrote Martha Gellhorn, "is not a hell-hole, not a visible disaster. It is worse. It is a jail"(*Atlantic Monthly*, October 1961). The outline of the refugee problem is sharp and clear-

---

[12] *How Many Refugees?* (London, 1959); *The Legend of the Arab Refugees* (Tel Aviv, 1967). The figures here given are from the more recent study (p. 45).

[13] In Lebanon, the one exception, rehabilitated refugees were in fact struck off the relief rolls; but Lebanon is a minor "host" country.

cut. Many of them in the parts of western Palestine annexed by Jordan in 1950, in Syria, and in Lebanon took affairs into their own hands and became more or less self-supporting though, like many hundreds of thousands of their neighbors who had never been refugees in any sense, they continued to supplement their earnings by the free food, free medical supplies, and even the free, if inferior, shelter provided by UNRWA.[14]

The remainder—either unwilling or unable to work or forcibly prevented (in Gaza) from establishing themselves —together with their progeny numbered less than 400,000 on the eve of the Six Day War.

Having established the image of a major problem, the Arab governments maintained and projected it. The fact that the vast majority of the Arabs who had actually left the Israeli part of Palestine had integrated into the life of their host country (or had emigrated to seek prosperity in Kuwait or elsewhere) did not disturb the myth. The governments had only to block any *official* scheme for resettlement of the refugees, so that the relief rolls never decreased, and to insure the continued existence of camps which could be photographed, showing people labeled "refugees" living in circumstances of various degrees of sordidness and squalor.

In the early years after 1948, Arab governments did from time to time pretend to consider plans for the integration of refugees put forward by the United Nations. In 1952 Jordan, Egypt, and Syria, all signed agreements with UNRWA for the execution of a plan for integration which was to cost the United Nations $200 million. The plan was adopted by the General Assembly of the UN on January 26, 1952. They never took any steps however to implement the plan. Not a single one of the projects it envisaged was ever launched.

---

[14] "There are numerous instances of full-time Government employees remaining on ration rolls because of the high income scale," states a laconic UNRWA report in 1952. UN Document A/2171, p. 16.

In the years that followed, other schemes were proposed. Any plan that involved resettlement of the refugees was automatically rejected. The Arab states agreed on one form of aid only—charity, the annual United Nations grant for relief, most of which was spent on people who had no need of it or who had never in any sense been refugees.

If there had in fact been even as many as a million refugees, their integration could have been effected in a few years. In this period vast international experience accumulated in integrating and resettling refugees. Since the Second World War there have been some forty million refugees in the world. The vast majority were either driven physically from their homes—where in some cases their families had lived for hundreds of years—or fled under the immediate threat of physical danger or political oppression.

Immediately after the Second World War some twelve million Germans were physically driven into Germany— West and East—from Poland, Czechoslovakia, the Soviet Union, Hungary, and Romania. They left all their property behind. The transfer from Poland, Czechoslovakia, and Hungary was carried out with the prior approval of the three great powers participating in the Potsdam Conference—the Soviet Union, the United Kingdom, and the United States—in the summer of 1945. The expulsion under these international auspices was carried out in such a way that many hundreds of thousands of refugees died in the process.[15] Their property was confiscated; nobody even suggested paying them compensation. The territory of Germany had been reduced by some 20 percent; now its population was forcibly increased by twenty percent.

In the months of chaos which followed the end of the war in Germany, when hunger and suffering predominated, there was for a while some talk of returning at least part of the refugees to Poland and Czechoslovakia. Liber-

---

[15] The dead numbered two million according to the West German authorities; "well under a million" according to Elizabeth Wiskemann in her *Germany's Eastern Neighbours* (London, 1956).

al President Eduard Beneš of Czechoslovakia replied on May 9, 1947: "If somebody should get the idea that this question has not been definitely settled, we would resolutely call the whole nation to arms." Soviet Foreign Minister Vyacheslav Molotov was no less explicit. "The very idea," he said, "of involving millions of people in such experiments [of reversing the process of eviction of Germans from Poland] is unbelievable, quite apart from the cruelty of it both toward the Poles and the Germans themselves."

The French Foreign Minister, Georges Bidault, added his government's opinion. "Poland's new frontier and the transfer of population are accomplished facts," he told the Council of Foreign Ministers in London in November 1947, "and it is no use thinking they can be reversed now."[16]

The West German government, confronted with gigantic physical, political, and psychological problems of reconstruction, did not hasten to accept the long-term implications of absorbing millions of refugees. Even five years after the end of the war voices were still raised in the West from time to time, complaining of tardiness in their resettlement. Thereafter the German government set in motion vast housing, education, and labor programs for the reintegration of fellow Germans into the national economy and society. It received no outside help; no international fund was set up; the United Nations Organization never sought, nor was it asked, to deal with the deliberate uprooting—sometimes forcible, always against their will—of twelve million human beings or with the problems attendant on their rehabilitation.

When, at the other end of the world, India was partitioned in 1947, fourteen million people became refugees within a few months. No international agency showed any sign of agitation at the terror-stricken flight of eight million Hindus from Pakistan and of six million Moslems

---

16 Molotov in interview with Polish News Agency (PAT), September 17, 1946. Bidault and Beneš quoted in Schechtman, The Refugee in the World (New York, 1963), pp. 29–30.

from their homes in India. The Indian and Pakistani leaders made vain appeals to their peoples to stay where they were. They were certainly not to blame for the two-way exodus or for the bloody riots that preceded it. But both the Indian and Pakistani governments at once set about giving the refugees succor and homes. They first of all used the homes forsaken by the refugees who had fled in the opposite direction.

The exchange of populations in itself came to be seen on all sides as a perfectly natural—indeed, as the best—solution to the problem of communal relations in the two states. Neither Pakistan nor India are wealthy countries, and the efforts of both peoples to solve the problem of absorption and integration went on for years. They received no international help; no special funds were set up to help them.

In 1947, after the Second World War, Finland was compelled to give up almost one-eighth of her territory and at the same time to receive nearly half a million Finnish refugees expelled by the Soviet Union. In 1950 the Bulgarians expelled 150,000 Turks, with whom they had last fought a war two generations earlier. These refugees, their property confiscated, were allowed to take personal belongings up to a value of two dollars when they were sent across the frontier into Turkey. The Turkish government, neither the richest nor most efficient government in the world, planned and carried out an absorption program which was completed in two years.

Tens of millions of refugees were thus absorbed by their own people, speaking the same language, with basically similar cultural backgrounds. Some were absorbed by foreign countries which owed them nothing except common humanity. A minority—rather more than a million—was settled in a variety of countries through the efforts of the International Refugee Organization.

The perpetuation of the Arab refugee problem by the Arab states has the same central purpose as its creation: to bring about the destruction of the State of Israel. No Arab leader has ever tried to hide or obscure this aim. All have repeatedly made it clear that their refusal to absorb refugees into their large, empty, and population-hungry territories stems from their insistence on the right of the refugees "to return to their home," a "right" held to be identical with the right of the Arab people to Palestine. A natural corollary of this right is the destruction of Israel as a state. The perpetuation of the "refugee problem" is part of the same policy that refuses to concede Israel's very right to exist.

"Any discussion aimed at a solution of the Palestine problem not based on assuring the refugees' right to annihilate Israel will be regarded as a desecration of the Arab people and an act of treason," stated a resolution of the Refugee Conference held at Homs, Syria, in 1957. "If Arabs return to Israel—Israel will cease to exist," Gamal Abdel Nasser himself said in an interview in *Züricher Woche,* September 1, 1961.

The Arab states hoped to achieve the right to introduce into Israel an army (labeled refugees) to blow it up from within as they have failed to destroy it from without.

The cause of the Arab refugees has been maintained with the help of the Western nations and the manipulation of the United Nations Organization by the Arabs and their supporters.

United Nations decisions are based on the quintessence of the interests of the participating nations or, in many cases, on the simple principle of buying political credit. Where a specfic issue does not affect a country's interests directly, it votes for the side from which it expects some political benefit tomorrow—such is the basic law of nations. The Arab states would be assured of forty votes at the United Nations even if (as Mr. Abba Eban once pointed out) they introduced a resolution proclaiming that the earth is flat. This circumstance has been exploited to the full by the Arabs. Though they have not taken a stand on the shape of the earth, their successes are impressive nonetheless.

Having set up the United Nations Relief and Works Agency, the international statesmen received its yearly reports, ostensibly read them, ignored the falsehoods and fraud they reflected, deplored the plight of the refugees, and passed a new vote of funds which served to perpetuate the problem.

Never was a problem less deserving of international aid—certainly not from the governments who have not considered lifting a finger even in charity for the tens of millions of innocent refugees driven or forced from their homes in all parts of the world—from the Finns in 1945, to the Biafrans in 1967-1969, to the Nilotic Negroes in Sudan and the ten million East Bengalis who fled to India while this book was in preparation. Except for the Germans in Czechoslovakia and Poland whom Hitler used as an excuse for war and who on his defeat were forced into the restricted area of postwar Germany—the Arabs are the only people whose refugees are the product of their own aggression. That aggression, moreover, was designed to nullify a resolution of the United Nations itself. And they are the only people, not excepting the Germans, who deliberately created a refugee problem with the intent to destroy another people.

It was no great problem for the Arab people, with its vast territory and resources, to absorb the 400,000 Arabs who left Israeli territory in Palestine. Even a million would have presented no insuperable problem. In fact, the vast majority of the refugees have been absorbed. The fantastically wealthy oil state of Kuwait has taken in large numbers of Palestinian Arabs who fled, as well as many Arabs who simply emigrated. From Judea and Samaria, the part of western Palestine controlled by Jordan in the years 1948-1967, some 400,000 Arabs emigrated voluntarily, without aid.

The guilt of collusion goes even deeper. The Western statesmen have turned a blind eye to the fact that the Arab states, when they failed to destroy the Jewish state at birth, expelled or forced out large numbers of the Jewish citizens of their own countries. Of 900,000 Jews who were so driven out—and whose property was confiscated—Israel took in and absorbed nearly three-quarters of a million.

All these Jews were private citizens, most of them members of families that had lived in those countries for many generations, some of them for hundreds of years before their Arab oppressors. A central ethnic feature of the whole of what is now called the Middle East and of the North African coast for more than 2,000 years has been the continuity there of Jewish life.

At the time of the rebirth of Jewish statehood in Palestine, approximately one million Jews were living in this area. Arab propagandists usually claim that the Arabs treated "their" Jews with tolerance. This is, generally speaking, untrue. But except in Yemen, it is only comparatively recently that the Arabs became the rulers who could decide on the "treatment" of Jews or of other minorities in their states. That treatment was sad and horrifying. Yet the oppression and discriminatory practices of the period before 1948 are for the most part insignificant in the light of what happened to the Jews of those countries after 1948.

Their agony was not uniform. In Yemen (where Jewish origins are lost in antiquity but certainly go back 2,600 years) the Jews lived for generations as second-class citizens in a primitive, medieval society. Restriction, discrimination, and humiliation had been their lot since the Middle Ages, an era which in Yemen has not yet come to an end. Though they were not expelled after 1948, the danger to their safety was so blatant that the exodus of the whole community was organized from Israel in one large-scale operation in 1949, with the passive consent of the Yemen authorities. Arriving at the transit camps by bus, on foot, or on donkeys from every corner of the mountainous and ragged kingdom, often after much harassment on the way, 48,000 Jews, most of them emaciated and sick and suffering from endemic eye diseases, were evacuated and flown to Israel in what became known as Operation Magic Carpet.

In other Arab countries a much more savage tale unfolded. The years 1948-1960 may well prove to have been the blackest period in the annals of the Jewish communities in the Arab countries. Humiliation and discrimination were the Jews' daily lot, then violence and looting and murder, then the closing of the borders to prevent their escape, only to have them suddenly opened again to engender the inevitable hasty empty-handed flight—such in varying degrees of intensity was the pattern. Most gruesome of all was the Jewish experience in Iraq and Egypt which people in the West tend to treat as though they were civilized countries.

In Iraq, the range of repression of the Jews, growing in intensity from 1948, compares only with the worse excesses of the Nazi regime in the 1930's: violent searches, wanton vandalism, confiscation of goods, arbitrary extortion, often under torture; frequently, after release, rearrest and repetition of the process of threat, violence, and extortion. These "processes of law" were covered by the Iraqi Proclamation of Martial Law of May 1948. Its refinements were considerably extended two months later by the simple expedient of adding "Zionism" to the list of capital crimes. Under this amendment to the Iraqi Criminal Code it was sufficient for two Moslems to swear that they knew someone to be sympathetic to Zionism to render him liable to hanging. Though few hangings were in fact carried out, a wave of terror against the Jews followed. In consonance with the spirit of the time, Jews were ousted overnight from government service, deprived of licenses as doctors, and prevented from obtaining new clerical posts. The schools and universities were "cleansed" of Jewish students. Severe restrictions were imposed on Jewish merchants and banks.

For nearly two years this comprehensive persecution continued. At the same time any attempt by a Jew to leave the country for Israel was declared a capital offense. Sentences of hanging, long imprisonment, and—in most cases—confiscation of property were imposed on a large number of Jews who were thus caught. To round out the picture, even Jews who had left in earlier years were tried *in absentia* and sentenced.

Suddenly, in March 1950, the government hastily pushed through the Iraqi Parliament a law enabling Jews to leave the country, provided they renounced their Iraqi citizenship. Emigrants were allowed to take only small cash sums; the property they left behind in Iraq, however, remained legally theirs. This omission was corrected a year later. In March 1951, after all but a handful of the 130,000 Jews of Iraq had registered for emigration and a substantial number had already left the country, the property of all of them was confiscated.

In Egypt before May 1948 the severities of economic repression and the ousting of people from hardly won positions and status in commerce and the professions were only theoretically mitigated for the Jewish community by the fact that in their early stage they were claimed to be directed against all foreigners and minorities. It was mainly Jews, however, who were the sufferers. Then a law was passed enabling the government to take over the property of anyone whose activities were deemed "prejudicial to the safety and security of the state" or who had been placed "under surveillance." Though this regulation could apply to everyone, it was in fact applied almost exclusively to Jews.

Indiscriminate arrest and imprisonment followed—as well as pogroms in the streets of Cairo, with their inevitable crop of murder and destruction. Here, too, in order to insure the maximum impact of terror, the gates were barred to departure and then suddenly opened in August 1949. Repression was relaxed until 1954, when Abdul Nasser, in the second phase of the "Egyptian revolution," took over power and brought down a new black night on the Jews of Egypt.

Thereafter the regime of oppression, discrimination, and confiscation in a framework of police surveillance spread and deepened. Introduction of the techniques of Nazi Germany was facilitated by the generous employment of former officials of the Nazi regime who had fled retribution. Arbitrary confiscation of property was legalized and emigration was encouraged. The policy was accompanied by automatic sequestration. These measures, too, were directed against a few foreigners, but the victims were predominantly Jews born in Egypt.

A conference of World Jewish organizations in January 1957 described how Jews were encouraged to leave Egypt:

> Large number of Jews of all nationalities have either been served with orders of expulsion, or were subjected to ruthless intimidation to compel them to apply for permission to depart. Hundreds who have reached lands of refuge have testified that they were taken in shackles from prison and concentration camps to board ships. In order to ensure that this deliberate creation of a new refugee problem should not evoke protests from international public opinion, documents proving expulsion were taken away from expellees before departure. Furthermore they were compelled to sign statements certifying that they left voluntarily. The victims of this barbaric process were deprived of their possessions.[17]

By 1960 some 80 percent of the 85,000 Jews in Egypt had emigrated, leaving most of their property behind.[18] Most of the rest followed before the Six Day War, and a smaller number emigrated after 1967. Israel absorbed about 50,000.

In varying degrees of harshness some 900,000 human beings were arbitrarily driven or forced out from these and the remaining Arab countries—notably Syria, Algeria, and Morocco. Their number is thus about double that of the Arabs who abandoned their homes in Palestine in 1948. Some 700,000 of them were brought to Israel and were absorbed into the country. Almost all came penniless. Their property, which certainly far exceeded the

---

[17] *Alliance Review,* New York April 1957.

[18] A convention of former Egyptian Jews held in Paris in July 1971 recommended that legal suits for compensation be filed by all those who had been incarcerated and deported because of the Egyptian-Israel wars of 1948, 1956, and 1967. The estimated claims for personal compensation, for confiscated communal property, and for religious articles amount to $1,000 million. Jerusalem *Post,* August 13, 1971.

abandoned property of Arabs in Israel, simply enriched the states which had driven them out.

Could an Orwell or a Kafka really have done justice to the monstrous fiction called the "Arab refugee problem?"

# 3

# The Origin of the Dispute

On November 29, 1947—the day the United Nations Assembly decided to recommend the partition of Palestine into an Arab and a Jewish state—there were no Arab refugees. The area allotted to the Jewish state was much smaller even than that established by the Armistice Lines of 1949 (which lasted until June 5, 1967), to which Israel is now urged to withdraw. At that time Israel had no "occupied territories" from which to withdraw.

It was against that embryo state that the Arabs declared and waged their war. Its total area, amounting to little more than half of western Palestine, was roughly 15,000 square kilometers (about 6,000 square miles), including the semi-arid Negev. (See Map No. 2). The Arabs were thus assured of seven-eighths of the totality of Palestine on both sides of the Jordan as it was recognized at the end of the First World War by all the nations of the world as the territory for the Jewish National Home (see Map No. 3).

The seven Arab states in existence in 1947—Egypt, Iraq, Syria, Lebanon, Saudi Arabia, Yemen, and Transjordan (see Map No. 4)—whose leaders decided to prevent the birth of Israel, contained an area 230 times larger than the projected Jewish state and a population 60 times that of its Jewish inhabitants, who numbered only a little more than half a million.

The Arab appetite would be satisfied with nothing less than the remainder. It was, moreover, characteristic that the secretary of this confederation of invader states, Azzam Pasha, in forecasting the success of the invasion,

38

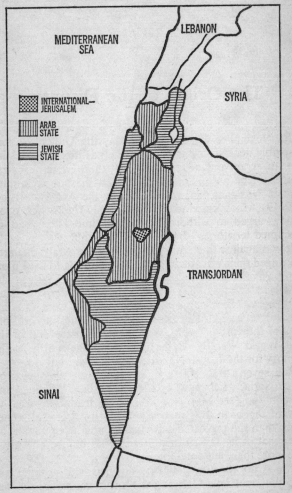

MEDITERRANEAN
SEA

LEBANON

SYRIA

INTERNATIONAL—
JERUSALEM

ARAB
STATE

JEWISH
STATE

TRANSJORDAN

SINAI

MAP NO. 2: The partition proposed by the United Nations (1947)

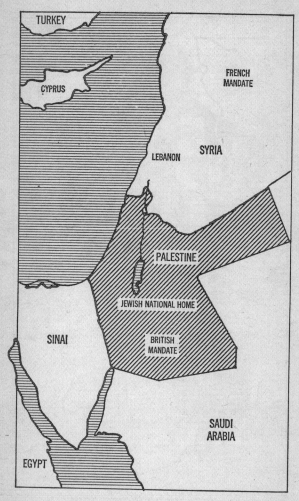

MAP NO. 3:   Palestine according to the British Mandate

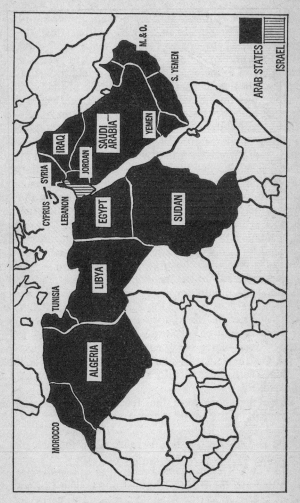

MAP No. 4: The Arab States and Israel

invoked the memory of the massacres by the Mongols and the Crusaders.

Such was the attitude of the Arabs in 1947, when they had in their hands all, and more than, the territory they are now demanding from Israel. At that time they violently refused to share Palestine with the Jews in a territorial ratio of 7 to 1. They refused to recognize the Jewish claim to the country or to the smallest part of it; to acquiesce in the international recognition of that claim; or to abate this one jot of their designs on the whole of the area that had once been the Moslem Empire in Asia.

Less than thirty years earlier, the "historic rights" to Palestine of the Arabs, allegedly existing for a thousand years, had not yet been discovered. In February 1919 the Emir Faisal, the one recognized Arab leader at the time, then still striving for the creation of Arab political independence in Syria (of which he was briefly king) and Iraq (over which he and his house subsequently ruled for forty years), signed a formal agreement with Dr. Chaim Weizmann, representing the Zionist Organization. This provided for cooperation between the projected Arab state and the projected reconstituted Jewish state of Palestine. Borders were still to be negotiated, but Faisal had already described the Zionist proposals as "moderate and proper." The borders proposed by the Zionists included what subsequently became Mandatory Palestine on both banks of the Jordan as well as northwestern Galilee up to the Litany River—later included in southern Lebanon—part of the Golan Heights—later included in Syria—and part of Sinai—left under British administration in Egypt (see Map No. 5).

When and how were the Jewish rights, historic and recognized, "transferred" to the Arabs?

The key to this question is reflected in the behavior of the British in 1947. When, in that year, the Arabs rejected the partition of Palestine and refused to set up the projected Arab state, the British administration, then still governing Palestine under the Mandate, refused to carry out the recommendations of the United Nations to implement the partition plan. The British government made it plain that

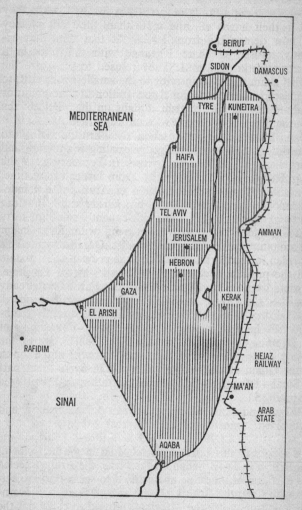

MAP NO. 5:   Proposal of the World Zionist Organization
to the Paris Peace Conference (1919)

it would do all in its power to prevent the birth of the Jewish state. Britain announced that she would not—and indeed, she did not—carry out the orderly transfer of any functions to the Jewish authorities in the interim before the end of the Mandate on May 15, 1948. Everything was left in a state of disorder. This was Britain's first contribution to the burden of the nascent state.

When, immediately after the United Nations Assembly decision, the Palestinian Arabs launched their preliminary onslaught on the Jewish community, the British Army gave them considerable cover and aid. It obstructed Jewish defense on the ground; it blocked the movement of Jewish reinforcements and supplies to outlying settlements; it opened the land frontiers for the entry of Arab soldiers from the neighboring Arab states; it maintained a blockade in the Mediterranean and sealed the coast and ports through which alone the outnumbered Jews could expect reinforcements; it handed over arms dumps to the Arabs. When Jaffa was on the point of falling to a Jewish counterattack, it sent in forces from Malta to bomb and shell the Jewish force. Meanwhile it continued to supply the Arab states preparing to invade across the borders with all the arms they asked for and made no secret of it.

The British government was privy to the Arab plans for invasion;[1] and on every diplomatic front, and especially in the United Nations and in the United States, it pursued a vigorous campaign of pressure and obstruction to hinder and prevent help to the embattled Zionists and to achieve the abandonment of the plan to set up a Jewish state. When the state was declared nevertheless, the British government exerted every effort to bring about its defeat by the invading Arab armies. It was not by chance that one of the last operations in the war between Israel and the Arab states in January 1949 was the shooting down on the Sinai front of five British RAF planes which had flown across the battle lines into Israeli-held territory. This was the culmination of a policy developed and pursued by the British throughout their administration of the Mandate

---

[1] See Elie Kedourie, *The Chatham House Version and Other Middle Eastern Studies* (London, 1970), pp. 231–233.

—surely not the least of the great betrayals of the weak by the strong in the twentieth century. The policy of Foreign Minister Ernest Bevin, who was severely criticized, was no more than the logical, if extreme, evolution of the policies of Anthony Eden, who inspired the creation of the Arab League in 1945; of Malcolm MacDonald, the colonial secretary who presided over the declaration of death to Zionism in the White Paper of 1939, and of their predecessors who shaped the "Arab Revolt" of 1936, who made possible the "disturbances" of 1929, and who were responsible for the pogrom in Jerusalem in 1920.

It is impossible and, indeed, pointless and misleading to explain, analyze, or trace the development of Arab hostility to Zionism and the origins of Arab claims in Palestine without examining the policy of the British rulers of the country between 1919 and 1948.

One of the great objects of British diplomacy as the conflict in Palestine deepened during the Mandate period was to create the image of Britain as an honest arbiter striving only for the best for all concerned and for justice. In fact, Britain was an active participant in the confrontation. She was indeed more than a party. The Arab "case" in Palestine was a British conception. It took shape and was given direction by the British Military Administration after the First World War. The release in recent years of even a part of the confidential official documents of the time has strengthened the long-held suspicion that the Arab attack on Zionism would never have begun had it not been for British inspiration, tutelage, and guidance.

In the end, it is true, British sympathy, assistance, and cooperation came to be auxiliary to Arab attitudes and actions. Those attitudes, however, had their beginnings and their original motive power as a function of British imperial ambitions and policy. The two intertwined progressively throughout thirty years, until their open cooperation after 1939. At the last, in 1947-1949, they consummated an imperfectly concealed alliance for the forcible prevention of the establishment of the Jewish state.

British policy in the Middle East was not confined to

Palestine. Its purpose, though now a defeated anachronism, informs British attitudes even today. It had its genesis in a historic misrepresentation: the inflation, out of all relation to the reality, of the so-called Arab Revolt during the First World War. This hoax was part of the intricate maneuvers of the great powers at the end of that war. It was at first directed against France.

Early in the First World War, after the defeat at Gallipoli, a group of senior British officials serving in the countries on the fringe of the Ottoman Empire—in Egypt and the Sudan—conceived the idea of bringing the vast Arab-speaking areas of the Ottoman Empire under British control after the war. In the words of the then Governor General of the Sudan, Sir Reginald Wingate, they envisaged "a federation of semi-independent Arab States under European guidance and supervision ... owing spiritual allegiance to a single Arab primate, and looking to Great Britain as its patron and protector."[2]

The early disaster to British arms in the Gallipoli Campaign in 1915 provided the impulse. The British government called on its agents with contacts in the Arab-speaking countries to make an effort to detach the Arabs from the Turks. The men on the spot in Cairo and Khartoum decided that Hussein ibn-Ali, Sherif of Mecca, Guardian of the Moslem Holy Places, a semi-autonomous chieftain in Hejaz (Arabia proper), was the suitable candidate for levering all the Arabs out of the Turkish war machine. While London was interested in immediate military relief, the Arabists in Cairo and Khartoum contrived to steer and manipulate the relations with Hussein toward their own more grandiose schemes. Hussein asked a high price for his participation in liberating his people from Turkish rule, even at one stage threatening to fight on the side of the Turks. He demanded all the territory in Asia that had ever been in the Moslem Empire. He was of course employing the accepted Oriental

---

[2] In a letter to Lord Hardinge, August 26, 1915. Wingate Papers, School of Oriental Studies, Durham University; quoted by Kedourie, p. 17.

gambit in a bout of bargaining: he asked for much more than he expected to get. Moreover the negotiators were warned from London that the British government had made other commitments in the area, concerning Palestine, Lebanon, and the Mosul area in Mesopotamia (Iraq). In return for the promise of liberation in his own territory and the gift of part of the other Arabic-speaking areas, together with vast sums of money (in gold) and considerable quantities of arms, Hussein launched his revolt, led in the field by his son Faisal.

Toward the end of the First World War, and increasingly after the war, it became common knowledge and part of the popular literature of the age that in the defeat of the Turks a specific and notable part was played by the Arab revolt and that its leaders had enjoyed the indispensable cooperation and advice of a brilliant young British officer named Thomas Edward Lawrence. This revolt, according to the account, began in Arabia, displacing the Turks, spread over into Syria, and reached a climax in the capture of Damascus. In the end, so the story ran, the promises to the Arabs were broken. The Arabs based their later vociferous propaganda—and their claim to vast additions of territory, including Palestine—on this account.

The major part of this story of the revolt was a fabrication, largely created in Lawrence's imagination. It grew and grew and was not exposed for many years. It suited the makers of British policy at the time so well that Lawrence, who was a yarn-spinner of quite extraordinary proportions[3] was able to impose himself, and to be imposed, on the British public, and on the world, as one of the great heroes and as one of the most brilliant brains of the First World War. Lawrence's monumental book on the subject, *The Seven Pillars of Wisdom* (of which *Revolt in the Desert* was an abridged popular edition), was published and publicized and widely accepted as authentic history. In fact, it was largely a work of fiction. On the basis of this fiction, however, the British government was

---

[3] "The truth about Lawrence—the phrase is almost a contradiction in terms," notes the British pro-Arab writer, Christopher Sykes. Introduction, in Richard Aldington, *Lawrence of Arabia*, 2nd ed. (London, 1969).

able to initiate and pursue its predominant policy in the Middle East and fight for it in the international arena. Directed at first primarily against France, much of its momentum and later fury was concentrated against the Jewish restoration in Palestine. It was the Lawrence fiction that for many years provided the main propaganda ammunition for the Arabs.

The Lawrence legend was finally demolished in 1955 in a remarkable "biographical enquiry" by the British writer Richard Aldington. His findings on the political and military facts were based on an exhaustive study of all the available sources, especially Lawrence's own copious writings and those he inspired and encouraged. They have been amplified and deepened by the research since made possible by the release of secret British documents of the period. It has consequently become fashionable in Britain today to write with contempt and denigration of Lawrence and to speculate in psychoanalytical overtones on the reasons for his aberrations.

Though the myth has been exploded, the exposure has not yet brought any recognition of the implications, historical and political, of the myth as a central pillar of British policy. The admission in Britain of the Lawrence myth is a confession of the tricking of the French after the First World War and of the falsehoods and fabrications employed to promote the betrayal of the British trust in Palestine and of Britain's undertakings to the Jewish people. That betrayal had far-reaching consequences in fostering and reinforcing the pan-Arab attack on the Jewish restoration, with all the resultant suffering and bloodshed that continue to this day.

The aid given to the Allied campaign against the Turks by the Arab Revolt was minor and negligible; Lawrence himself, in one of his outbursts of near-penitence, once described it as "a sideshow of a sideshow." Though the Sherif Hussein did send out his call for an Arab rising throughout the Ottoman Empire, in fact no such rising took place. Nor was there a mutiny by Arabs anywhere in the Turkish Army; on the contrary, the Arabs fought enthusiastically in the cause of their Turkish overlords.

The operations of the "Arab Army" can be summed up in Aldington's words: "To claim that these spasmodic and comparatively trifling efforts had any serious bearing on the war with Turkey, let alone on the greater war beyond is . . . absurd"(p. 209).

Aldington further explains that the revolt was limited to the distant Hejaz, an area that was relatively unimportant to the Turks, and to "desert areas close to the British army, from which small raids could be made with comparative immunity. Beyond those areas, where there was real danger to be found and real damage to be done, the Arabs did nothing but talk and conspire" (p. 210). The operations in the Hejaz itself were not conclusive. A few weakly held Turkish positions were taken, but the Turks were not driven out; they held out in Medina for two years. In consequence, "much of the effort of the Arab forces—say 20,000 to 25,000 tribesmen plus the little regular army of 600 . . . was diverted to hanging around on the outskirts of Medina and to attacks on that part of the Damascus-Medina railway which was of least importance strategically" (p. 177).

These demolition raids on the Hejaz Railway became the most famous operation of the Arab Revolt. Their avowed object was to eliminate the Turkish supply line to Medina, but in fact they did nothing of the sort. Any damage they caused was quickly repaired; its extent was no greater than the damage inflicted on the same railway by the same Bedouin tribesmen in peacetime as part of their customary marauding activities. When General Allenby decided really to put the railway out of commission, he sent British General Dawnay, with a British force, for the purpose; Dawnay demolished it beyond repair.

During the final phase of the war the British conquered southern Palestine. The prospect of victory over the Turks appeared over the horizon. Soon there would be an accounting of what had and what had not been achieved, and by whom. Now therefore came the last fantastic phase of the "Revolt."

Allenby's great breakthrough in September 1918 provided [the Arabs] with sitting targets which nobody could miss, and the chance to race hysterically into towns which they claimed to have captured after the British had done the real fighting. [Aldington, p. 178]

There was calculated purpose in this behavior. It was part of an agreement between the makers of British policy and their Arab collaborators. The Arab Revolt had obviously failed as a major or even a significant enterprise. Outside of Husein's own area of Arabia, it had not attracted any significant assistance from Arabs. In spite of efforts at persuasion by Faisal and Lawrence, the tribes of Syria had refused to join the war effort. No Arab had risen even in the rear of the advancing British troops in southern Palestine. The Hejaz regular force was numerically insignificant, and the Bedouin tribesmen, traditionally well versed in the primitive techniques of looting forays, could contribute nothing to Allenby's offensive through Palestine and Syria. The discussion on the future of the area thus threatened to remain a dialogue between Britain and France, who had reached agreement earlier on the division of the spoils.

Herein lay the British dilemma. French control of part of the area, to which London had previously agreed, ruled out the later plan by Cairo and Khartoum for British control of the whole area. Thus the objective of British policy now became to find a way to "biff the French out of all hope of Syria" (in Lawrence's words) or, in the blunter terms used—disapprovingly—in the British Cabinet by Lord Milner, "to diddle the French out of Syria."[4] This could only be done, if at all, by establishing a plausible Arab claim.

In June 1918 an ingenious solution was accepted by the British government. Osmond Walrond, an intelligence officer attached to the Arab Bureau in Cairo, read out to "seven Syrians" living in that city a statement in which the British government officially pledged itself to recognize in the areas not yet conquered the "complete and sovereign

---

[4] *Letters of T. E. Lawrence* (London, 1938), p. 196; Milner cited in David Lloyd George, *The Truth about the Peace Treaties* (London, 1936), p. 1047.

independence of any Arab area emancipated from Turkish control *by the action of the Arabs themselves.*"[5]

On this principle Lawrence and the Sherifians now hastened to operate in order to establish the "facts" they required. As an Arab historian has summed it up: "Wherever the British Army captured a town or reduced a fortress which was to be given to the Arabs it would halt until the Arabs could enter, and the capture would be credited to them."[6] Hence the wild chase that followed to raise the Arab flag in towns from which the Turks had already been driven by the British. Dera'a and Aleppo were two such easy conquests. At Damascus there was a serious difficulty, and the maneuver did not succeed.

The capture of Damascus, the ancient seventh-century capital of the Arab Umayyad dynasty, was to have been the climax of the revolt, installing Faisal as the indigenous king of Syria before the French could object. General Allenby, the British Commander-in-Chief, ordered the officers in command of the combined British, Australian, and French forces advancing on Damascus not to enter the city. It was assumed that the retreat of the Turks could be completely cut off north of the city. Only the Sherifian troops were to be allowed to pass into the city, to announce its capture and set up an administration. All this was worked out in advance between the British War Office, Allenby, and Lawrence. Because Faisal's 600 soldiers were not adequate for the required pomp of his entry, one of his Syrian supporters was sent to recruit Druze and Houranians to march in with what was now called the Northern Arab Army (it was, in fact, the southern contingent gone north).

Two unforeseen circumstances upset the plan. The Australian Commander, Brigadier Wilson, finding that he could not cut off the Turks' retreat without entering the

---

[5] This document was never published officially but was presumably to be held "available" in case of French reactions. It is quoted by George Antonius, *The Arab Awakening* (London, 1938), p. 271. (Italics added)

[6] Muhammed Kurd Ali, *Khitab el Sham* (Damascus, 1925) Vol. III, p. 154, quoted in E. Kedourie, *England and the Middle East* (London, 1956), p. 21.

city, therefore went in, and so it was to the Australians that Damascus was in fact surrendered.[7] Later a British force under Col. Bourchier also went in to quell a rising against the British and against the planned installation of Faisal. It was put down only by the application of considerable force.

Nevertheless, a Sherifian administration was installed, and the fiction was then promoted that the Arabs had captured Damascus.

From this scramble to claim territory by "right of conquest" Palestine was excluded. No such effort was made by the Sherifian forces on either side of the Jordan. Coming as it did a year after the publication of the Balfour Declaration on the Jewish National Home in Palestine, this restriction underlines the fact that the Arab leaders felt no urge to oppose or obstruct the establishment of a Jewish National Home in Palestine.

In Syria the clash between French claims, accepted by the British in the Sykes-Picot Agreement of 1915, and Arab claims, conceived and fostered by the British after 1916, was not finally resolved until 1945. In Palestine the French effectively gave up their claims as early as 1918.

The Sykes-Picot Agreement, providing for an international administration in Palestine (see Map No. 6), was the original reason for the exclusion of Palestine from the promises made to Hussein. But in 1917 the British government published the Balfour Declaration for the establishment of the Jewish National Home in Palestine. To achieve this promise of support in the restoration of their ancient homeland, issued after much negotiation and deep consideration, the Jews made a significant contribution to the British war effort. Whatever fantastic interpretations were later put on it, the British intention was clear and was understood clearly at the time. A Jewish state was to be established, not at once, but as soon as the Jewish

---

[7] See Kedourie, *Chatham House Version*, p. 51; Muhammad Kurd Ali, quoted in *Chatham House Version*, p. 40; W. T. Massey, *Allenby's Final Triumph* (London, 1920), p. 230.

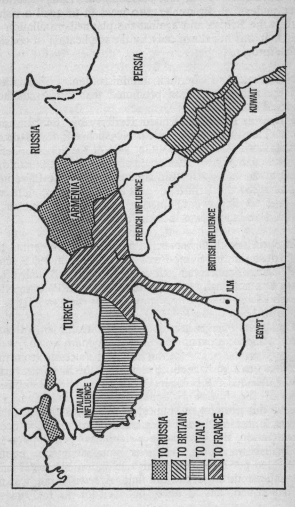

MAP No. 6: Territories delineated by the Sykes-Picot Agreement (1915)

people by immigration and development became a majority in the still largely derelict and nearly empty country with its then half-million Arabs and 90,000 Jews.

This plan would require the tutelage of a major power. The mandate system of the then infant League of Nations seemed to apply perfectly to the situation. British overall control could be achieved by granting a mandate to Britain. With a group of Arab states in Arabia, Syria, and Mesopotamia—"semi-independent," with British mentors and advisers in Jedda, Damascus, and Baghdad (not to mention the British-controlled administration in Cairo and Khartoum)—and with, now, a British Mandatory Administration in Palestine, Britain would have unhampered control of the whole Middle East, from the Mediterranean clear to the borders of India. Zionist diplomacy was now exploited by the British to achieve the consent of France to, in effect, her own elimination from any direct influence in Palestine. This was not an easy matter, especially in view of obvious British efforts to "biff" her out of Syria as well. The French, however, were also sensitive during the war to American opinion and had already acquiesced in the Balfour Declaration. In order to insure the establishment of the Jewish National Home, the French agreed, in the end (and not without some mining and sapping), to waive their claims in Palestine by acceding to the grant of the mandate over Palestine to Britain. Considerable pressure had to be exerted on France over the question of the borders: in the north she did hold out successfully for the inclusion in "her" zone of the area enclosing the main water sources of Palestine (which remained largely unexploited). Northwestern Galilee was included in Lebanon, and Mount Hermon and the Golan Heights in Syria.

The claim to eastern Palestine—Transjordan—on the other hand was, after a struggle, relinquished by France. Characteristic of the argument brought to bear by the British to persuade her was a leading article in the London *Times,* in those days an authentic spokesman for the British government. The paper called for the inclusion of Eastern Palestine as essential to the Jewish state and urged a "good military frontier" for Palestine to the east of the river Jordan "as near as may be to the edge of the desert."

The Jordan, noted the *Times* on September 19, 1919, "will not do as Palestine's eastern boundary. Our duty as Mandatory is to make Jewish Palestine not a struggling State but one that is capable of a vigorous and independent national life." France consented; eastern Palestine remained part of the area designed for the Jewish National Home and thus passed into British control.

A dovetailed Middle East, with Arab client states and a Jewish client state coexisting and cooperating under a completely British umbrella, provided the motive power of official British policy in the period 1917-1920. On December 2, 1917, Lord Robert Cecil had said at a large public meeting in London, "The keynote of our meeting this afternoon is liberation. Our wish is that the Arabian countries shall be for the Arabs, Armenia for the Armenians and Judea for the Jews."[8]

The Zionists, moreover, helped the Arabs and the British in the great diplomatic campaign that went on around the Paris Peace Conference and used their influence in Washington to urge the Arab claims. The Emir Faisal was not overstating when he wrote on March 3, 1919, to Felix Frankfurter; "Dr. Weizmann has been a great helper of our cause, and I hope the Arabs may soon be in a position to make the Jews some return for their kindness."

France, pressing her claim to Syria and Lebanon, was granted control over them by the Peace Conference. In defiance of this decision, a so-called General Syrian Congress offered the throne of Syria to Faisal; he was subsequently installed in Damascus, where he set up an administration. The Supreme Allied Council in Paris retorted by formally granting the mandate over Syria and Lebanon to France. This duality could not last. In July 1920 the French ordered Faisal out of the country.

Faisal, bereft of the Syrian crown, for which Lawrence and the Arab Bureau had labored so hard, was instead offered the throne of Iraq by the British, though it had

---

[8] There was indeed close diplomatic cooperation between Armenians and Zionists, especially between Weizmann and Aaron Aaronson on the Zionist side and the Armenians Nubar Pasha and James Malcolm. The efforts failed—the Armenians did not gain their independence.

previously been earmarked for Faisal's younger brother Abdullah ibn-Hussein, who was thus left without a throne.

At the end of October 1920 Abdullah therefore collected some 1,500 Turkish ex-soldiers and Hejaz tribesmen, seized a train on the Hejaz Railway, and entered eastern Palestine. Here he announced that he was on his way to drive the French out of Syria and called on the Syrians to join him. There was no response, nor was Abdullah given any encouragement by the handful of inhabitants of Transjordan itself.

His continued encampment in eastern Palestine created a dilemma for the British. They had not yet set up any administrative machinery in what was largely empty territory—its 90,000 square kilometers were estimated to hold at most 300,000 inhabitants, most of them nomads. The British feared, or were induced to fear, that the French, angered by Abdullah's threats, would invade eastern Palestine. They therefore casually suggested to Abdullah that he forget about Syria and instead become a representative of Britain in administering eastern Palestine on behalf of the mandatory authority. Whereupon Abdullah generously resigned himself to the French presence in Syria and took up office in Transjordan, and in time accepted it as a substitute.

The British government then recalled that eastern Palestine was part of the area pledged to the Jewish people. They thereupon inserted an alteration in the draft text of the mandate (then not yet ratified by the League of Nations) which gave Britain the right to "postpone or withhold" the provisions of the mandate relating to the Jewish National Home "in the territories lying between the Jordan and the eastern boundary of Palestine as ultimately determined." The Zionist leaders were stunned by this threatened lopping off of three-quarters of the area of the projected Jewish National Home; its establishment had, after all, been Britain's warrant for being granted the mandate. But the British government countered with the proposal that, if the Zionists did not accept the situation, Britain would decline the mandate altogether and thus withdraw her protection from the Jewish restoration. The Zionist leaders—struggling with the material problem of building a country out of a desert and restoring a people, largely impoverished, from the four corners of the world—were moreover inadequately equipped with political experience to judge the emptiness of the British threat. They did not feel strong enough to resist this blow to the integrity and security of the state-in-building and to their faith in the sanctity of compacts.[9]

Thus, as a purely British manufacture, filched from the Jewish National Home, torn out of Palestine of which it had always been an integral part, there was brought into being from the empty waste what subsequently became a spearhead in the "Arab" onslaught on the Jewish state—the Emirate of Transjordan, later expanded across the river and renamed the Hashemite Kingdom of Jordan (see Map No. 7).

The elimination of eastern Palestine in 1921-1923 was only the first act—though stark, dramatic, and momentous—in a developing effort by the British to frustrate and emasculate the Jewish restoration which began in Palestine immediately after the British occupation. At first British policy was confined to the military administration in Palestine itself.

In colonial politics nothing seems to succeed like repeated error and miscalculation and failure. The Cairo-Khartoum school of British officials in 1916 had grossly overestimated the influence of the Sherif Husein of Hejaz on the Arabs outside his own area. His "revolt" proved a damp squib and had to be retrieved and embellished by a large fraud. But these officials did not give up their dream of a large Arab state or federation of states, extending from the Persian Gulf to the Mediterranean and from the borders of Turkey to the southern seaboard of Arabia and supervised by Britain. It was the men of this school who continued from Cairo to direct overall British policy for the occupied territory and who came into Palestine with Allenby, or in the wake of his victory in 1918, to form the

---

[9] The claim to eastern Palestine was unanimously reiterated by the Zionist Congress in 1923 and remained part of the program of the Revisionist Party under Vladimir (Zeev) Jabotinsky and of the Socialist Achdut Avodah Party.

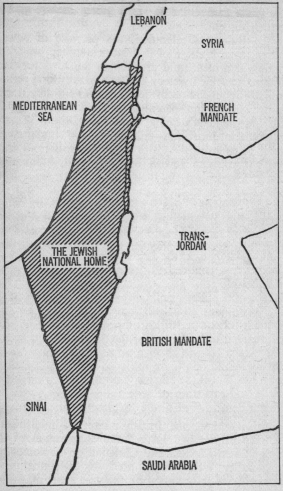

MAP No. 7:  The First Partition: Eastern Palestine
(Transjordan) excluded from the Jewish National Home
(1923–1946)

Military Administration in Palestine. They were stricken to the heart by their government's deviation from what they had conceived as the correct policy to be followed in the Fertile Crescent.

But the Balfour Declaration, the promise of Jewish restoration, even if shorn of its historical sweep, was seen by London as a clear quid pro quo to the Jews for their contribution to Allied victory and as a great moral reason for France's renunciation of her claim. The policy it embodied became the indispensable (or unavoidable) condition for the mandate's being granted to Britain. To the ruling group in Jerusalem—almost wholly composed of leaders or disciples of the Cairo school—the Balfour Declaration guaranteeing Jewish restoration represented an intolerable interference in their plans. They set out to undermine it. Just as they continued trying to "biff the French out of Syria," they applied themselves to biffing the Zionists out of Palestine. While their government was still canvassing international support to grant Britain the mandate in order to implement the Zionist policy, and while the Zionists were urging Britain's claims, the first British administration in Palestine was busily engaged in open defiance of its government's declared policy.

It was this group, all-powerful on the spot, that inspired and mobilized and established organized Arab resistance to the Jewish restoration. It used its power and authority as a military regime to establish facts, to create events, and to control them. It was this group whose views progressively pervaded the subsequent mandate regime.

That is the background of the sudden appearance in 1919 of a militant Arab "movement." In the circumstances of the time, the British military administration should have invited and insured the cooperation of the local population, Moslem and Christian, in implementing London's policy. What was required was dissemination of clear and concise information on the vast areas of Arabia and Mesopotamia that had been liberated by the British and their Allies and were to become Arab or predominantly Arab states; on the contribution made by the Jews to the liberation of Palestine, their ancient and unrelinquished homeland; and on the undertaking made to them in the Balfour Declaration and the safeguards in that declaration for the civil and religious rights of the non-Jewish communities in Palestine. It might have been made clear that the Sherif Hussein had called on the Moslems to welcome the Jews to Palestine: information should have been spread about the cordial meetings between Faisal and Dr. Chaim Weizmann and the agreement they had signed; and last but not least, the determination of the British government to carry out its Zionist policy should have been confirmed. Such a declaration would without a doubt have created the right climate for launching that policy. "The Military Administration ruled the country which waited on its very nod," wrote a contemporary observer. "It would consequently have required the maximum of moral courage, enmity or external support, deliberately to go in the teeth of the policy of the Administration—above all in the Levant where the whole population is so singularly sensitive to every nuance of tyranny and of intrigue."[10]

The popularization of the Jewish National Home policy was, however, furthest from the minds of the Military Administration. For more than two years it neither published nor allowed the publication of the Balfour Declaration in Palestine. This act of omission was backed by a specific prohibition from headquarters in Cairo. The Declaration, wrote the Chief Political Officer to the Chief Administrator in Jerusalem on October 9, 1919, "is to be treated as extremely confidential and is on no account for any publication."[11]

The group in power in Jerusalem made no secret of its hostility to Zionism. The whole of its administration, even down to its social occasions, was permeated with an anti-Jewish atmosphere which reminded some Jewish observers of the tsarist regime in Russia. Indeed Zeev Jabotinsky, then serving as a lieutenant in the Jewish Legion which he

---

[10] Horace B. Samuel, *Unholy Memories of the Holy Land* (London, 1930), p. 51.

[11] Pal. Govt. File Pol/2108, in Israel State Archives. Quoted in Kedourie, *Chatham House Version*, p. 57.

had founded, and himself a native of Russia, wrote "Not in Russia nor in Poland had there been seen such an intense and widespread atmosphere of hatred as prevailed in the British Army in Palestine in 1919 and 1920."[12]

Nor did the administration wait on events. They worked hard, simultaneously on two fronts, the second being in Syria, against the French. In July 1919 a "Syrian National Congress" demanded the unity of Syria (that is, to include Palestine) and the installation of Faisal as king. The French expressed a fear that this sudden materialization from nowhere of a Syrian national movement and the reversal of the popular feeling against the Sherifians was the result of a British intrigue. The British replied with denials and reassuring statements. In fact, Allenby in Cairo and his subordinates in Palestine, G.O.C. General Bols and his Chief of Staff Col. Waters Taylor, were secretly pressing their home government to "accept the situation": to jettison their government's pact with the French, to abandon the Zionists, and to give Syria and Palestine to Faisal.

The plan, however, could not be pursued as a bald British purpose. In the face of London's official Zionist policy, it had to be covered by an Arab cloak, and quickly. The military administration began itself creating an Arab organization which could then be presented as the authentic voice and representative of "the Arabs" in rejecting and combating the Zionists and the Zionist policy of the British government. Here began the history of the first Arab political organization, the Moslem Christian Association (MCA). Its first branch, in Jaffa, was organized at the inspiration of the District Military Governor Lt. Col. J. E. Hubbard—who had formally proposed to his superiors in the administration the setting up of an Arab organization—and under the personal direction of the district

---

[12] *The Story of the Jewish Legion* (New York, 1945), p. 171. Jabotinsky's book contains (pp. 168–77) a description of the policy and motives of the military administration in 1919 and 1920. More detail still is in Richard Meinertzhagen: *Middle East Diary 1917–1956* (London, 1959). Horace B. Samuel, *Unholy Memories of the Holy Land*. See also Chaim Weizmann, *Trial and Error*, (London, 1949).

head of British intelligence, Captain Brunton. Not insignifi-
cantly, the most active and disproportionately numerous
early recruits were Christian Arabs. Years later a leading
member of the Military Administration, Sir Wyndham
Deedes, admitted that from its inception the Moslem
Christian Association had enjoyed the support and financial aid of the British administration.[13]

The purposes of the administration were now pursued
by a stream of memoranda of protest and demands by the
several branches of the MCA, dutifully forwarded to London with accompanying evaluations of their originality,
spontaneity, sincerity, and the representative character of
their signatories.

Memoranda, however, were not enough to generate
quick action; a "situation" had to be created. Col. Waters-
Taylor maintained contact with Faisal in Damascus, urging upon him action to assume power in Syria from the
French. He assured him that the Arabs of Palestine were
behind him and would welcome him as king of a "united
Syria"—that is, including Palestine. He urged him, moreover, "to stand up against the British Government for his
principles." Early in 1920 this general effort at persuasion
gave way to more specific inducement; money and arms
were provided for the planned coup.[14]

In Jerusalem, Waters-Taylor and Col. Ronald Storrs,
one of the original members of the Cairo school and now
governor of the city, established and maintained regular
contact with the handful of militant Sherifians, notably
Haj Amin el Husseini, the young brother of the Mufti of
Jerusalem, and Aref el Aref. In early 1920 Waters-Taylor
suggested to his and Storrs' Arab contacts the desirability
of organizing "anti-Jewish riots to impress on the Administration the unpopularity of the Zionist policy." A detailed critical report of all these activities was submitted to
General Allenby by the political officer of the Palestine

---

[13] J. E. Hubbard to Occupied Enemy Territory Administration,
November 20, 1918. Israel State Archives, Pal. Govt. Secretariat
File No. 40. Quoted in Y. Porat, *Tsemihat Hatenua Ha'aravit
Hapalestinait, 1918–1929* (Tel Aviv, 1971), p. 24.
[14] Samuel, *Unholy Memories.* p. 9.

Administration, Col. Richard Meinertzhagen. Allenby told him he would take no action.[15]

The spring of 1920 was chosen for action. In March the coup was carried out in Damascus and Faisal was installed as king. In order to achieve a sizable riot in Palestine, the country (in the words of the subsequent military Court of Enquiry) was "infested with Sherifian officers"[16] who carried on a lurid agitation against the Jews. As the court noted euphemistically, the administration took no action against them.

On the Wednesday before Easter, Col. Waters-Taylor had a meeting in Jerusalem with Haj Amin el Husseini and told him "that he had a great opportunity at Easter to show the world that the Arabs of Palestine would not tolerate Jewish domination in Palestine; that Zionism was unpopular not only with the Palestine Administration but in Whitehall; and if disturbances of sufficient violence occurred in Jerusalem at Easter, both General Bols and General Allenby would advocate the abandonment of the Jewish Home" (Meinertzhagen, pp. 81–82).

That year Easter coincided with the Moslem festival of Nebi Musa. Its celebration included a procession starting in Jerusalem, where the crowd was addressed by the Sherifians and told to fall on the Jews "in the name of King Faisal." For doubters there was an even more convincing argument: *A'dowlah ma'ana*—the government is with us. This was a demonstrable fact; all but a remnant of the Jewish regiments that had helped liberate Palestine had been disbanded over the preceding months; the few remaining soldiers were confined to camp at Sarafand. On the day of the outbreak, all British troops and Jewish police had been removed from the Old City; only Arab policemen were left.

The mob in the Old City, armed with clubs and knives, first looted shops. Then it caught and beat up or killed Jews and raped Jewish women. The Court of Enquiry— itself a creation of the administration—summed up: "The

---

[15] Meinertzhagen, *Middle East Diary 1917–1956* (London, 1959), pp. 55–56.

[16] Report of Court of Enquiry, FO 371/5121, p. 38.

Jews were the victims of a peculiarly brutal and cowardly attack, the majority of the casualties being old men, women and children" (p. 76).

Zeev Jabotinsky and Pinchas Rutenberg had in the preceding days hastily organized a Jewish self-defense unit. Their way into the Old City was barred at the gates by British troops.

In the first flush of enthusiasm a British military court compounded the offense in traditional fashion: the defenders were punished. Jabotinsky was sentenced to fifteen years' imprisonment and twenty of his followers were given lesser terms. But Haj Amin and el Aref had operated too openly for any government publicly to ignore their guilt. Though they escaped across the Jordan, they were sentenced *in absentia* to ten years' imprisonment each.

The British government, however much whitewash it was willing to splash over the events in Jerusalem, had to react to the outcry that went up in Europe and the United States at the phenomenon of a pogrom in Jerusalem. Nor could it ignore the factual inside information it received. Meinertzhagen, as a representative of the Foreign Office, sent a new, detailed report derived from an independent intelligence unit he had established. This time he bypassed Allenby and wrote directly to the Foreign Office.

As a result, the sentence on Jabotinsky was quashed, the most obvious conspirators, including Bols and Waters-Taylor, were removed; the military regime was replaced by a civil administration. Storrs, more subtle than his colleagues, remained, and he was not alone.[17] The Arabist purpose of the Cairo school did not change, but was carried over into the civil administration of Palestine and pervaded and finally dominated the mandatory regime.

It did not succeed in creating an Arab "nation" in Palestine. In 1918, at the height of his campaign to register Arab achievements, Colonel Lawrence himself had cautiously confessed in one of his confidential reports:

---

[17] Henrietta Szold, the American Zionist leader, described Storrs as "an evil genius, who despises Jews." Marvin Lowenthal, *Henrietta Szold* (New York, 1942), pp. 186–187.

"The phrase Arab Movement was invented in Cairo as a common denominator for all the vague discontents against Turkey which before 1916 existed in the Arab provinces. In a non-constitutional country, these naturally took on a revolutionary character and it was convenient to pretend to find a common ground in all of them. They were most of them very local, very jealous, but had to be considered in the hope that one or the other of them might bear fruit."[18]

In 1919 and 1920, despite the historic transformation that had taken place around them, the Arabs had not changed. When in July 1920 the French in Syria decided on a firm stand and ordered Faisal to leave the country, he meekly complied. The popular forces which his British sponsors attributed to him did not show themselves. In Jerusalem that Easter even the Arab mob in the market-place, before they attacked Jews, had to be fired by religious incitement, by the invocation of a living king, by the visible evidence that their victims were defenseless, and by the assurance that their violence would be welcomed by the British rulers.

The political officer to the administration went even further: "Arab national feeling," he wrote, "is based on our gold and nothing else" (Meinertzhagen, p. 83).

In the early years of the civil administration there was still a running policy conflict between the British statesmen who had been responsible for, or associated with, the negotiations with the Zionists and the undertakings made to them and the purveyors of Laurentian pan-Arabism. The Laurentians, however, contrived to fill key posts in the Palestinian administration, and some of them were inevitably recruited to fill the posts in the Middle Eastern Department of the Colonial Office, which in 1921 took over responsibility for Palestine.

The Cairo-Khartoum school, moreover, found an unexpected ally in the first chief of the civil administration, Sir Herbert Samuel. Samuel, precisely because he was a Jew,

---

[18] T. E. Lawrence, *Secret Despatches from Arabia* (London, 1939), p. 158.

soon found himself in the position of either following the advice of his subordinates or being considered insufficiently British. In striking contrast to his English soldier-successor, Lord Plumer, who adhered as best he could to the status quo and to the brief he had from Whitehall, Samuel allowed his administration to develop naturally the anti-Zionist themes of the military administration it had replaced. An anti-Zionist official named Ernest T. Richmond, in government employ as an architect, was maneuvered by Storrs (as is now made clear by the British Government archives) into the post of assistant secretary (political), whose duties were formally those of chief adviser to the High Commissioner on Moslem affairs.[19]

Richmond, receiving a salary to carry out the London government's official policy, openly spent his time in the administration on efforts to undermine it. He gave advice to the Arab agitator-leaders. He became their intermediary and self-appointed spokesman. It was at the initiative and under the tutelage of Richmond, Storrs, and their colleagues, and under their inspiration, that the Sherifian instigators of the pogrom of 1920 were now brought back into the arena to build up a political machine, so that they could claim to speak for the "Arabs of Palestine."

Haj Amin el Husseini was hiding across the Jordan to avoid serving his jail sentence. Since no other candidate for this kind of leadership had appeared among the Arabs, Samuel was persuaded by Storrs to pardon Haj Amin —and his colleague Aref el Aref—as a "gesture"; and they returned to Jerusalem. When the incumbent Mufti of Jerusalem died soon afterward, the Moslem religious leaders convened as an electoral college to recommend a short list of three candidates from whom the High Commissioner would have to make the appointment. Haj Amin entered the contest. He had no special qualification to be the head of the Moslem community in the city. He was twenty-five years old and his education must have been over well before he was twenty-one, since he had served in the Turkish Army certainly before 1917. In the poll he re-

[19] FO 371/5267 file E 9433/8343/44; FO 371/5268 files E 11720/8343/44, 11835/8343/44.

ceived the lowest number of votes and thus could not be included in the recommended list of three.

Richmond launched an energetic campaign to get Samuel to appoint him nevertheless. He urged upon him the "expert" view that the poll was unimportant, that Haj Amin was the man the "Moslem population" insisted on. A virulent agitation was let loose within the Moslem community against the successful candidate, Sheikh Jurallah, who was described, among other things, as a Zionist who intended to sell Moslem holy property to the Jews. Samuel gave way. He did not in fact send Haj Amin the letter of appointment and it was never gazetted. Haj Amin simply "became" the Mufti of Jerusalem. Thus this man, imposed on the Moslem community, became and remained for most of the crucial years of the Mandate the director and spearhead of the war on Zionism. The Moslem dignitaries, whom even the backward Turks had not accustomed to such outrageous interference or dictation, nevertheless took the hint. They knew now beyond any doubt what the British power expected of them.

When he started on his career, however, Haj Amin's followers were few, and he had no sources of finance for the political task projected for him. This too had been thought of. The administration then set up a body called the Supreme Moslem Council. Haj Amin, now clothed with the authority of mufti and authentic favorite of the British, was elected its president without difficulty. His position was entrenched: the appointment was for life, so that no opposition could ever unseat him democratically. He and his pliant subordinates became the arbiters of all Moslem religious endowments and expenditure. Many Moslems became dependent on him for their livelihood. He controlled an annual income of more than £100,000, for which he was not accountable. (By today's values this would be equivalent in purchasing power to about $2 million.) Such was the origin of the organized "national movement" of the "Arabs of Palestine."

The means of organizing propaganda and violence against Zionism and the pattern of its organization were thus assured. A short localized attack took place in 1921 and simultaneous onslaught in several areas in 1929. This latter attack was again distinguished by the choice of helpless, defenseless people as its target—in Hebron the bulk of the community of rabbis and yeshiva students and their wives and children were slaughtered—and by the blatantly benevolent neutrality of the British forces of law and order, one of whose first acts was to disarm the Jewish villages. In 1936 came the last and most protracted offensive, officially organized by an informal political body called the Arab Higher Committee; it was led by Haj Amin el Husseini, still mufti and still president of the Moslem Supreme Council.

In the intervening years the men of the Cairo school—as they progressively increased their dominance in Palestine as well as over the central policies in the Colonial Office and the Foreign Office—were able to deepen and diversify their campaign against Zionism. During those years their propaganda identified Zionism with Bolshevism—an image carrying instant demonic conviction with devout Christians as well as devout Moslems. During those years the Lawrence myth was built into the popular history of the age, and with it the story of the "Arab Revolt" gained credence. Now the Arabs, and even the Arabs of Palestine, gradually came to play a major role in the liberation of the country from the Turks. Now, too, the claim promoted by Lawrence and embellished by Oriental imagination about how the Arabs had been "let down" by the British was broadcast as historic truth. The very real and significant Jewish share in Allenby's campaign in Palestine on both sides of the Jordan was not mentioned. The Balfour Declaration was somehow twisted at one and the same time into a discreditable transaction and a meaningless document which promised the Jews nothing. During those years, in order to match the unique relationship of the Jewish people to the Land of Israel, the "rights of the Palestine Arabs" were manufactured and endowed with the fictitious historical continuity which serves as the substance of present-day Arab propaganda.

In Palestine the measures to confine and restrict Jewish reconstruction slowly tightened. The British government was not free to make drastic changes, since Britain had no sovereignty in Palestine. She was there constitutionally to fulfill the Mandate and was answerable to the League of Nations for her actions. As long as the League had prestige in the world, it served as a restraining influence on the deepening tendency in London to turn the purpose of the Mandate from the "reconstitution of the Jewish National Home" to the creation of an Arab-dominated dependency of Great Britain. Informed public opinion could not be disregarded, nor that part of the British establishment that fought back, though ever less effectively, against the Arabist erosion of its obligation to the Jewish people.

But while the Colonial Office and the administration in Palestine reduced the essentials of the Mandate, the League of Nations grew progressively less effective; its influence waned gradually in the 1920s, speedily after its show of impotence over the Japanese seizure of Manchuria in 1931. In sum, Zionism was fought on every possible front: economically, in the social services, in the police and public service. The administration was so filled with officials hostile to the purpose of the Mandate that the exceptions became famous. The progress of Jewish restoration was retarded as much as possible.

The central and most effective weapon in the British armory was the control of immigration, and this was used with ever increasing severity. In justification, economics were invoked; a principle called "economic absorptive capacity" was the guiding criterion. With the help of "experts" who asserted that there simply was little or no cultivable land left for development, the government's control of Jewish immigration—administered by a system of quotas—became ever more restrictive. (At that time there were less than a million people in Western Palestine; today there are 4 million, with still undefined possibilities of growth.) Through the country's back door, in quiet defiance of its Mandate, it also allowed an incessant inflow of Arabs. These came mainly from Syria and Transjordan, who were attracted by the progress and prosperity which the Jews were bringing to Palestine. In a constant atmosphere of Jewish crisis and tragedy, in the twenty-six years of the Mandate period, the British allowed the entry of approximately 400,000 Jews into their national home and hounded and punished, and in the end drove back or deported Jews who were trying to steal in. In that same period, crossing the Jordan with ease, probably 200,000 Arabs came in to swell the "existing non-Jewish population."[20]

Yet, though the effort was sustained for a whole generation, from the early 1920s to 1948, neither the British rulers nor Haj Amin el Husseini with the machine he had built for propaganda and indoctrination, ever succeeded in converting the Arab population of Palestine into a nationally conscious entity, moved and animated by a hunger for "liberation," proclaiming and asserting itself as a people with a positive aim. The fundamental reason is that it was—and is still—no such thing. A nation cannot be "created" in a generation or even in two, certainly not when essential ingredients are lacking. It was difficult to distinguish an Arab people altogether, not only in Palestine. A sense of fraternal solidarity did exist in the Arab family, in its economics, in its sense of honor. It existed in the clan that might grow out of the individual family. It might exist in the village. Beyond these loyalties there was only a religious sense, a sense of community in Islam. Even that, with the considerable sectarian fragmentation, never proved itself in modern times as an effective force. There was little sense of belonging to "Arabdom." To the degree that such a feeling ultimately did take root, it was expressed by an affinity to the large Arab people as a whole. Such an affinity could at least refer back to the ancient glory of a vast Arab Empire. This very frame of reference emphasized the absence of a "Palestinian" consciousness—which had, in fact, never existed and which could not be conjured up. Whenever, therefore, a reaction was to be provoked in the more militant, or more unruly, section of the Arab population, it was the vaguer generality of Islam or of pan-Arabism that was invoked.

---

[20] See the report of the Royal Commission on Palestine (H. M. Stationery Office, 1937). Also Y. Shimoni: Arviyei Eretz Yisrael (Tel Aviv, 1947); the UNRWA Review, Inf. Paper No. 6 (September 1952) on illegal Arab immigration during the Second World War.

Thus the disturbances in 1929 were organized on a religious pretext—the alleged designs of the Zionists on the Moslem Holy Places and an Arab assertion of Moslem ownership of the Western Wall (of the Jewish Temple) which abuts the Temple Mount where the Moslems built their mosques. These disturbances, marked by the resolute permissiveness of the British authority, were characterized by outbursts of sheer slaughter. The massacre of the scholarly Jewish community of Hebron remained unrepeated elsewhere because of the defense provided by the newly effective Jewish Haganah organization.

The "Arab Revolt" of 1936-1939, developed by British and Arab cooperation into an expression of pan-Arab policy, was far more ambitious. It was intended—and indeed came to be—the herald of Britain's final abrogation of her pact with the Jewish people. For between 1929 and 1936 a drastic and dire change had occurred in the world.

The Nazis had come to power in Germany. The campaign of the German state against the Jewish people in Germany and throughout the world, the wave of anti-Semitism engulfing the Jews of Eastern Europe and poisoning the wells of the West, had created an unprecedented pressure on the gates of their national home. During the three years after 1933, when the official anti-Jewish terror in Germany began, some 150,000 Jews had entered Palestine by taking advantage of remaining loopholes in the immigration regulations. The plight of the Jews remaining in Germany and of the persecuted, increasingly desperate, five million Jews in Eastern Europe was arousing considerable international attention. Opening the gates of Palestine, though the obvious solution, would have meant the defeat of the Arabists' purpose. A few more years of large-scale Jewish immigration would have placed the Jews in a majority. If the Jews could proclaim a state, the Arab population—for the most part probably prepared to resign itself to a Jewish regime if it did not interfere with its way of life—might well make peace with it; and the British presence would come to an end. The pressure of Jewish need and world sympathy could be countered only by a more powerful, irresistible force which would prove that it was impossible to achieve the Mandate's original purpose, that Arab resistance was too strong, too determined. The Arab "Revolt" was the result.

It was not a revolt at all but a campaign of violence directed against the Jews. Haj Amin's resources, after fifteen years of organization, were adequate to give it a countrywide—though still primitive and improvisational—character. In 1920 the pogroms had been inspired and connived at by the military administration in an effort to nip its home government's Zionist policy in the bud. In 1936 the Arab campaign of violence was a move calculated to further the British home government's intention of finally burying Zionism. The policy laid down in 1939 in the White Paper was the preordained purpose for which the 1936 outbreak was needed.

The permissive attitude of the Palestine government to the campaign of violence was evident from the outset. The outbreak was signaled months in advance. Inciting speeches by Arab political and religious notables and inflammatory articles in the Arab newspapers were the order of the day. It was common talk among both Jews and Arabs that the Arab villages (as in 1920) were "infested with agitators" who were inciting the population to violence against the Jews and that once again the people were being assured that *a'dowlah ma'ana*. This process was not disturbed by a single overt act, nor by any public statement, nor any warning of preventive or punitive action by the government.[21]

When, in the face of this astonishing forbearance, warnings were addressed to the High Commissioner and to the Colonial Office in London of the signs of the imminence of Arab violence, the reply was that the situation was under control. Similar reassuring statements were made after the first day's toll of seventeen Jews killed by Arab mobs in the public streets of Jaffa under the nose of the British authority (Katz, pp. 4-5).

---

[21] A description of the developing situation three months before the outbreak began is contained in Samuel Katz, *Days of Fire* (London, 1968), p. 3–4.

Had the campaign been in fact a spontaneous Arab outbreak, and had the government been determined to maintain law and order, the outbreak would have lasted no more than a few days and would have made little impact. A completely typical illustration of the administration's solution to the problem of pretending to be putting down the "rebellion" is provided by the description by a British soldier on the spot, given in the London journal *New Statesman and Nation*, September 20, 1936:

> At night, when we are guarding the line against the Arabs who come to blow it up, we often see them at work but are forbidden to fire at them. We may only fire into the air, and they, upon hearing the report, make their escape. But do you think we can give chase? Why, we must go on our hands and knees and find every spent cartridge-case which must be handed in or woe betide us.

In a similar spirit the general strike proclaimed by the Arab Higher Committee (the self-appointed leadership of the Arab community, headed by Haj Amin el Husseini) and imposed on the Arab masses as the central weapon and symbol of the campaign was not resisted by the administration. It refused to declare the strike illegal, in flagrant contrast to its swift crushing of an earlier strike in nonviolent protest—by the Jews against Jabotinsky's arrest after the pogrom of 1920.

When, subsequently, the "rebels," mistaking British permissiveness for Arab strength, went beyond attacks on Jewish villages and on Jewish life and property and attacked British personnel, effective measures were taken, and the "rebels" were firmly suppressed.

The revolt, widely publicized, served its purpose. The British government proclaimed in its famous White Paper of 1939 its abandonment of the Zionist policy. After the introduction of 75,000 more Jews into Palestine during the ensuing five years, the gates would be closed. The way would thus be opened for that ultimate semidependent Arab state which would complete the British pan-Arab dream in the Middle East.

This document was rejected as inconsistent with the Mandate by the supervising body of the League of Nations, the Permanent Mandates Commission. But the League of Nations was dying, and Britain treated it with appropriate contempt. Four months later, the Second World War broke out; and the British government executed the White Paper policy as if Palestine had been a British possession and the White Paper an act of Parliament. Unnumbered Jews thus were trapped in Nazi-occupied Europe when, but for the rigid and unrelenting application of the provisions of the White Paper, they could have escaped to Palestine even during the war.

It may be that this grim consequence of British policy is the reason why the British government later willfully destroyed so many of the documents which could have provided direct evidence of the Palestine government's behavior. After thirty years the British state archives were, in accordance with custom, opened to the research of writers and historians. The entire correspondence between the Palestine administration and its chiefs at the Colonial Office in London relating to the records of the meetings of the Executive Council (in effect the Cabinet) of the Palestine government had been "destroyed under statute." Another obviously important file so destroyed was that relating to the Haganah Organization—which, if it had not been hamstrung by the government, was itself capable of putting a swift end to the Arab attacks. Yet another file destroyed was on "Propaganda Among the Arabs"—the incitement against the Jews—which the Palestine government had often been charged with inspiring, sponsoring, or at least facilitating.[22]

The sanctity of the minutes of the British Cabinet in London has, however, saved one item of direct documentary evidence on the British government's relationship to the "revolt" and to the "rebels." The disturbances were not even mentioned when the Cabinet met soon after they

---

[22] Files CO 793/27/75269; CO 793/27/75402; and CO 793/27/75528/25.

broke out. Nor was the outbreak discussed at the next meeting or the one after that. Indeed, five meetings went by before the Cabinet discussed any aspect of the situation in Palestine. At the meeting of May 11, 1936—three weeks and a day after the outbreak—the Secretary of State for the Colonies presented the Cabinet with a memorandum, not indeed proposing or even announcing measures for putting an end to the violence, but reporting that

> the High Commissioner recommended that the most helpful means now open to His Majesty's Government of preventing the present disorders from spreading and increasing in violence would be for an immediate announcement of a Royal Commission with wide terms of reference, with power to make recommendations for lessening animosities and for establishing a feeling of lasting security in Palestine. [Cab. 23/84]

The Secretary of State "did not," the minutes continue, "ask for a decision on the Terms of Reference to, or composition of the proposed Royal Commission which would require careful consideration, but merely for permission to tell the High Commissioner that His Majesty's Government was favorable to the proposal *so that he could sound the Arabs* and report further" (italics added).

Nevertheless, in spite of this collusion, the development of the "revolt" was made possible and given shape and thrust only by the introduction of help by Arabs from outside Palestine. One of the outstanding features of the "revolt" was the failure of the Arabs of Palestine themselves to act appropriately.

The Palestinian Arabs were comfortably aware of the existence around them, in addition to their original homeland in Arabia, of six more Arabic-speaking countries, five of them predominantly Moslem, all part of the same sprawling territory which many centuries ago had been won and lost by the invaders from Arabia. Those Arabs who had dealings with the Jews got on well with them, and even if they did not like the idea of Jews, rather than Turks or British, ruling the country, they could not conjure up enough hostility to fight them. In 1929 the Mufti had incited them by distributing postcards which showed the El Aksa mosque flying the Zionist flag—an effective essay in photomontage. In 1936 the bulk of Palestinian Arabs still remained cold to the urgings of Haj Amin. A minority carried out the street knifings, the sniping at Jewish transport, the throwing of bombs in cinemas and marketplaces. The general strike was maintained only by the constant threat of force by the Mufti's organization; and the threat was made more persuasive by the refusal of the administration to declare the strike illegal.

The effort of the Palestine Arabs was not enough to impress the world. After the first phase of sniping, of attacks by street mobs, of individual bomb throwing, of shooting at transport on the main roads, there came a relaxation even of this effort. "Rebels" were consequently imported. A Syrian, Fawzi Kaukji, led a mixed band of Syrian and Iraqi mercenaries in the extended campaign directed mainly against the Jewish villages.[23] The Palestine Arab population on the whole refused to cooperate with these liberators, often even denying them shelter. The outcome was a campaign of murder against the Palestinian Arabs. When Arab villages appealed to the British administration for arms to defend themselves against Kaukji's invading bands, they were refused. In the end more Arabs than Jews were killed by the rebels.[24]

The intervention by Arabs from the neighboring countries was a reflection of the Cairo school's dream. To its members Palestine was only part of the larger scheme; it was needed only to complete the homogeneity of a large

---

[23] The Colonial Office files of correspondence on the "Participation of Syrian Arabs" in the Disturbances (CO 793/27/75528/48), and "Activities of Fawzi Kaukji" (Co 793/27/75528/82) have been "Destroyed Under Statute."

[24] A critical detailed analysis, legal and administrative, of the British measures during the first phase of the 1936 revolt is given in Horace B. Samuel, *Revolt by Leave* (London, 1937). For a comprehensive picture and summing up, see Chaim Weizmann, *Trial and Error* (London, 1949) and Katz, *Days of Fire.*

Arab "world" under British tutelage. That dream was not abandoned. Indeed, the British government worked energetically to create a form of unity, or at least a framework of cooperation, among the Arab states. In an Arab world riven with disagreements and jealousies, the Palestine issue was the ideal instrument to bring about such cooperation. To appear, without much effort as the champions of their brothers in Palestine and at the same time to nourish the hope that the Fertile Crescent might become homogeneously Arab—this was a prospect that appealed to the Arab states.

As early as 1936 the real or nominal heads of the Arab states or states in embryo were called in by the administration and generously agreed to "secure" from the Mufti and his Arab Higher Committee a temporary cessation of the revolt so as to enable an investigation of grievances. When the Mufti in his turn graciously consented, the government permitted the main body of Fawzi Kaukji's terrorists to go back across the Jordan, where they could rest and reorganize. Thereafter it became a self-understood facet of British policy that the Arab states had acquired a right to intervene in the affairs of Palestine. As though they were parties to the "dispute," with a claim and interests in the country—and in flagrant flaunting of the origin, the concept, the letter and the spirit of Britain's own defined mandate—the Arab rulers were invited in 1939 to a so-called Round Table Conference. The predetermined failure of this conference (where the Arab representatives refused to meet the Jews face to face) was enshrined in the White Paper that followed immediately.

Looking ahead, through the storms of the war that followed to the final consummation of the White Paper, the British government took active steps to create a formal instrument of pan-Arabism. Thus the Arab League was born. After Anthony Eden first mentioned it publicly in 1941, the then British Foreign Secretary presided over the necessary diplomatic exchanges and negotiations which brought about the formal establishment of the League in 1945. The pan-Arab dream had meanwhile also assumed that large economic importance which had been part of its inspiration. The oil fields of Iraq proved to be but a small portion of a vast potential in Iraq itself and, even more, in Saudi Arabia and the British dependent sheikhdoms on the Persian Gulf. In their exploitation British commercial interests played a large part.

Thus, after thirty years, an Arab entity consisting of seven countries—Egypt, Syria, Iraq, Lebanon, Yemen, Saudi Arabia, and Transjordan, formally independent, semi-dependent, or on the way to formal independence, and providing substantial dividends to an impoverished British economy—promised to realize the dream, conceived in 1915, of an Arab confederation which would "look to Britain as its patron and protector." Western Palestine was still lacking to complete the picture, but its inclusion seemed imminent. It remained only to give the finishing stroke to Zionism. That should not be difficult after the battering the Jewish people had suffered from the Nazis.

Zionism, however, refused to die. On the contrary: with a drive and a passion that may have been unexpected by the British, a Jewish resistance sprang up, determined now, after six million Jews had been exterminated, to take what seemed the last chance to restore the Jewish independence that Britain had been pledged to establish and had now betrayed. In varying degrees of intensity before the end of the Second World War, at increased and increasing pitch after the war, the Jews were locked in struggle with the mandatory regime. Large military forces were poured into the country by Britain.

Now at last the time had come for the assertion of a "Palestinian" Arab entity. The Arabs could theoretically have joined the Jews in a classic war of liberation from a foreign ruler and established a claim to partnership in the ensuing independence. Or, more credibly, the British having already promised them in fact independence which the Jewish resistance was endangering, they might have rushed in to help the British in crushing the Zionists. In fact, faced with the two alternatives, they chose a third:

they did nothing. The Arab population of Palestine sat by while the Jewish resistance movement brought about the end of British rule.

The claim has in fact been made that the Arabs' restraint was calculated: "let" the Jews get rid of the British, then "settle" with the Jews. The facts prove otherwise. When the United Nations General Assembly decided on November 29, 1947, to recommend the partition of Palestine and the establishment of two states, the Arabs did launch a countrywide attack on the Jews. But this too was carried out only with considerable aid from the British who maintained their presence in the country for another six months. Clearly also the attacking Arabs were a minority of the people, while the majority remained passive or evacuated in order to leave the field to the invading Arab states, who promised to drive the Jews into the sea. The Palestine Arabs were truly a people of noncombatants; they contributed very little manpower to the ensuing full-scale war which was supposed to be a life-and-death struggle for them. The British statistics gave the Arabs a population of 1,200,000 in western Palestine. Even if, as is likely, this figure is an exaggeration, there must still, at a highly conservative estimate, have been 100,000 men of military age. The report of the Iraqi Government Commission which subsequently inquired into the cause of the defeat[25] established that the total number of Palestinian Arabs who took part in the war was 4,000. The Jews, altogether some 650,000, *lost* one-and-a-half times that number.

This confrontation of figures is symbolic of the affinity to Eretz Israel of the Jewish people and of the real Arab relationship to the country. The Arabs of Palestine were under no physical compulsion when their vast majority deliberately left their homes unguarded and exposed and moved off across the Jordan or into Syria or Lebanon or to those parts of western Palestine that fell under the control of the Arab invaders. The Jews—most of them the

---

[25] Published in Hebrew translation in *Behind the Curtain* (Maarakhot Tel Aviv, 1954).

first and second generation of the organized return to their ancestral country—stood and fought and died for every inch of the land. This stark confrontation of affinities has its deep roots in the history of the land and the people.

# 4

# The Jewish Presence in Palestine

Promoted by two such powerful forces as Soviet assertions and Arab propaganda, the claim of Arab historical rights has become a central element in the international debate. By sheer weight of noise it has impressed many otherwise knowledgeable and well-meaning people. The facts of history are thus a vital element in understanding the conflict over Palestine and for placing it in its proper perspective. They are all readily ascertainable.

In our day we are witnessing an astonishing phenomenon demonstrating and dramatizing the depth of attachment to the land of Israel in the heart by Jews long alienated from it both physically and spiritually: the explosion of Zionism among the Jewish youth of the Soviet Union.

For fully fifty years the Soviet state, clothed with totalitarian authority, by its very nature brooking no other ideology, has labored to indoctrinate its people with the Communist faith. Hostile to all religions, the Soviet regime has made a special, purposeful effort to eradicate Judaism. It has achieved the closing down of most of the synagogues in the country; there are no Jewish religious schools or classes in the Soviet Union. After thirty, forty, fifty years, as the third generation of Soviet-educated, Soviet-indoctrinated young Jews grew up, only faint remnants of Jewish religious observance survived.

The idea of the return of the Jewish people to Palestine was outlawed by the Soviet regime. For nearly thirty years Zionism was denounced as an instrument of British imperialism and of international capitalism, as an enemy of the Soviet state and of Communism. It was a crime in the Soviet code. At different times tens of thousands of Jews were jailed or toiled and suffered—and often died—in Siberian exile, for no other reason than that they were declared or suspected Zionists. Hostility to Zionism has found ever more violent expression in concentrated enmity to the State of Israel.

By its very nature and content, Soviet education not only insured that young Jews should not be taught the faith of their fathers, but also subjected them throughout their formative years to a curriculum of hatred and contempt for the ideas, values, and achievements of Zionism.

While the first generation of Jews in the era of the Bolshevik Revolution may have been able to inspire some spiritual resistance in the hearts of its sons, that little had all but evaporated when, after the creation of the Jewish state, the sons were faced with the task of rearing the third generation. No wonder, then, that twenty-five years ago many of us in the West assumed that the Soviet Union had probably succeeded in forcing assimilation on the Jews of the USSR, that where indoctrination and suppression had not entirely succeeded in the first generation, sheer ignorance in the second and third would complete the process.

In fact, under the surface a completely different spiritual transformation was taking place. It came to fulfillment precisely in the third generation—whose parents were born and reared in the embrace of the Soviet state. It incubated and grew slowly. Only from time to time were there public signs of nonconformism. It became explosive after the Six Day War.

In the years since 1967, the Jewish community in the Soviet Union has become a boiling cauldron. The third generation, the sons of the "lost" generation are visibly restless with longing for this land they have never seen and of which they know very little. They have made manifest a fierce sense of alienation from the society that reared them and a passion of oneness with the Jewish people against whom their whole education and the culture of their upbringing has nurtured them. A movement has spread throughout the Soviet Union in spite of the totalitarian repression of the regime. This movement is one of young people, challenging the very core of Soviet indoctrination.

It started in the secret study of Hebrew, which was frowned upon, in copying and spreading literature about Israel, which was by definition forbidden, in word-of-mouth dissemination of news gleaned from foreign radio broadcasts. Many of the young Jews emerged from their anonymity. At the very moment that the Soviet Union exchanged its long-standing policy of arming and backing the forces arrayed against Israel for a policy of direct physical intervention on their behalf, these young Soviet Jews boldly addressed the authorities, proclaiming their renunciation of identification with the Soviet state. They demanded the fulfillment of their right—formally entrenched in the Soviet Constitution but denied by Soviet policy—to leave the Soviet Union and to join the Jewish people in their homeland. They also drew many of their parents out of their timidity; the Soviet Home Office was flooded with numerous applications by whole families in the tens of thousands. Defying the state's capacity for retribution and its potential for punishment, they declared their desire to give up their Soviet citizenship, give up all they have in the Soviet Union, and go, "on foot if necessary," to join their people in the State of Israel.

For a variety of alleged offenses committed in the process many of them have been sent to jail or, in a few cases, to mental homes. This response, far from deterring others, has spurred them on to more and more defiant action. An unsuccessful attempt to hijack a Soviet plane and thus fly to freedom; unprecedented demonstrations of protest by groups of Jews inside Soviet government offices; the passion that alone could make possible such an explosion of defiance—are all powerful indications that a form of Zionist rebellion is in progress inside the Soviet Union.

The emergence and the progressive intensification of Jewish national identification in the Soviet Union has seemed miraculous even to many historically minded people. It is, in fact, merely an expression sharpened, deepened, and concentrated by the circumstances of the central fact of 3,500 years of Jewish history: the passion of the Jewish people for the land of Israel. The circumstances in which the Jewish people, its independence crushed nineteen centuries ago and large numbers of its sons driven into exile, maintained and preserved its connection with the land are among the most remarkable facts in the story of mankind. For eighteen centuries the Zionist passion—the longing for Zion, the dream of the restoration, and the ordering of Jewish life and thought to prepare for the return—pulsed in the Jewish people. That passion finally gave birth to the practical and political organizations which, amid the storms of the twentieth century, launched the mass movement for the return to Zion and for restored Jewish national independence.

The Jews were never a people without a homeland. Having been robbed of their land, Jews never ceased to give expression to their anguish at their deprivation and to pray for and demand its return. Throughout the nearly two millenia of dispersion, Palestine remained the focus of the national culture. Every single day in all those seventy generations devout Jews gave voice to their attachment to Zion.

The consciousness of the Jew that Palestine was his country was not a theoretical exercise or an article of theology or a sophisticated political outlook. It was in a sense all of these—and it was a pervasive and inextricable element in the very warp and woof of his daily life. Jewish prayers, Jewish literature are saturated with the love and the longing for and the sense of belonging to Palestine. Except for religion and the love between the sexes, there is no theme so pervasive in the literature of any other nation, no theme has yielded so much thought and feeling and expression, as the relationship of the Jew to Palestine in Jewish literature and philosophy. And in his home on family occasions, in his daily customs on weekdays and Shabbat, when he said grace over meals, when he got married, when he built his house, when he said words of comfort to mourners, the context was always his exile, his hope and belief in the return to Zion, and the reconstruction of his homeland. So intense was this sense of affinity that, if in the vicissitudes of exile he could not envisage that restoration during his lifetime, it was a matter of faith that with the coming of the Messiah and the Resurrection he would be brought back to the land after his death.

Over the centuries, through the pressures of persecution—of social and economic discrimination, of periodic death and destruction—the area of exile widened. Hounded and oppressed, the Jews moved from country to country. They carried Eretz Israel with them wherever they went. Jewish festivals remained tuned to the circumstances and conditions of the Jewish homeland. Whether they remained in warm Italy or Spain, whether they found homes in cold Eastern Europe, whether they found their way to North America or came to live in the southern hemisphere where the seasons are reversed, the Jews celebrated the Palestinian spring and its autumn and winter. They prayed for dew in May and for rain in October. On Passover they ceremonially celebrated the liberation from Egyptian bondage, the original national establishment in the Promised Land—and they conjured up the vision of a new liberation.

Never in the periods of greatest persecution did the Jews as a people renounce that faith. Never in the periods of greatest peril to their very existence physically, and the seeming impossibility of their ever regaining the land of Israel, did they seek a substitute for the homeland. Time after time throughout the centuries, there arose bold spirits who believed, or claimed, they had a plan, or a divine vision, for the restoration of the Jewish people to Palestine. Time after time a wave of hope surged through the ghettos of Europe at the news of some new would-be Messiah. The Jews' hopes were dashed and the dream faded, but never for a day did they relinquish their bond with their country.

There were Jews who fell by the wayside. Given a choice under torture, or during periods of civic equality and material prosperity, they foresook their religion or turned their backs on their historic country. But to the people, the land—as it was called for all those centuries: simply *Ha'aretz*, the Land—remained the one and only homeland, unchanging and irreplaceable. If ever a right has been maintained by unrelenting insistence on the claim, it was the Jewish right to Palestine.

Widely unknown, its significance certainly long ungrasped, is the no less awesome fact that throughout the eighteen centuries between the fall of the Second Jewish Commonwealth and the beginnings of the Third, in our time, the tenacity of Jewish attachment to the land of Israel found continuous expression in the country itself. It was long believed,—and still is—even in some presumably knowledgeable quarters, that throughout those centuries there were no Jews in Palestine. The popular conception has been that all the Jews who survived the Destruction of 70 C.E. went into exile and that their descendants began coming back only 1,800 years later. This is not a fact.[1] One of the most astonishing elements in the history of the Jewish people—and of Palestine—is the continuity, in the face of the circumstances, of Jewish life in the country.

It is a continuity that waxed and waned, that moved in kaleidoscopic shifts, in response to the pressures of the foreign imperial rulers who in bewildering succession imposed themselves on the country. It is a pattern of stubborn refusal, in the face of oppression, banishment, and slaughter, to let go of an often tenuous hold in the country, a determined digging in sustained by a faith in the ultimate full restoration, of which every Jew living in the homeland saw himself as caretaker and precursor.

This people that was "not here"—the Jewish community in Palestine, its history continuous and purposeful—in fact played a unique role in Jewish history. Too often lacking detail and depth, the story of the Jewish presence in Palestine, threaded together from a colorful variety of sources and references, pagan and Christian, Jewish and

---

[1] James Parkes, the Christian scholar who has done much to explode the myth, writes: "[The Zionists'] real title deeds were written by the . . . heroic endurance of those who had maintained a Jewish presence in the Land through the centuries, and in spite of every discouragement." *Whose Land? A History of the Peoples of Palestine* (London, 1970), p. 266.

Moslem, spread over the whole period between the second and the nineteenth centuries, is a fascinating and compelling counterpoint to the dominating theme of the longing-in-exile.

Only when they had crushed the revolt led by Simon Bar Kochba in 135 C.E.—over sixty years after the destruction of the Second Temple—did the Romans make a determined effort to stamp out Jewish identity in the Jewish homeland. They initiated the long process of laying the country waste. It was then that Jerusalem, "plowed over" at the order of Hadrian, was renamed Aelia Capitolina, and the country, denied of the name Judea, was renamed Syria Palestina. In the revolt itself—the fiercest and longest revolt faced by the Roman Empire—580,000 Jewish soldiers perished in battle, and an untold number of civilians died of starvation and pestilence; 985 villages were destroyed.[2]

Yet even after this further disaster Jewish life remained active and productive. Banished from Jerusalem, it now centered on Galilee. Refugees returned; Jews who had been sold into slavery were redeemed. In the centuries after Bar Kochba and Hadrian, some of the most significant creations of the Jewish spirit were produced in Palestine. It was then that the Mishnah was completed and the Jerusalem Talmud was compiled; and the bulk of the community farmed the land.

The Roman Empire adopted Christianity in the fourth century; henceforth its policy in Palestine was governed by a new purpose: to prevent the birth of any glimmer of renewed hope of Jewish independence. It was, after all, basic to Christian theology that loss of national independence was an act of God designed to punish the Jewish people for their rejection of Christ. The work of the Almighty had to be helped along. Some emperors were more lenient than others, but the minimal criteria of oppression and restriction were nearly always maintained.

---

[2] Dio Cassius, *History of the Romans;* Theodor Mommsen, *Provinces of the Roman Empire.* Both quoted in Jacob De Haas, *History of Palestine, the Last Two Thousand Years* (New York, 1934), pp. 52.

Nevertheless, even the meager surviving sources name forty-three Jewish communities in Palestine in the sixth century: twelve towns on the coast, in the Negev, and east of the Jordan and thirty-one villages in Galilee and in the Jordan valley.

The Jews' thoughts at every opportunity turned to the hope of national restoration. In the year 351 they launched yet another revolt, provoking heavy retribution. When, in 438, the Empress Eudocia removed the ban on Jews' praying at the Temple site, the heads of the Community in Galilee issued a call "to the great and mighty people of the Jews" which began, "Know then that the end of the exile of our people has come"![3]

In the belief of restoration to come, the Jews made an alliance with the Persians who invaded Palestine in 614, fought at their side, overwhelmed the Byzantine garrison in Jerusalem, and for three years governed the city.[4] But the Persians made their peace with the Emperor Heraclius. Christian rule was reestablished, and those Jews who survived the consequent slaughter were once more banished from the city. A new chapter of vengeful Byzantine persecution was enacted, but as it happened, it was short-lived. A new force was on the march. In 632 the Moslem Arab invaders came and conquered. By the year 640 Palestine had become a part of the emerging Moslem empire.

The 450-year Moslem rule in Palestine was first under the Omayyads (predominantly Arab), who governed tolerantly from Damascus; then under the Abbasid dynasty (predominantly Turkish), in growing anarchy, from Baghdad; and finally, in alternating tolerance and persecution, under the Fatimids from Cairo. The Moslem Arabs took from the Jews the lands to which they had clung for twenty generations after the fall of the Jewish state. The Crusaders, who came after them and ruled Palestine or parts of it for the better part of two centuries, massacred the Jews in the cities. Yet, under the Moslems openly,

---

[3] Avraham Yaari, *Igrot Eretz Yisrael* (Tel Aviv, 1943), p. 46.

[4] A. Malamat, H. Tadmor, M. Stern, S. Safrai: *Toledot Am Yisrael Bi'mei Kedem* (Tel Aviv, 1969), p. 348. Recent archaeological finds in Jerusalem suggest that the period was five years.

under the Crusaders more circumspectly, the Jewish community of Palestine, in circumstances it is impossible to understand or to analyze, held on by the skin of its teeth, somehow survived, and worked, and fought. Fought. Along with the Arabs and the Turks, the Jews were among the most vigorous defenders of Jerusalem against the Crusaders. When the city fell, the Crusaders gathered the Jews in a synagogue and burned them. The Jews almost single-handedly defended Haifa against the Crusaders, holding out in the besieged town for a whole month (June-July 1099). At this time, a full thousand years after the fall of the Jewish state, there were Jewish communities all over the country. Fifty of them are known to us; they include Jerusalem, Tiberias, Ramleh, Ashkelon, Caesarea, and Gaza.

During more than six centuries of Moslem and Crusader rule periods of tolerance or preoccupied indifference flickered fitfully between periods of concentrated persecution. Jews, driven from the villages, fled to the towns. Surviving massacre in the inland towns, they made their way to the coast. When the coastal towns were destroyed, they succeeded somehow in returning inland. Throughout those centuries war was almost continuous, whether between Cross and Crescent or among the Moslems themselves. The Jewish community, now heavily reduced, maintained itself in stiff-necked endurance.

Moslem and Christian records report that they pursued a variety of occupations. The Arab geographer Abu Abdallah Mohammed—known as Mukadassi—writing in the tenth century, describes the Jews as the assayers of coins, the dyers, the tanners, and the bankers in the community. In his time, a period of Fatimid tolerance, many Jewish officials were serving the regime. While they were not allowed to hold land in the Crusader period, the Jews controlled much of the commerce of the coastal towns during times of quiescence. Most of them were artisans: glassblowers in Sidon, furriers and dyers in Jerusalem.

In the midst of all their vicissitudes and in the face of all change, Hebrew scholarship and literary creation went on flourishing. It was in this period that the Hebrew grammarians at Tiberias evolved their Hebrew vowel-pointing system, giving form to the modern study of the language; and a large volume of *piyutim* and *midrashim* had their origin in Palestine in those days.

After the Crusaders there came a period of wild disturbance as first the Kharezmians—an Asian tribe appearing fleetingly on the stage of history—and then the Mongol hordes, invaded Palestine. They sowed new ruin and destruction throughout the country. Its cities were laid waste, its lands were burned, its trees were uprooted, the younger part of its population was destroyed.

Yet the dust of the Mongol hordes, defeated by the Mamluks, had hardly settled when the Jerusalem community, which had been all but exterminated, was reestablished. This was the work of the famous scholar Moses ben Nachman (Nachmanides, the "RaMbaN"). From the day in 1267 when RaMbaN settled in the city, there was a coherent Jewish community in the Old City of Jerusalem until it was driven out, temporarily as it proved, by the British-led Arab Legion from Transjordan nearly seven hundred years later.

For two and a half centuries (1260–1516) Palestine was part of the Empire of the Mamluks, Moslems of Turkish-Tartar origin who ruled first from Turkey, then from Egypt. War and uprisings, bloodshed and destruction flowed in almost incessant waves across their domain. Though Palestine was not always involved in the strife, it was frequently enough implicated to hasten the process of physical destruction. Jews (and Christians) suffered persecution and humiliation. Yet toward the end of the rule of the Mamluks, at the close of the fifteenth century, Christian and Jewish visitors and pilgrims noted the presence of substantial Jewish communities. Even the meager records that survived report nearly thirty Jewish urban and rural communities at the opening of the sixteenth century.

By now nearly fifteen hundred years had passed since the destruction of the Jewish state. Jewish life in Palestine had survived Byzantine ruthlessness, had endured the discriminations, persecutions, and massacres of the variegated Moslem sects—Arab Omayyads, Abbasids, and Fatimids, the Turkish Seljuks, and the Mamluks. Jewish life had by some historic sleight-of-hand outlived the Crusaders, its mortal enemy. It had survived Mongol barbarism.

More than an expression of self-preservation, Jewish life had a purpose and a mission. It was the trustee and the advance guard of restoration. At the close of the fifteenth century the pilgrim Arnold Van Harff reported that he had found many Jews in Jerusalem and that they spoke Hebrew. They told another traveler, Felix Fabri, that they hoped soon to resettle the Holy Land.[5]

During the same period Martin Kabatnik (who did not like Jews), visiting Jerusalem during his pilgrimage, exclaimed:

> The heathens oppress them at their pleasure. They know that the Jews think and say that this is the Holy Land that was promised to them. Those of them who live here are regarded as holy by the other Jews, for in spite of all the tribulations and the agonies they suffer at the hands of the heathen, they refuse to leave the place.[6]

At the height of their splendor, in the first generations after their conquest of Palestine in 1516, the Ottoman Turks were tolerant and showed a friendly face to the Jews. During the sixteenth century there developed a new effervescence in the life of the Jews in the country. Thirty communities, urban and rural, are recorded at the opening of the Ottoman era. They include Haifa, Sh'chem, Hebron, Ramleh, Jaffa, Gaza, Jerusalem, and many in the north. Their center was Safed; its community grew quickly. It became the largest in Palestine and assumed the recognized spiritual leadership of the whole Jewish world. The luster of the cultural "golden age" that now developed shone over the whole country and has inspired Jewish

---

[5] *The Pilgrimage of Arnold van Harff* (London, 1946) p. 217; *The Wanderings of Felix Fabri* (London, 1897) p. 130.

[6] Justin V. Prasek, *Martin Kabatnik* (Prague). Quoted in Michael Ish-Shalom, *Masaei Notzrim Be'eretz Yisrael*, p. 265.

spiritual life to the present day. It was there and then that a phenomenal group of mystic philosophers evolved the mysteries of the Cabala. It was at that time and in the inspiration of the place that Joseph Caro compiled the Shulhan Aruch, the formidable codification of Jewish observance which largely guides orthodox custom to this day. Poets and writers flourished. Safed achieved a fusion of scholarship and piety with trade, commerce, and agriculture. In the town the Jews developed a number of branches of trade, especially in grain, spices, and cloth. They specialized once again in the dyeing trade. Lying halfway between Damascus and Sidon on the Mediterranean coast, Safed gained special importance in the commercial relations in the area. The 8,000 or 10,000 Jews in Safed in 1555 grew to 20,000 or 30,000 by the end of the century.[7]

In the neighboring Galilean countryside a number of Jewish villages—from Turkish sources we know of ten of them—continued to occupy themselves with the production of wheat and barley and cotton, vegetables and olives, vines and fruit, pulse and sesame.[8]

The recurrent references in the sketchy records that have survived suggest that in some of those Galilean villages—such as Kfar Alma, Ein Zeitim, Biria, Pekiin, Kfar Hanania, Kfar Kana, Kfar Yassif—the Jews, against all logic and in defiance of the pressures and exactions and confiscations of generation after generation of foreign conquerors, had succeeded in clinging to the land for fifteen centuries.[9] Now for several decades of benevolent Ottoman rule, the Jewish communities flourished in village and town.

The history of the second half of the sixteenth century illustrates the dynamism of the Palestinian Jews—their prosperity, their progressiveness, and their subjugation: In 1577 a Hebrew printing press was established in Safed.

---

[7] H. H. Ben-Sasson, *Toledot Hayehudim Bi-mei Habeinayim* (Tel Aviv, 1969), pp. 239–240.

[8] Bernard Lewis, *Notes and Documents from the Turkish Archives* (Jerusalem, 1952), p. 15ff.

[9] Yitzhak Ben-Zvi, *She'ar Yashuv* (Jerusalem, 1966), p. 10.

The first press in Palestine, it was also the first in Asia. In 1576, and again in 1577, the Sultan Murad III, the first anti-Jewish Ottoman ruler, ordered the deportation of 1,-000 wealthy Jews from Safed, though they had not broken any laws or transgressed in any way. They were needed by Murad to strengthen the economy of another of the Sultan's provinces—Cyprus. It is not known whether they were in fact deported or reprieved.[10]

The honeymoon period between the Ottoman Empire and the Jews lasted only as long as the empire flourished. With the beginning and development of its long decline in the seventeenth century, oppression and anarchy made growing inroads into the country, and Jewish life began to follow a confused pattern of persecutions, prohibitions, and ephemeral prosperity. Prosperity grew rarer, persecutions and oppressions became the norm. The Ottomans, to whom Palestine was merely a source of revenue, began to exploit the Jews' fierce attachment to Palestine. They were consequently made to pay a heavy price for living there. They were taxed beyond measure and were subjected to a system of arbitrary fines. Early in the seventeenth century two Christian travelers, Johann van Egmont and John Hayman, could say of the Jews in Safed: "Life here is the poorest and most miserable that one can imagine." The Turks so oppressed them, they wrote, that "they pay for the very air they breathe."[11]

Again and again during the three centuries of Turkish decline the Jews so lived and bore themselves that even hostile Christian travelers were moved to express their astonishment at their pertinacity—despite suffering, humiliation, and violence—in clinging to their homeland.

The Jews of Jerusalem, wrote the Jesuit Father Michael Naud in 1674, were agreed about one thing: "paying heavily to the Turk for their right to stay here. . . . They prefer being prisoners in Jerusalem to enjoying the freedom they could acquire elsewhere. . . . The love of the Jews for the Holy Land, which they lost through their betrayal [of

---

[10] Lewis, p. 28–33.
[11] Travels: (London 1759) quoted by Ish-Shalom, p. 388.

Christ], is unbelievable. Many of them come from Europe to find a little comfort, though the yoke is heavy."[12]

And not in Jerusalem alone. Even as anarchy spread over the land, marauding raids by Bedouins from the desert increased, and the roads became further infested with bandits, and while the Sultan's men, when they appeared at all, came only to collect both the heavy taxes directed against all and the special taxes exacted from the Jews, Jewish communities still held on all over the country. During the seventeenth and eighteenth centuries travelers reported them in Hebron (where, in addition to the regular exactions, threats of deportation, arrests, violence, and bloodshed, the Jews suffered the gruesome tribulations of a blood libel in 1775); Gaza, Ramleh, Sh'chem, Safed (where the community had lost its preeminence and its prosperity), Acre, Sidon, Tyre, Haifa, Irsuf, Caesarea, and El Arish; and Jews continued to live and till the soil in Galilean villages.

But as the country itself declined and the bare essentials of life became inaccessible, the Jewish community also contracted. By the end of the eighteenth century historians' estimates put their number at between 10,000 and 15,000. Their national role, however, was never blurred. When the Jews in Palestine had no economic basis, the Jews abroad regarded it as their minimum national duty to insure their physical maintenance, and a steady stream of emissaries brought back funds from the Diaspora. In the long run this had a degrading effect on those Jews who came to depend on these contributions for all their needs. But the significance of the motive and spirit of the aid is not lessened: the Jews in Palestine were regarded as the guardians of the Jewish heritage. Nor can one ignore the endurance and pertinacity of the recipients, in the face of oppression and humiliation and the threat of physical violence, in their role of "guardians of the walls."

However determined the Jews in Palestine might have been, however deep their attachment to the land, and

---

[12] R. P. Michael Naud: *Voyage Nouveau de la Terre-Sainte* (Paris 1702) pp. 58, 563.

however strong their sense of mission in living in it, the historic circumstances should surely have ground them out of physical existence long before the onset of modern times.

Merely to recall the succession of conquerors who passed through the country and who oppressed or slaughtered Jews, deliberately or only incidentally to their struggle for power or survival, raises the question of how any Jews survived at all, let alone in coherent communities. Pagan Romans, Byzantine Christians, the various Moslem imperial dynasties, (especially during the Seljuk Turkish interlude, before the Crusaders), the Crusaders themselves, the Kharezmians and the Mongols, the Ottoman Turks—all these passed over the body of the Jewish community. How then did a Jewish community survive at all? How did it survive as an arm of the Jewish people, consciously vigilant for the day of national restoration?

The answer to these questions reflects another aspect of the phenomenal affinity of the Jewish people to the Land of Israel. In spite of bans and prohibitions, in spite of the most improbable and unpromising circumstances, there was never a period throughout the centuries of exile without Jewish immigration to Palestine. *Aliyah* ("going up") was a deliberate expression and demonstration of the national affinity to the land. A constant inflow gave life and often vigor to the Palestinian community. By present-day standards the numbers were not great. By the standards of those ages, and in the circumstances of the times, the significance and weight of that stream of *aliyah*—almost always an individual undertaking—matches the achievements of the modern Zionist movement.

Modern Zionism did indeed start the count of the waves of immigration after 1882, but only the frame and the capacity for organization were new: the living movement to the land had never ceased.

The surviving records are meager. There was much movement during the days of the Moslem conquest. Tenth century appeals for *aliyah* by the Karaite leaders in Jerusalem have survived. There were periods when immigration was forbidden absolutely; no Jew could "legally" or safely enter Palestine while the Crusaders ruled. Yet precisely in that period Yehuda Halevi, the greatest Hebrew poet of the exile, issued a call to the Jews to immigrate: and many generations drew active inspiration from his teaching. (He himself died soon after his arrival in Jerusalem in 1141, crushed, according to legend, by a Crusader's horse.) A group of immigrants who came from Provence in France in the middle of the twelfth century must have been scholars of great repute, for they are believed to have been responsible for changing the Eretz Israel tradition of observing the New Year on only one day; ever since their time, the observance has lasted two days. There are slight allusive records of other groups who came after them. Among the immigrants who began arriving when the Crusaders' grip on Palestine had been broken by Saladin was an organized group of three hundred rabbis who came from France and England in the year 1210 to strengthen especially the Jewish communities of Jerusalem, Acre, and Ramleh. Their work proved vain. A generation later came the destruction by the Mongol invaders. Yet no sooner had they passed than a new immigrant, Moses Nachmanides, came to Jerusalem, finding only two Jews, a dyer and his son; but he and the disciples who answered his call reestablished the community.

Though Yehuda Halevi and Nachmanides were the most famous medieval preachers of *aliyah*, they were not the only ones. From the twelfth century onward, the surviving writings of a long series of Jewish travelers described their experiences in Palestine. Some of them remained to settle; all propagated the national duty and means of individual redemption of the "going up" to live in the homeland.

The concentrated scientific horror of the holocaust in twentieth-century Europe has perhaps weakened the memory of the experience of the people to whom, year after year, generation after generation, Europe was purgatory. Those, after all, were the Middle Ages; those were the centuries when the Jews of Europe were subjected to the whole range of persecution, from mass degradation to death after torture. For a Jew who could not and would not hide his identity to make his way from his own familiar city or village to another, from the country whose language he knew through countries foreign to him, meant to expose himself almost certainly to suspicion, insult, and humiliation, probably to robbery and violence, possibly to murder. All travel was hazardous. For a Jew in the thirteenth, fourteenth, or fifteenth century (and even later) to set out on the odyssey from Western Europe to Palestine was a heroic undertaking, which often ended in disaster. To the vast mass of Jews sunk in misery, whose joy it was to turn their faces eastward three times daily and pray for the return to Zion, that return in their lifetime was a dream of heaven.

There were periods, moreover, when the Popes ordered their adherents to prevent Jewish travel to Palestine. For most of the fifteenth century the Italian maritime states denied Jews the use of ships for getting to Palestine, thus forcing them to abandon their project or to make the whole journey by a roundabout land route, adding to the initial complications of their travel the dangers of movement through Germany, Poland, and Southern Russia or through the inhospitable Balkans and a Black Sea crossing before reaching the comparative safety of Turkey. In 1433, shortly after the ban was imposed, there came a vigorous call by Yitzhak Tsarefati, urging the Jews to come by way of then tolerant Turkey. Immigration of the bolder spirits continued. Often the journey took years, while the immigrant worked at the intermediate stopping places to raise the expenses for the next leg of his journey or, as sometimes happened, while he invited the local rich Jews to finance his journey and to share vicariously in the *mitzvah* of his *aliyah*.

Siebald Rieter and Johann Tucker, Christian pilgrims visiting Jerusalem in 1479, wrote down the route and stopping places of a Jew newly arrived as an immigrant from Germany. He had set out from Nuremberg and traveled to Posen (about 300 miles). Then

| Posen [Poznan] to Lublin | 250 miles |
| Lublin to Lemberg [Lvov] | 120 miles |
| Lemberg to Khotin | 150 miles |
| Khotin to Akerman | 150 miles |
| Akerman to Samsun | 6 days |

| Samsun to Tokat | 6–7 days |
|---|---|
| Tokat to Aleppo | 15 days |
| Aleppo to Damascus | 7 days |
| Damascus to Jerusalem | 6 days |

The Ottoman Sultans had encouraged Jewish immigration into their dominions. With their conquest of Palestine, its gates too were opened. Though conditions in Europe made it possible for only a very few Jews to "get up and go," a stream of immigrants flowed to Palestine at once. Many who came were refugees from the Inquisition. They comprised a great variety of occupations; they were scholars and artisans and merchants. They filled all the existing Jewish centers. That flow of Jews from abroad injected a new pulse into Jewish life in Palestine in the sixteenth century.

As the Ottoman regime deteriorated, the conditions of life in Palestine grew harsher, but waves of immigration continued. In the middle of the seventeenth century there passed through the Jewish people an electric current of self-identification and intensified affinity with its homeland. For the first time in eastern Europe, which had given shelter to their ancestors fleeing from persecution in the West, rebelling Cossacks in 1648 and 1649 subjected the Jews to massacre as fierce as any in Jewish history. Impoverished and helpless, the survivors fled to the nearest refuge—now once more in Western Europe. Again the bolder spirits among them made their way to Palestine.

That same generation was electrified once more by the advent of Shabbetai Zevi, the self-appointed Messiah whose imposture and whose following among the Jews in both the East and the West were made possible only by the unchanged aspirations of the Jews for restoration. The dream of being somehow wafted to the land of Israel under the banner of the Messiah evaporated, but again there were determined men who somehow found the means and made their way to Palestine, by sea or by stages overland through Turkey and Syria.

The degeneration of the central Ottoman regime, the anarchy in the local administration, the degradations and exactions, plagues and pestilence, and the ruin of the country continued in the eighteenth and well into the nineteenth century. The masses of Jews in Europe were living in greater poverty than ever. Yet immigrants, now also in groups, continued to come. Surviving letters tell about the adventures of groups who came from Italy, Morocco, and Turkey. Other letters report on the steady stream of Hasidim, disciples of the Baal Shem-Tov, from Galicia and Lithuania, proceeding during the whole of the second half of the eighteenth century.

It is clear that by now the state of the country was exacting a higher toll in lives than could be replaced by immigrants. But the immigrants who came shut their eyes to the physical ruin and squalor, accepted with love every hardship and tribulation and danger. Thus in 1810 the disciples of the Vilna Goan who had just immigrated, wrote:

> Truly, how marvelous it is to live in the good country. Truly how wonderful it is to love our country. . . . Even in her ruin there is none to compare with her, even in her desolation she is unequaled, in her silence there is none like her. Good are her ashes and her stones.[13]

These immigrants of 1810 were yet to suffer unimagined trials. Earthquake, pestilence, and murderous onslaught by marauding brigands were part of the record of their lives. But they were one of the last links in the long chain bridging the gap between the exile of their people and its independence. They or their children lived to see the beginnings of the modern restoration of the country. Some of them lived to meet one of the pioneers of restoration, Sir Moses Montefiore, the Jewish philanthropist from Britain who, through the greater part of the nineteenth century, conceived and pursued a variety of practical plans to resettle the Jews in their homeland. With him began the gray dawn of reconstruction. Some of the children of those immigrants lived to share in the enterprise and purpose and daring that in 1869 moved a group of

---

13 Avraham Yaari, p. 330.

seven Jews in Jerusalem to emerge from the Old City and set up the first housing project outside its walls. Each of them built a house among the rocks and the jackals, in the wilderness that ultimately came to be called Nahlat Shiva (Estate of the Seven). Today it is the heart of downtown Jerusalem, bounded by the Jaffa Road, between Zion Square and the Bank of Israel.

In 1878 another group made its way across the mountains of Judea to set up the first modern Jewish agricultural settlement at Petah Tikva, which thus became the "mother of the settlements." Eight years earlier, the first modern agricultural school in Palestine had been opened at Mikveh Yisrael near Jaffa. As we see it now—and they in 1810 would not have been surprised, for this was their faith and this was their purpose—the long vigil was coming to an end.

But the conception and application of practical modern measures for the Jewish restoration was preceded by a fascinating interlude: Zionist awakening in the Christian world.

The affinity of the Jewish people for Palestine, unique in the historic circumstances, had become an integral part, inextricably entwined in the texture of Western culture. It was a commonplace of all education. The persistence of the Jewish people as an entity, kept alive for century after century of monstrous persecution by a faith in ultimate restoration to its Homeland was congenial to some Christians, unpalatable to others. The Christian Churches had their share in perpetuating the forced exile of the Jewish people. To Catholics it was a matter of duty as God's servants to enforce the Jewish dispersion; they therefore could not even countenance Jewish restoration to their land. It was part of his apostasy that in 464 the Emperor Julian announced his intention of rebuilding the Temple. With the splits and schisms in the Church, the coming of the Reformation, and the evolution of the various Protestant sects, voices were heard proclaiming it as a Christian act to help the Jewish people regain its homeland. Palestine, however, was in the hands of the

Ottoman Turks, and there was no means of translating Christian feeling into action.

In practical Christian minds this situation began rapidly to change during the early nineteenth century. The first catalytic agent may have been Napoleon Bonaparte. On launching his campaign for the conquest of Palestine in 1799, he promised to restore the country to the Jews. Though Napoleon was forced to withdraw from Palestine, the prospect he opened may have been instrumental in setting off a chain of developments, primarily in Britain, which grew in intensity and significance as the nineteenth century wore on.

A distinguished gallery of writers, clerics, journalists, artists, and statesmen accompanied the awakening of the idea of Jewish restoration in Palestine. Lord Lindsay, Lord Shaftesbury (the social reformer who learned Hebrew) Lord Palmerston, Disraeli, Lord Manchester, George Eliot, Holman Hunt, Sir Charles Warren, Hall Caine—all appear among the many who spoke, wrote, organized support, or put forward practical projects by which Britain might help the return of the Jewish people to Palestine. There were some who even urged the British government to buy Palestine from the Turks to give it to the Jews to rebuild.

Characteristic of the period were the words of Lord Lindsay:

> The Jewish race, so wonderfully preserved, may yet have another stage of national existence opened to them, may once more obtain possession of their native land. . . . The soil of "Palestine still enjoys her sabbaths, and only waits for the return of her banished children, and the application of industry, commensurate with her agricultural capabilities, to burst once more into universal luxuriance, and be all that she ever was in the days of Solomon.[14]

In 1845 Sir George Gawler urged as the remedy for the desolation of the country, "Replenish the deserted towns

---

[14] A. W. C. Crawford, Lord Lindsay, *Letters on Egypt, Edom and the Holy Land* (London, 1847), Vol. II, p. 71.

and fields of Palestine with the energetic people whose warmest affections are rooted in the soil."[15]

There were times when this concern took on the proportions of a propaganda campaign. In 1839 the Church of Scotland sent two missionaries, Andrew Bonar and Robert Murray M'Cheyne, to report on "the conditions of the Jews in their land." Their report was widely publicized in Britain and it was followed by a Memorandum to the Protestant Monarchs of Europe for the restoration of the Jews to Palestine. This memorandum, printed verbatim by the *London Times,* was the prelude to many months of newspaper projection of the theme that Britain should take action to secure Palestine for the Jews. The *Times,* in that age the voice of enlightened thought in Britain, urged the Jews simply to take possession of the land. If a Moses became necessary, wrote the paper, one would be found.

Again and again groups and societies were projected or formed to promote the restoration. The proposals and activities of Moses Montefiore found a wide echo throughout Britain. Many Christians associated themselves practically with his plans; others brought forward plans and projects of their own and even took steps to bring them to fruition. What was probably the first forerunner in modern times of the Jewish agricultural revolution in Palestine was the settlement established in 1848 in the Vale of Rephaim by Warder Cresson, the United States consul in Jerusalem; he was helped by a Jewish-Christian committee formed in Britain for the Jewish settlement of Galilee.

The ideas of Col. George Gawler, a former governor of South Australia, before and after the Crimean War, when he formed the Palestine Colonisation Fund; of Claude Reignier Conder, who, with Lieutenant Kitchener, carried out a survey of Palestine and brought to public notice the fact that Palestine could be restored by the Jews to its ancient prosperity; of Laurence Oliphant, the novelist and politician, who worked out a comprehensive plan of restoration and a detailed project for Jewish settlement of Gilead east of the Jordan; of Edward Cazalet, who pro-

---

[15] George Gawler, *Tranquillisation of Syria and the East* (London, 1845), p. 6.

posed equally detailed projects—all were broached and propagated against a background of widespread Christian support.

By the middle of the century the concept of Jewish restoration began to be considered in responsible quarters in Britain as a question of practical international politics. In August 1840 the *Times* reported that the British government was feeling its way in the direction of Jewish restoration. It added that "a nobleman of the Opposition" (believed to be Lord Ashley, later Lord Shaftesbury) was making his own inquiries to determine:

1. What the Jews thought of the proposed restoration.
2. Whether rich Jews would go to Palestine and invest their capital in agriculture.
3. How soon they would be ready to go.
4. Whether they would go at their own expense, requiring nothing more than assurance of safety to life and property.
5. Whether they would consent to live under the Turkish government, with their rights protected by the five European powers (Britain, France, Russia, Prussia, Austro-Hungary).

Lord Shaftesbury pursued the idea with Prime Minister Palmerston and his successors in the government and was incidentally instrumental in the considerable assistance and protection against oppression that Britain henceforth extended to the Jews already living in Palestine.

The Crimean War and its aftermath pushed the ideas and projects into the background, but they soon came to life again. In 1878 the Eastern Question reached its crisis in the Prusso-Turkish War, and the Congress of Berlin gathered to find a peaceful solution. At once reports spread throughout Europe that Britain's representatives, Lord Beaconsfield (Benjamin Disraeli) and Lord Salisbury, were proposing as part of the peace plan to declare a protectorate over Syria and Palestine and that Palestine would be restored to the Jews.

Though these reports were unfounded, the idea again caught the imagination of political thinkers in Britain. It was widely supported in the newspapers, which saw it as both a solution to the Jewish problem and a means of eliminating one of the perennial causes of friction between the powers. So popular was the idea with the British public that the weekly *Spectator* on May 10, 1879, in criticizing Beaconsfield for not having adopted it, wrote: "If he had freed the Holy Land and restored the Jews, as he might have done instead of pottering about Roumelia and Afghanistan, he would have died Dictator."

No less significant is the fact that the idea of Jewish restoration, when it was presented in the form of practical projects, was not rejected by the Moslem authorities. In 1831 Palestine was conquered from the Turks by Mehemet Ali, who ruled it from Egypt for the next nine years, introducing a comparatively pleasant interlude in the life of the country. It was at this time that Sir Moses Montefiore began developing his practical plans. In 1839 he visited Mehemet Ali in Egypt and put forward a large-scale scheme for Jewish settlement which would regenerate Palestine. Mehemet Ali accepted it. Montefiore was in the midst of discussing practical details with him when Mehemet was forced to withdraw from Palestine, which returned to Turkish rule.

Forty years later the Turks themselves were presented with practical plans for Jewish colonization and autonomy in a part of Palestine. The most important of these plans was that carefully and conscientiously worked out by Laurence Oliphant, who demonstrated to the Turks that it was in their own interest, as well as in Britain's, to help fulfill a Jewish restoration in Palestine. His detailed plan for the settlement of Gilead was supported and recommended to the Turkish government by the leading personalities in Britain: the Prime Minister Lord Beaconsfield, the Foreign Secretary Lord Salisbury, and even the Prince of Wales (later King Edward VII). The French government, through its Foreign Minister Waddington, also added its encouragement.

The Sultan showed considerable interest in the plan, the Turkish Foreign Office even proposed some amendments for further discussion. But again events intervened. In 1880, a general election drove Beaconsfield—considered by Turkey as her friend—from office, to be replaced by William Ewart Gladstone. To the Turks, Gladstone was an enemy. The Oliphant scheme, based on Turco-British cooperation as well as a similar scheme proposed by the British industrialist Edward Cazalet were shelved and faded into history.

By now the effervescence among the Jewish people began to find its outlets.

Jewish organizations were now launched. The result was a wave of immigration, to be known later as the First Aliyah, which laid the solid foundation of the new Jewish agriculture. The advent of Theodore Herzl was only fifteen years away, and with it the beginning of the modern political frame for the return to Zion: the World Zionist Organization.

Throughout the ages, and now in the nineteenth century when the restoration of the Jewish people to Palestine and the restoration of Palestine to the Jewish people was discussed in growing intensity, when scores of books and pamphlets and innumerable articles published in Europe, America, and Britain put forward both ideological motivation and practical projects for the consummation of the idea, never once was it suggested openly or covertly that the Holy Land could not, or should not, be restored to the Jews because it had become the property of others. There were many who disliked the Jews; there were Christians who objected on theological grounds to the very idea of reversing the "edict" of exile. Imagine what would happen to the Catholic dogma of the inadmissability of Jewish restoration if a Jewish State were suddenly to arise! They had enough reason to seek grounds and means of resistance to the spread of the idea. Yet nothing led anyone to believe or to suggest that there was any other nation which had a claim, or had established an affinity or connection, or had made such a contribution in sweat or in blood, to have and to hold the country for its own.

No such nation existed, nor any such claim. The claim

of historic association, of historic right, of historic ownership by the Arab people or by a "Palestinian entity" is a
fiction fabricated in our own day.

After the Jews had been absent as a nation for eighteen
centuries, this was a self-evident truth, which is also part
of the historic record.

"No nation has been able to establish itself as a nation
in Palestine up to this day," wrote Prof. Sir John William
Dawson in 1888, "no national union and no national
spirit has prevailed there. The motley impoverished tribes
which have occupied it have held it as mere tenants at
will, temporary landowners, evidently waiting for those
entitled to the permanent possession of the soil."[16]

There was another fact that gave immediate practical
impact to the logic and justice of Jewish restoration. Palestine was a virtually empty land.

When Jewish independence came to an end in the year
70, the population numbered, at a conservative estimate,
some five million people. (By Josephus' figures, there were
nearer seven million.)

Even sixty years after the destruction of the Temple, at
the outbreak of the revolt led by Bar Kochba in 132,
when large numbers had fled or been deported, the Jewish
population of the country must have numbered at least
three million, according to Dio Cassius' figures. Seventeen
centuries later, when the practical possibility of the return
to Zion appeared on the horizon, Palestine was a
denuded, derelict, and depopulated country. The writings
of travelers who visited Palestine in the late eighteenth and
throughout the nineteenth century are filled with descriptions of its emptiness, its desolation. In 1738 Thomas
Shaw wrote of the absence of people to till Palestine's
fertile soil. In 1785 Constantine François Volney described the "ruined" and "desolate" country. He had not
seen the worst. Pilgrims and travelers continued to report
in heartrending terms on its condition. Almost sixty years

---

[16] Modern Science in Bible Lands (New York, 1890), pp. 449–
450.

later Alexander Keith, recalling Volney's description, wrote, "In his day the land had not fully reached its last degree of desolation and depopulation."[17]

In 1835 Alphonse de Lamartine could write:

Outside the gates of Jerusalem we saw indeed no living object, heard no living sound, we found the same void the same silence . . . as we should have expected before the entombed gates of Pompeii or Herculaneam . . . a complete eternal silence reigns in the town, on the highways, in the country . . . the tomb of a whole people.[18]

Mark Twain, who visited Palestine in 1867, wrote of what he saw as he traveled the length of the country:

Desolate country whose soil is rich enough, but is given over wholly to weeds—a silent mournful expanse. . . . A desolation is here that not even imagination can grace with the pomp of life and action. We reached Tabor safely. . . . We never saw a human being on the whole route.

And again:

There was hardly a tree or a shrub anywhere. Even the olive and the cactus, those fast friends of a worthless soil, had almost deserted the country.

So overwhelming was his impression of an irreversible desolation, that he came to the grim conclusion that Palestine would never come to life again. As he was taking his last view of the country, he wrote:

Palestine sits in sackcloth and ashes. Over it broods the spell of a curse that has withered its fields and fettered its energies. Palestine is desolate and unlovely. . . . Palestine

---

[17] Thomas Shaw, *Travels and Observations Relating to Several Parts of Barbary and the Levant* (London, 1767), p. 331ff; Constantine François Volney, *Travels Through Syria and Egypt in the Years 1783, 1784 and 1785* (London, 1787); Alexander Keith, *The Land of Israel* (Edinburgh, 1844), p. 465.

[18] *Recollections of the East*, Vol. I (London, 1845) pp. 268, 308.

is no more of this workday world. It is sacred to poetry
and tradition, it is dreamland.[19]

By Volney's estimates in 1785, there were no more
than 200,000 people in the country.[20] In the middle of the
nineteenth century the estimated population for the whole
of Palestine was between 50,000 and 100,000 people.[21]

It was the gaping emptiness of the country, the specta-
cle of ravages and neglect, the absence of a population that
might be dispossessed and the growing sense of the country's having "waited" for the "return of her banished
children" that lent force and practical meaning to the
awakening Christian realization that the time had come
for Jewish restoration.

What is the Arab historical connection with Palestine?
What is the source of their fantastic claims?

The Arabs' homeland is Arabia, the southwestern peninsula of Asia. Its 1,027,000 square miles (2,630,000
square kilometers) embrace the present-day Saudi Arabia,
Yemen, Kuwait, Bahrein, Qatar, Trucial Oman on the
Persian Gulf, Muscat and Oman, and South Yemen.
When in the seventh century, with the birth of the new
Islamic religion, the Arabs emerged from the desert with an
eye to conquest, they succeeded in establishing an empire
that within a century extended over three continents, from
the Atlantic Ocean to the border of China. Early in their
phenomenal progress they conquered Palestine from the
Byzantines.

Purely Arab rule, exercised from Damascus by the
Omayyad dynasty, lasted a little over a century. The Omayyads were overthrown in 750 by their bitter antagonists,
the Abbasids, whose two centuries of government was
increasingly dominated first by Persians, then by Turks.
When the Abbasids were in their turn defeated by the
Fatimids, the Arabs had long had no part in the govern-

---

[19] *The Innocents Abroad* (New York, 1966), pp. 351, 375, 401,
441.
[20] Vol. II, p. 219.
[21] De Haas, p. 39n.

ment of the empire, either at the center or in the provinces.

But the Arabs had one great lasting success: throughout a large part of the subjugated territories Arabic became the dominant language and Islam the predominant religion. (Large scale conversions were not on the whole achieved by force. A major motive in the adoption of Islam by "nonbelievers" was the social and economic discrimination suffered by non-Moslems.) This cultural assimilation made possible the so-called golden age of Arabic culture.

"The invaders from the desert," writes Professor Philip K. Hitti, the foremost modern Arab historian, "brought with them no tradition of learning, no heritage of culture to the lands they conquered. . . . They sat as pupils at the feet of the peoples they subdued." What we therefore call "Arabic civilization" was Arabian neither in its origins and fundamental structure nor in its principal ethnic aspects. The purely Arabic contribution in it was in the linguistic and to a certain extent in the religious fields. Throughout the whole period of the caliphate the Syrians, the Persians, the Egyptians, and others, as Moslem converts or as Christians or Jews, were the foremost bearers of the torch of enlightenment and learning.

The result was a great volume of translation from the ancient writings of a host of cultures in East and West alike, from Greece to India. Most of the great works in mathematics, astronomy, medicine, and philosophy were rendered into Arabic and in many cases were thus saved for Europe. The translation period was followed by the even brighter glow of great original works in Arabic on all these subjects, as well as on alchemy, pharmacy, and geography.

"But when we speak of 'Arab medicine' or 'Arab philosophy' or 'Arab mathematics'," notes Hitti, "we do not mean the medical science, philosophy or mathematics that are necessarily the product of the Arabian mind or developed by people living in the Arabian peninsula, but that body of knowledge enshrined in books written in the

Arabic language by men who flourished chiefly during the caliphate and were themselves Persians, Egyptians or Arabians, Christian, Jewish or Moslem.

"Indeed, even what we call 'Arabic literature' was no more Arabian than the Latin literature of the Middle Ages was Italian. . . . Even such disciplines as philosophy, linguistics, lexicography and grammar, which were primarily Arabian in origin and spirit and in which the Arabs made their chief original contribution, recruited some of their most distinguished scholars from the non-Arab stock."[22]

Whatever the precise definitions of the cultural historians, the Arab Empire certainly ushered in a cultural era that illuminated the Middle Ages. In this golden age Palestine played no part at all.

The history books and the literature of the period fail to reveal even a mention of Palestine as the center of any important activity or as providing inspiration or focus for any significant cultural activity of the Arabs or even of the Arabic-speaking people.[23]

On the contrary: anyone seeking higher learning, even in specifically Moslem subjects, was forced to seek it at first in Damascus, later in the centers of Moslem learning in various other countries. The few known Palestinian scholars were born and may have died in Palestine, but they studied and worked in either Egypt or Damascus.

Palestine was never more than an unconsidered backwater of the empire. No great political or cultural center ever arose there to establish a source of Arab, or any other non-Jewish, affinity or attachment. Damascus, Baghdad, Cairo—these were the great, at times glittering, political and cultural centers of the Moslem empire. Jerusalem, where a Moslem Holy Place was established on the site of the ancient Jewish Temple, never achieved any political or even cultural status.

---

[22] Philip K. Hitti, *History of the Arabs*, 9th ed. (New York, 1967), pp. 174, 240, 402.

[23] See, for example: R. A. Nicholson, *A Literary History of the Arabs* (London, 1930).

To the Arab rulers and their non-Arab successors, Palestine was a battleground, a corridor, sometimes an outpost, its people a source of taxes and of some manpower for the waging of endless foreign and internecine wars. Nor did a local non-Jewish culture grow. In the early Arab period immigrants from Arabia were encouraged, and later they were given the Jewish lands. But the population remained an ethnic hodgepodge. When the Crusaders came to Palestine after 460 years of Arab and non-Arabic Moslem rule, they found an Arabic-speaking population, composed of a dozen races (apart from Jews and Druzes), practicing five versions of Islam and eight of heterodox Christianity.

"With the passing of the Umayyad empire ... Arabianism fell but Islam continued."[24] The Persians and the Turks of the Abbasid empire, the Berbers and the Egyptians of the Fatimid empire had no interest at all in the provincial backwater except for what could be squeezed out of it for the imperial exchequer or the imperial army.

To the Mamluks who, in 1250, followed the Crusader Christian interregnum, Palestine had no existence even as a subentity. Its territory was divided administratively, as part of a conquered empire according to convenience. Its variegated peoples were treated as objects for exploitation, with a mixture of hostility and indifference. Some Arab tribes collaborated with the Mamluks in the numerous internal struggles that marked their rule. But the Arabs had no part or direct influence in the regime. Like all the other inhabitants of the country, they were conquered subjects and were treated accordingly.

Their state did not improve under the Ottoman Turks. The fact of a common Moslem religion did not confer on the Arabs any privileges, let alone any share in government. The Ottomans even replaced Arabic with Turkish as the language of the country. Except for brief periods, the Arab inhabitants of Palestine had cause to dislike their

---

[24] Hitti, pp. 286–287.

Turkish rulers just one degree less than did the more heavily taxed Jews.

The Arabs did, however, play a significant and specific role in one aspect of Palestine's life: they contributed effectively to its devastation. Where destruction and ruin were only partly achieved by warring imperial dynasties—by Arab, Turkish, Persians, or Egyptians, by the Crusaders or by invading hordes of Mongols or Kharezmians—it was supplemented by the revolts of local chieftains, by civil strife, by intertribal warfare within the population itself. Always the process was completed by the raids of Arabs—the Bedouins—from the neighboring deserts. These forays (for which there were endemic economic reasons) were known already in the Byzantine era. Over fifteen centuries they eroded the face of Palestine.

During the latter phase of the Abbasids and in the Fatimid era, Bedouin depredations grew more intense. It was then that Palestine east of the Jordan was laid waste.

Starting in the thirteenth century, with the entry of the Mamluks, all the instruments of ruin were at work almost continuously. The process went on even more colorfully under Ottoman misrule. Bedouin raiders, plundering livestock and destroying crops and plantations, plagued the life of the farmer. Bedouin encampments, dotting the countryside, served as bases for highway attacks on travelers, on caravans carrying merchandise, on pilgrim cavalcades.

Count Volney, describing the Palestinian countryside, in 1785, wrote:

> The peasants are incessantly making inroads on each other's lands, destroying their corn, durra, sesame and olive-trees, and carrying off their sheep, goats and camels. The Turks, who are everywhere negligent in repressing similar disorders, are the less attentive to them here, since their authority is very precarious; the Bedouin, whose camps occupy the level country, are continually at open hostilities with them, of which the peasants avail themselves to resist their authority or do mischief to each other, according to the blind caprice of their ignorance or the interest of the moment. Hence arises an anarchy, which is still more dreadful than the despotism that pre-

vails elsewhere, while the mutual devastation of the contending parties renders the appearance of this [the Palestinian] part of Syria more wretched than that of any other. . . . This country is indeed more frequently plundered than any other in Syria for, being very proper for cavalry and adjacent to the desert, it lies open to the Arabs.[25]

Neither history books nor reports of travelers, whether Christian, Moslem, or Jewish, report on any other permanent feature of the Arabs' historical relationship with Palestine. In the tenth century the Arab writer Ibn Hukal had written: "Nobody cares about building the country, or concerns himself for its needs." This was a mild foretaste of the ruination of a country, carried out over hundreds of years. There is no reason to blame the handful of Arabs who were part of the medley of peoples that made up the settled population of Palestine.[26] They were merely subject residents, usually downtrodden, of this or that village or this or that town. The remote central authority in Constantinople stretched out its conscripting hand to take away their sons, the local tax farmer sucked them dry; the village over the hill, and the rival tribe, had to be guarded against or fought in a cycle of mutually destructive retaliation. The Bedouin nomads tore up their olive trees, destroyed their crops, filled their wells with stones, broke down their cisterns, took away their livestock—and were sometimes called in as allies to help destroy the next village.[27]

Thus it was that by the middle of the nineteenth century, when hundreds of years of abuse had turned the country into a treeless waste, with a sprinkling of emaciated towns, malaria-ridden swamps in its once-fertile northern valleys, the once-thriving South (Negev) now

[25] Volney, vol. II, pp. 196–197.

[26] "In a peaceful interlude, in the seventeenth century," writes de Haas (p. 16), "one visitor claimed that seventy-seven languages are in use in Jerusalem." For a detailed analysis of the Palestine non-Jewish population, see also James Parkes, *Whose Land?*

[27] James Finn, *Stirring Times* (London, 1878), pp. 315–316.

a desert, the population too had dwindled almost to nothing.

There was never a "Palestinian Arab" nation. To the Arab people as a whole, no such entity as Palestine existed. To those of them who lived in its neighborhood, its lands were a suitable object for plunder and destruction. Those few who lived within its bounds may have had an affinity for their village (and made war on the next village), for their clan (which fought for the right of local tax-gathering) or even for their town. They were not conscious of any relationship to a land, and even the townsmen would have heard of its existence as a land, if they heard of it at all, only from such Jews as they might meet. (Palestine is mentioned only once in the Koran, as the "Holy Land"—holy, that is, to Jews and Christians.)

The feeling of so many nineteenth-century visitors that the country had been waiting for the return of its lawful inhabitants was made the more significant by the shallowness of the Arab imprint on the country. In twelve hundred years of association, they built only a single town, Ramleh, established as the local subprovincial capital in the eighth century. The researchers of nineteenth-century scholars, beginning with the archaeologist Edward Robinson in 1838, revealed that hundreds of placenames of villages and sites, seemingly Arab, were Arabic renderings or translations of ancient Hebrew names, biblical or Talmudic. The Arabs have never even had a name of their own for this country which they claim. "Filastin" is merely the Arab transliteration of "Palestine," the name the Romans gave the country when they determined to obliterate the "presence" of the Jewish people.

Sir George Adam Smith, author of the *Historical Geography of the Holy Land,* wrote in 1891: "The principle of nationality requires their [the Turks'] dispossession. Nor is there any indigenous civilization in Palestine that could take the place of the Turkish except that of the Jews who ... have given to Palestine everything it has ever had of value to the world"[28] This blunt judgment was entirely normal; it aroused no objections and offended no one. It was a simple statement of a unique and irrefutable fact. The Arabs' discovery of Palestine came many years later.

---

[28] Quoted by Herbert Sidebotham in *England and Palestine* (London, 1918), p. 174.

# 5

# Beginning to Restore the Land

The land, unloved by its rulers and uncared for by most of its handful of inhabitants, whose silences Lamartine had likened to those of ruined Pompeii, and which Mark Twain had compassionately consigned to the world of dreams, began to come to life again with the blossoming of Jewish restoration in the nineteenth century. Now, instead of having to adapt the pattern of their living, as they had done for centuries, to the frozen mould of Ottoman stagnation, the Jewish immigrants were able to put down their own fresh roots. In the latter half of the nineteenth century, under the pressure and inspiration of the European powers—especially Britain and France, who were supporting the Sultan's regime against collapse and his empire against Russian penetration—the Ottoman government introduced a series of reforms. Though imperfectly implemented, they restored a degree of law and order in the country and introduced a revolutionary change in the communal law: non-Moslems were henceforth to enjoy equality before the law with Moslems.

This reform was bitterly opposed by the Moslems. Non-Moslems had always been second-class citizens under Moslem rule; and Moslems regarded as sacred the inequality in their favor. It was considered natural law that Moslems should be treated as superior beings.[1] During the middle

---

[1] Ahmed Cevdet, *Tezakir* (Ankara, 1953), vol. 1, p. 68. Quoted in Shimeon Shamir, *Toledot Ha'aravim Bamizrah Hatichon Bazeman Hehadash* (Tel Aviv, 1968), vol. I, p. 243.

of the century, in protest against the new equality, there were many anti-Christian outbreaks, even massacres, in Syria, Mesopotamia, and Arabia. In Lebanon, French troops came in, and at Jidda French and British warships had to be sent to intervene on behalf of the victims.

Empty coffers in Constantinople brought about a reform of even more far-reaching consequence: it became possible to buy land from the Sultan. Tracts of land, mostly in Syria, much of it altogether unworked, were bought by a small number of families.

Hence the renewal of Jewish agriculture. Land could be bought from the new landowners. The Turkish government, however, after the brief flicker of hope of cooperation in 1880, became antagonistic to the Jewish restoration. Faced with the organized movement Hoveve Zion (Lovers of Zion), an Eastern European forerunner of the Zionist Organization, preaching and practising immigration and settlement in Palestine, the Turks imposed a dual prohibition on Jews: they forbade their entry for permanent residence in the country and their purchase of land. The growing number of immigrants thus came into the country as pilgrims, while land was usually acquired by subterfuge and at appreciably higher prices. The ravaged desolation of the land caused many of its non-Jewish inhabitants to leave it, thus bringing on more desolation and denudation. For the returning Jews it held a challenge and a call for care and love.

The struggle of that generation of pioneers in the 1880s and the two generations that followed them was carried on in a harsh climate, on toughened, treeless soil, while waging an often losing battle with malaria, which came up from the swamps and the undrained rivers, and resisting Bedouins, whose marauding habits persisted even into the twentieth century. The process of reviving the country was to be a long one; it continues to this day. But by 1914 Jewish villages dotted the countryside. As for the towns, the Jews became a majority in Jerusalem by mid-century; then they developed the city outside the walls. They began to give new shape to Haifa, Safed, and Tiberias, and in 1909, expanding the borders of Jaffa, they founded what was to become the first modern all-Hebrew city: Tel Aviv.

The non-Jewish inhabitants of the country were the passive beneficiaries of these developments. The Ottoman reforms were followed by the opening up of the area to European and American influences. The Christian Churches established schools in Syria and Lebanon, of which both Christians and Moslems took advantage. The new Jewish immigrants directly or indirectly helped to improve their peasant neighbors' farming methods and to raise their standard of living.

Thus at the eleventh hour, with the onset of the new century, the long process of flight and disintegration of the non-Jewish population in Palestine was halted.

With the founding of the Zionist Organization in 1897 by Theodor Herzl, the longing for the return to Zion for the first time in over seventeen centuries achieved a serious and comprehensive political frame of reference. Herzl's logical policy of working directly and openly for an arrangement with the Sultan's government to create the legal instrument for Jewish colonization on a large scale failed in his short lifetime. Equally unsuccessful were later efforts to establish rapport with the revolutionary Young Turks. Zionism's political progress was blocked, but the physical movement of immigration and restoration continued, in the face of endless difficulties erected by the decrepit, backward and corrupt administration and the physical hardships and perils presented by the ravaged country.

The war that broke out in 1914 provides the most striking confrontation between the passionate Jewish affinity to Eretz Israel, and the absence of any awareness of Palestine in the consciousness of the Arab people in general or the Arab community in the country itself.

To the new and young exponents of the Zionist dream, the meaning of Turkey's entry into the war on the side of Germany was clear from the outset. It was a historic opportunity: defeat of the Turkish Empire could break its hold on Palestine. The Jews, they decided, must range themselves on the side of Turkey's enemies, to help bring about the dismemberment which would make possible

Jewish restoration. In the result, the Jewish people played a part far beyond its weight and size in winning the war. The Jews had no sovereign power and no national base of operations, they were a collection of minorities scattered over the world, and they were in fact fighting as citizens in all the armies on both sides. Yet out of the vast panorama of the first World War and its carnage, and the range of peoples that took part in it, there emerges the phenomenon of an additional, superimposed contribution, a unique voluntary engagement, and a willing sacrifice which sprang from the Jewish passion for Eretz Israel and a now urgent hunger for independence.

The Zionist effort in its various ramifications was spread far and wide. It revolved primarily around the work of three men: Chaim Weizmann, Zeev Jabotinsky, and Aaron Aaronson. Each independently came to the conclusion that Jewish restoration could be built only on the ruins of the Ottoman Empire. Each in his own way sought to provide Britain and her allies with help to win the war.

The question of taking sides was not simple for the Jewish people at large. Considerable numbers of Jews lived in the German and Austro-Hungarian Empires. Their condition was tolerable, certainly incomparably better than the state of the Jews in Russia; tsarist Russia—the ally of Britain and France—was unspeakably, endemically anti-Semitic. In nineteenth- and early-twentieth-century Europe it played the role that a generation later was filled, more directly and thoroughly and scientifically, and with devastating effect, by Nazi Germany. Not the least of the factors weighing in the United States and in its Jewish community for neutrality in the war, or even for support for Germany, was the deep and widespread disgust for the Russian regime and the knowledge that a victory for the Allies would mean a victory for tsarist tyranny.

Moreover, there was now a substantial Jewish population in Palestine, as well as sizable communities in other parts of the Ottoman Empire. All these would be potentially in jeopardy if the Jewish people were to be identified as anti-Turkish. The disadvantages and the dangers of identification with the allied cause were clear.

Fear of Turkish reprisals and hatred of Russia were overcome, however, by a more powerful emotion—the urge to national regeneration.

Under Weizmann's lead the Zionists developed a consistent pro-Allied propaganda in the United States. The issue was crucial—no more and no less than bringing influence to bear in the United States for the government to abandon its neutrality and to join the Allies in the war against Germany. This was amplified, as soon as Turkey entered the war, by the campaign launched by Jabotinsky to form a Jewish Legion in the British Army to fight for the liberation of Palestine. Though the idea of a Jewish military unit inevitably met with considerable opposition both from timid and assimilated Jews and from the British, it prevailed in the end. A Jewish auxiliary unit, the Zion Mule Corps, took part in the Gallipoli campaign. Jewish battalions consisting of volunteers from Britain, the United States, Canada, and Palestine itself took part in the latter stages of Allenby's campaign. They played an especially notable part in the defeat of the Turks on the Jordan River and in driving the Turks out of eastern Palestine (Transjordan).

The Australian General Sir Edward Chaytor told the Legionnaires:

> By your gallant capture of the Umm Es Shert Ford and defeat of the Turkish rearguard I was enabled to push my mounted men over the Jordan and so you contributed materially to the capture of Es Salt and Amman, the cutting of the Hedjaz Railway and the destruction of the Fourth Turkish Army, which helped considerably towards the great victory won at Damascus.[2]

Aaron Aaronson, the only one of the three leaders to live in Palestine at the time, made a major contribution to the conduct of the Allied campaign in Palestine. A brilliant and versatile man, Aaronson by 1914 had won

---

[2] Quoted in letter from Col. J. H. Patterson to British Royal Commission 1937. CO 733/319.

worldwide fame as a scientist, especially as the discoverer of wild wheat. He was chosen by the Turkish government to direct the campaign against the plague of locusts that ravaged the country during the first year of the war. Soon after the war began, Aaronson was afforded details of the extermination in cold blood by the Turks of some two million Armenian subjects of their empire. By this time the Jews in Palestine were already being subjected to terrorization, despoliation, and deportation. In the circumstances it seemed impossible to fight against the Turks. The leaders of the still modest Jewish community bowed their heads to the storm. Aaronson, convinced that a British victory was vital for the Jewish future, organized the Nili group—an intelligence service for the British behind the Turkish lines. He himself managed to find his way to Egypt, where, in addition to directing and maintaining contact with Nili, he became probably the most important adviser at British HQ for the forthcoming invasion of Palestine under the Commander-in-Chief, General Allenby. Aaronson's encyclopedic knowledge of the terrain in all its aspects—population, climatic vagaries, water problems, transport problems—was unique. In addition, a stream of essential current military information came from the Nili Organization. The price paid by Aaronson's group was high. In an attempt to reach Egypt overland by way of the Sinai desert, Aaronson's chief collaborator, Avshalom Feinberg, was killed by Bedouins. In September 1917 the Turks exposed the Nili network. Two of its leaders, Naaman Belkind and Yosef Lishansky, were hanged in Damascus; many of the others were imprisoned and tortured. Among these was Aaronson's sister Sarah, who had served as his deputy. During a respite from torture, she succeeded in shooting herself.[3]

---

[3] Literature on Aaronson, who died in an air crash in 1919, is sparse. See a recent biography by Eliezer Livneh, *Aaron Aaronson Ha'ish Uzmano* (Jerusalem, 1969), and Aaronson's diary notes, published as *Yoman 1916–1919* (Tel Aviv, 1970). See also Anita Engle, *The Nili Spies* (London, 1959), and E. Livneh, Y. Nedava, and Y. Efrati, *Nili Toledoteha Shel Heazah Medinit*, (*Nili: The Story of a Daring Political Venture*) (Tel Aviv, 1961). See also Chaim Weizmann's autobiography, *Trial and Error*, and Vladimir Jabotinsky, *Story of the Jewish Legion* (New York, 1945).

The Nili intelligence proved indispensable. British General Gribbon expressed the opinion that in the crucial battle for Beersheba alone it had saved 30,000 British lives. Even more explicit were Allenby's own words on Aaronson: "He was mainly responsible for the formation of my Field Intelligence Organization behind the Turkish lines."[4]

The significance of that intelligence service was summed up by General Sir George Macdonogh, Director of British Military Intelligence, in a professional lecture after the war:

> You will remember Lord Allenby's great campaign in Palestine in that year and you may have wondered at the audacity of his operations. It is true that in war you cannot expect a really great success unless you are prepared to take risks, but these risks must be reasonable ones. To the uninitiated it may sometimes have appeared that Lord Allenby's were not reasonable. That however was not the case because Lord Allenby knew from his Intelligence every disposition and movement of the enemy. Every one of his opponent's cards was known to him, and he was consequently able to play his own hand with the most perfect assurance. In those circumstances victory was certain.[5]

The Nili underground was surrounded by an atmosphere of perpetual terrorization by the Turkish authorities. From the very beginning of the war the governor, Djemal Pasha, had treated the Jews of Palestine as a potential enemy, since he realized that to the Jews the Turks were the alien occupiers of their country and that Zionism was now an active force in the world. In response to the practical manifestations of Jewish collaboration with the Allies—the Zion Mule Corps in Gallipoli 1915, the campaign in Britian to create Jewish regiments, the Zionist pro-Allied campaign in the United States and elsewhere—Djemal became ever more fierce in his repressions. Police brutality, economic discrimination, arbitrary ar-

---

[4] Letter to Dr. D. Eder, July 19, 1919. In Beit Aaronson files.
[5] Lecture at the Royal Artillery Institution, Woolwich, November 25, 1921. New York *World*, December 4, 1921.

rests, and deportations were the constant companions of the Jews throughout the war. Of a population estimated at some 90,000 at its outbreak, less than 60,000 remained when it ended.

The Arabs living in Palestine did not protest Turkish overlordship. When war came, they fought to perpetuate Turkish imperial rule. The Arabs of Palestine made no response to the call of Sherif Husein of Hejaz, the one zone where Arab action against the Turks developed, and they contributed nothing to even that marginal Arab contribution to the downfall of Turkey. Even when the British forces under Allenby, their path eased and smoothed by the Nili intelligence, finally swept into Palestine, there was no Arab rising behind the lines to help them rout the Turks.

Thus Djemal, commanding the Turkish force which in 1915 made its way through Sinai to attack the British on the Suez Canal, was able in his memoirs to emphasize the spirit of solidarity displayed by the Arab soldiers. "I can have no greater duty," he wrote, "than to offer a respectful tribute to these heroes. . . . In this force, composed of men of Arab and Turkish stock, a fine feeling of brotherly affection prevailed. This first campaign against the Canal was a brilliant revelation of the fact that the majority of the Arabs stood by the Khalifate with heart and soul. The Arabs, who composed the entire 25th division and the whole of the L. of C. Organization, did their duty with the greatest zeal and devotion."[6]

Even after the defeat of the Turks, the Arabs were unable to hide their feelings. British Col. Richard Meinertzhagen recorded in his diary on December 2, 1917:

The Arabs of Ramleh gave us an amusing incident yesterday which accurately reflects their attitude towards us. A large batch of Turkish prisoners were being marched through the village, but they were not preceded by their British Guard. The Arabs, thinking it was the return of the Turkish Army, turned out in force, yelling with delight and waving Turkish flags. [*Middle East Diary*, p. 7]

6 Ahmed Djemal, *Memories of a Turkish Statesman 1913–1919* (New York, 1922), p. 153.

After the war and at the beginning of the British mandatory regime in Palestine, Arabs, among themselves and in trying to engage the sympathies of the Moslem world, emphasized how loyal they had been to the Turks. Writing to the Mufti of Jerusalem on a visit to India in 1923, the Mufti of Haifa noted:

We found repugnance by every Moslem towards anyone who was called Arab. . . . They took him to be like the Sharif Husain of whom they say that he betrayed Islam. . . . We began to rebut this notion and to show all that Palestine had done in giving total aid to the Turkish army and how she fought to the end."[7]

This attitude and behavior were, in fact, natural and logical. Even in 1914 there were no more than the faintest glimmerings of any Arabic national consciousness. After 1908—the year of the Young Turkish revolution—an opposition had come into existence in the empire against the Young Turks' excessive administrative centralization and cultural Turkification. These oppositional groups worked for decentralization and for a recognized status for the Arabic language, but they made no impact on the population: throughout the area the membership of all the groups totaled 126. Of these 22 were from Palestine.[8]

There was no sign of anything remotely resembling a national movement, and a sense of nationality, of "ownership" of the country they lived in, of rejection of the Turks. As late as March 1917 T. E. Lawrence—the last person in the world to understate the Arab case—wrote in a confidential report in the *Arab Bulletin*:

The words Syria and Syrian are foreign terms. Unless he had learnt English or French, the inhabitant of these parts has no words to describe all his country. . . . *Sham* is Arabic for the town of Damascus. An Aleppine always calls himself an Aleppine, a Beyrouti a Beyrouti, and so down to the smallest villages. This verbal poverty indi-

---

[7] See Kedourie, *Chatham House Version*, p. 74.
[8] C. E. Dawn, "The Rise of Arabism in Syria," *Middle East Journal*, Vol. 16 (1962), pp. 148–149.

cates a political condition. There is no national feeling. [*Secret Despatches,* pp. 77-78]

The Arab leaders, before they became involved in the intrigues launched to resist the Jewish restoration, gave unequivocal recognition to the Jewish bond with Palestine and the Jewish right.

The Emir Faisal I, son of Hussein, Sherif of Mecca, who initiated the Arab Revolt, briefly King of Syria and later King of Iraq, signed a treaty with Dr. Chaim Weizmann in February 1919. In this treaty they outlined the relations between "the Arab state and Palestine." There was no mention of mutual "recognition"—in the context of the treaty it was superfluous. That an Arab state was about to arise (as it did) was taken for granted. It was equally taken for granted that Palestine was to be a Jewish state.

Before signing the 1919 treaty with Weizmann, Faisal had told Reuter's Agency: "Arabs are not jealous of Zionist Jews and intend to give them fair play, and the Zionist Jews have assured the nationalist Arabs of their intention to see that they too have fair play in their respective areas" (London *Times,* December 12, 1918).

What was the Zionist area? In a letter to Felix Frankfurter (March 3, 1919) Faisal wrote: "We Arabs, especially the educated among us, look with the deepest sympathy on the Zionist Movement. Our delegation here in Paris is fully acquainted with the proposals submitted yesterday by the Zionist Organization to the Peace Conference and we regard them as moderate and proper."

These proposals had called for the establishment of a Jewish state and specified its boundaries in detail. These took in all of Galilee (including the area up to the Litany River, later torn out of Palestine and transferred to the French zone of interest in Lebanon), the territory east of the Jordan (later torn out of Mandatory Palestine to become finally the Arab Kingdom of Transjordan) and part of the Sinai peninsula.

The treaty itself was couched in simple language:

The Arab State and Palestine in all their relations and undertakings shall be controlled by the most cordial

goodwill and understanding and to this end Arab and
Jewish duly accredited agents shall be established and
maintained in the respective territories.

In the establishment of the Constitution and Administration of Palestine all such measures shall be adopted as
will afford the fullest guarantees for carrying into effect
the British Government's (Balfour) declaration of 2 November 1917.

All necessary measures shall be undertaken to encourage and stimulate immigration of Jews into Palestine on a
large scale and as quickly as possible to settle Jewish
immigrants upon the land.[9]

The treaty further envisaged Jewish aid to the Arab
state. The Zionist Organization undertook to place at the
disposal of the Arab state a commission of experts to
study economic possibilities and to try to obtain economic
help.

A year earlier Faisal's father, Hussein (who in his negotiations with the British on the rewards for his revolt had
demanded all the Asian territory ever included in the
Moslem Empire, except Turkey, and who had been promised most of it—excepting Palestine) had written or inspired an article in the Mecca Newspaper *Al Qibla*
which is most revealing on the relative affinities of Arabs
and Jews to Palestine. It appeared on March 23, 1918,
while the war was still in progress, two months after Hussein had been officially informed of the British government's Balfour Declaration promising the establishment
of the Jewish Home in Palestine.

Hussein called upon the Arab population in Palestine to
welcome the Jews as brothers and to cooperate with them
for the common good.

---

[9] Faisal added in his handwriting in Arabic a clause which reads:
If the Arabs are established as I have asked in my manifesto
of January 4 addressed to the British Secretary for Foreign
Affairs, I will carry out what is written in this agreement. If
changes are made I cannot be answerable for failing to carry
out this agreement.
This was not necessarily an unreasonable reservation; in any case,
it does not affect Faisal's unreserved acceptance of Jewish sovereignty in Palestine.

The resources of the country are still virgin soil and will be developed by the Jewish immigrants. One of the most amazing things until recent times was that the Palestinian used to leave his country, wandering over the high seas in every direction. His native soil could not retain a hold on him, though his ancestors had lived on it for 1,000 years. At the same time we have seen the Jews from foreign countries streaming to Palestine from Russia, Germany, Austria, Spain, America. The cause of causes could not escape those who had the gift of a deeper insight. They knew that the country was for its original sons [abna'ihi-l-asliyin], for all their differences, a sacred and beloved homeland. The return of these exiles [jaliya] to their homeland will prove materially and spirtually an experimental school for their brethren who are with them in the fields, factories, trades, and in all things connected with toil and labor.

In that same year the leaders of the Moslem community in Palestine itself had an opportunity to give formal expression to their attitude toward the movement of Jewish restoration and its recognition by the British government. On July 24, 1918, the foundation stones of the Hebrew University were laid on Mount Scopus in Jerusalem. Christian and Moslem notables attended. The religious leader of the Moslems, Kamil el-Husseini, the Mufti of Jerusalem, laid one of the stones and signed the parchment buried under it. There the date was given as the twenty-first year after the first Zionist Congress and the first year of the Balfour Declaration "promising to grant a national home to the Jewish people in Palestine."

The twilight months of the end of the First World War were a dramatic moment in the history of Eretz Israel. As the 400-year-old Ottoman Empire, crumbling to its fall, released its hold on the country, it brought to a close the long succession of its foreign and—except for the Crusaders—imperial absentee rulers. For nearly two thousand years, though the Jews were powerless to prevent it, no other people had made Palestine its national home. And now Christians and Moslems, whatever resentments they might harbor, however much they might dislike or fear the Jewish return to the land—all now joined in recognition of the title of the Jewish people to be the land's master.

The myth of an Arab historic claim to the country was born later.

# 6

# A Garland of Myths

The distortion of history, ancient and modern, basic to the Arab-British resistance to Jewish restoration, had been fully articulated by 1948. After 1948 the Arabs added greater depth and vehemence in presentation and with it a theme of hatred of the Jews, comparable only to the demonology of medieval Christianity or the excesses of German Nazi propaganda in our own age. Inevitably the propaganda became even more intense and unrestrained after the Six Day War. As Hitler and Goebbels, the arch-propagandists of the century, discovered and taught, the greater the lie, the more likely it is to be believed.

The Arabs' version of history, of their and the Jews' relationship to Palestine, is not uniform. It is often accommodated to the tastes or prejudices of the audience. It not only fabricates; it ignores the known recorded facts and unblinkingly replaces the picture of public knowledge of even a year ago with a completely imagined substitute.

Thus one of the versions in its bold outline goes: Palestine was the Arab homeland even before the Arab-Moslem conquest in the seventh century. The Arabs were the original inhabitants and rulers of the country. The Canaanites were, in fact, Arabs; the Philistines were Arabs; the Amorites were Arabs. The Jews for their part were, in fact, the rulers of the country only briefly—for some eighty years in the days of David and Solomon. In any case, they disappeared and were subsequently swallowed up by the Arabs. The modern Jews are not the descendants of the ancient Jews. This version has not yet reached the point of suggesting that the modern Jews do not exist.

The Western powers—so goes the Arab version—as an act of recompense for the Christian persecution of the Jews, brought them to Palestine, where they drove out the Arab possessors of the country. The Western powers did this by promulgating the Balfour Declaration and the Mandate at the end of the First World War or, alternately, after the Nazi campaign of extermination during the Second World War.

The most startling item in the Arabs' propaganda is their usurpation of the Jewish patrimony of Jerusalem. Arab political propaganda claims that Jerusalem is an "Arab city," has been an Arab city for many centuries, is a holy city in Islam. There is only one small grain of truth in this claim, which on the whole is as false as the quite common description of Palestine as "a land holy to three faiths."

It is possible to call Palestine a land holy to two faiths: to Christianity as well as to Judaism. It was certainly never holy to Islam. Mohammed no doubt turns in his grave at the ignorant suggestion that Islam has a "holy land" other than Arabia. Palestine has no significance in the Moslem religion. It never existed as a country under Arab or any of the other Moslem administrations. Jerusalem does contain a place holy to Islam (and this too was borrowed from Judaism), but the city as such has no significance in Islam.

The known facts are fascinatingly simple. Mohammed, in establishing Islam in Arabia, hoped that both Jews and Christians would adopt the new religion. He called on them to accept him as the successor of both Moses and Jesus, whose original authority and sanctity he respected. To emphasize the affinity and religious continuity between the two older religions and Islam, he at first ordered that when praying the Moslem should adopt the Jewish custom of turning his face to Jerusalem (at that time still under Christian rule). When, however, there was no response by Christians or Jews to his claim or to his appeal, he rescinded the order eighteen months later. Moslems at prayer have ever since turned their faces to Mecca.

It was presumably the recognition by Mohammed of the sanctity of the Holy City of Judaism that gave birth to the Moslem tradition that the Temple Area was the site of his ascent to the seventh heaven. The Koran itself relates only that Mohammed in a single night was transported to heaven by Buraq, a horse with wings, a woman's face, and a peacock's tail. He was first taken to what the Koran called the "uttermost mosque"—*il masjad al aksa*. Jerusalem is not mentioned in the story, and there was, of course, no mosque in Jerusalem. After Mohammed's death the tradition—which did not pass unchallenged by an opposing school of thought—laid it down that the "uttermost mosque" meant the Temple Mount in Jerusalem.

It was not Mohammed's dream that conferred sanctity on the Temple Mount. On the contrary, it was the existing sanctity of the place—it had been holy to the Jews for nearly two thousand years before Mohammed—that inspired the weavers of the legend to choose it as lending a fittingly awesome station for Mohammed's ascent. The Buraq, as the Moslems call the site, is thus in fact a permanent memorial to Islam's recognition of the Jewishness of the Holy Place.

On this legend rests the Moslem claim to the Jewish Temple Mount as a Moslem Holy Place. The Dome of the Rock and the Al Aksa Mosque were subsequently built on the Mount. This, called Haram-A-Sharif, became the third-holiest place in Islam (after Mecca and Medina). It is not known that Mohammed in fact ever set foot in Jerusalem. Here begins and ends the religious significance of Jerusalem to Islam. It is fascinating to reflect what the Christian reaction would be if the Moslem theologians had chosen to declare the Church of the Holy Sepulchre as the station for Mohammed's ascent, then renamed it Buraq, and claimed the site as Moslem property. Christopher Sykes has put it pithily: "To the Moslems it is not Jerusalem, but a certain site in Jerusalem which is venerated . . . the majestic Dome of the Rock. To a Moslem there is a profound difference between Jerusalem and Mecca or

Medina. The latter are holy places containing holy sites. Apart from the hallowed rock, Jerusalem has no major Islamic significance."[1]

Nor were the Moslems overly impressed with Jerusalem's importance when they ruled in Palestine. When, on the fall of the city to the Crusaders in 1099, a Moslem delegation arrived in Baghdad, then the capital of the empire, to seek aid against the invading Christians, the Baghdadis shed tears and expressed sympathy but offered and took no action to help in the recovery of Jerusalem.[2] The city never played any part in the Arabs' political life. While in turn Damascus, Baghdad, and Cairo glittered with the luster of an imperial capital, Jerusalem stagnated as a remote provincial townlet. It never served even as a provincial capital, not even a subprovincial capital (an honor reserved for Ramleh). No less significantly, it was never a Moslem cultural center. No great school of Islamic lore was established nor any religious message proclaimed there. To the Moslems, Jerusalem, though the site of a Holy Place, was a backwater.

Nor did the Arabs attach any importance to living in Jerusalem. Even when the Moslems ruled, for long periods the majority was Christian. After the middle of the nineteenth century, soon after modern Jewish reconstruction began, the Jews attained a majority, which they have never relinquished. Successive Arab attacks, encouraged or permitted by the British, from 1920 onward, gradually squeezed the majority of the Jews out of the Old City and into the New. In 1948, when their ammunition ran out, the final remnant and the handful of defenders surrendered to the Jordanians. That was when the city was divided.

The Arab's slight and superficial relationship to the city has been only recently expanded into a claim of an uncompromising, even exclusive ownership. Just as they originally borrowed the sanctity of the Jewish Holy Place, they have now, in our generation, tried to simulate some-

---

[1] "Holy City," *Encounter,* February 1968.
[2] Hitti, p. 480.

thing of the unique and mystic passion of the Jewish people for their ancient and incomparable Holy City.

In the war of 1948 Abdallah's Arab League under British guidance, captured the eastern part of Jerusalem, including the Old City. The one significant change in the subsequent nineteen years of Jordan rule was the attempt to obliterate the Jewish presence and the signs of Jewish identity. All the synagogues were destroyed. In the ruins of the most famous of them—the Hurvah—an enterprising Arab citizen put together a small stable for his ass or his goat. The ancient Jewish cemetery on the Mount of Olives, overlooking the Old City, was torn up, some of its tombstones being used for paving and some for lavatory seats in Jordanian army camps.[3] The Arabs avoided hurting any Christian susceptibilities and as a result, the many Christian witnesses in the Old City kept silent about acts of desecration and destruction perpetrated against Jewish sites. Then, suddenly for the first time in history the Arabs discovered and revealed to the world, the vehement, passionate almost desperate accents of a deep-rooted and long-standing, undying attachment to Jerusalem.

This fabrication of an emotion which can after all so easily and manifestly be exposed—has yet, again because of the very intensity of its presentation, made at least some impression throughout the world. But it may be helpful in demonstrating a national characteristic of the Arabs which has assumed central importance in the confrontation between the Jewish and Arab peoples: the admitted capacity of the Arabs to manufacture facts, to deceive themselves into accepting them and to work themselves up into a public passion over what is in fact a nonexistent emotion. "What a people believes," writes Hitti about the Arabs, "even if untrue, has the same influence over their lives as if it were true" (p. 88).

What is commonly called the Oriental imagination has long been recognized. It is only in our day, however, that

---

[3] The vandalism in the Old City was described by many writers after the Six Day War. See, for example, Samuel Katz, "The Undivided City," *Israel Magazine* (Tel Aviv), no. 2 (April 1968), pp. 11–17.

it has played a striking part in shaping world events. The amplifying effects of modern communication media—radio and television—and the willing involvement of powerful world interests have presented the Oriental imagination with unprecedented influence. The use of lies in our time as a primary weapon of state policy by the two most powerful totalitarian states the world has known—Nazi Germany and the Soviet Union—has, moreover, set an example. It also introduced techniques whose application has sharpened the Oriental imagination into a highly effective political weapon.

Al-Ghazzali, the great eleventh-century Moslem theologian, wrote: "Know that a lie is not *haram* [wrong] in itself, but only because of the evil conclusions to which it leads the hearer, making him believe something that is not really the case. . . . If a lie is the only way of obtaining a good result, it is permissible. . . . We must lie when truth leads to unpleasant results."

Students of Islam and the Arabs—not least Moslem and Arab scholars—have devoted much attention to the significance and the consequences of the application of this precept. "Lying," writes the Arab sociologist Sania Hamady, "is a widespread habit among the Arabs and they have a low idea of truth. . . . The Arab has no scruples about lying if by it he obtains his objective. . . . He is more interested in feeling than facts, in conveying an impression than in giving a report. The Arab language, moreover, provides its users with the tool, for assertion [*tarokid*] and exaggeration [*mubalong*]."[4]

The result has been the creation of colorful rules in communication. "The Arabs are forced," writes another Arabic scholar, Eli Shouby "to overassert and exaggerate in almost all types of communication, lest they be misunderstood. If an Arab says exactly what he means without the expected exaggeration, his hearers doubt his stand or even suspect him of meaning the opposite."[5]

---

[4] *Character and Temperament of the Arabs* (New York, 1960), pp. 5, 36, 62–63.

[5] "The Influence of the Arabic Language on the Psychology of the Arabs," *Middle East Journal*, 5 (Summer 1951), pp. 284–320.

Falsifying history is not a new Arab art, and it was never confined to the marketplace. According to the whimsical description given by Hitti, "The Arabian genealogist, like his brother the Arabian historian, had a *horror vacui* and his fancy had no difficulty in bridging gaps and filling vacancies; in this way he has succeeded in giving us in most instances a continuous record from Adam or, in more modest compass, from Ishmael and Abraham" (p. 91).

As a major political weapon, however, complex fabrication has developed organically among the Arabs in the two generations of the struggle for Palestine. In their first encounter as a group with the modern world, the Arab leaders discovered how avidly foreign imperialists and other interested parties who were not Moslems and who were not Arabic-language specialists were ready to encourage, and exploit for their own ends, Arab fantasies and exaggerations. The Sherifian Arabs in the First World War and in its aftermath had the great good fortune to be allied with a British agent interested in precisely the kind of fabrication their own culture and custom encouraged. T. E. Lawrence found the appropriate partners for his historic adventure in mendacity.

Thus, for example, the Emir Faisal, in addressing the Paris Peace Conference in February 1918, turned the few train wreckings by his Bedouins into an "advance of 800 miles by the Arab army." The army (of 600 men) did, in fact, move about 800 miles northward, but most of the advance took place only after the British, Australian, and French forces (and in the latter stage a Jewish force) had already driven out the Turks. The size of the army, Faisal claimed, was 100,000, and it had suffered 20,000 casualties. To top it all, his army, he declared, had taken 40,000 prisoners. This tale, however, so suited the British interests at the time that it was only eighteen years later that the British Prime Minister, who had been present at Faisal's speech, described his figures as "Oriental arithmetic."[6]

---

[6] Lloyd George, The Truth About the Peace Treaties, p. 1041. In fact both Arab casualties and Turkish prisoners were only in the hundreds.

At the time the statement was woven into the fable, disseminated by the British and accepted by the world at large as a measure of the scope and impact of the "Revolt in the Desert."

The profit to the Arabs of the Laurentian fraud was not calculated to encourage them to restrain their own national failing and it made its continuous impact on the history of Palestine. It was brought home in incredible drama to millions of citizens throughout the world in June 1967.

The Arab's account of the events of the Six Day War consisted of a counterpoint utterly different to the events themselves. Their reports bore only minimal relation to what was happening—except for the two facts that a war was in progress and that its scene was the Middle East.

Even the identities of the combatants were distorted. The Egyptians and the other Arab states in their wake, repeatedly proclaimed the completely imaginary participation of American and British pilots and planes in the attacks on their airfields. The Egyptians Air Force—which, in fact, never left the ground—was said to be wreaking havoc in Tel Aviv, in Haifa, in Natanya. The Israeli Air Force (which came through the six days with a loss of nineteen planes on all fronts) lost, according to Arab communiqués, 160 planes on the first day alone. Gigantic tank battles in the Sinai desert, with huge Israeli losses, were waged in the Arab reports two and three days after the Israeli forces had overwhelmed the mass of Egyptian armor, and while tens of thousands of Egyptian soldiers were giving themselves up as prisoners or fleeing toward and across the Suez canal.

Some skeptical, case-hardened newspaper readers and television viewers, remote from the scene of conflict, were convinced that after allowing for wartime exaggeration, the war was going very well for Egypt and Jordan and badly for Israel. It could surely not all be untrue. Though it was no doubt untrue that Haifa and Natanya were in flames, they must have suffered some damage. If the Arabs claimed that Tel Aviv had suffered heavy casualties from bombing, some casualties there must no doubt have occurred. Allowing for exaggeration, twenty or thirty Israeli planes had surely been downed. In fact, neither Haifa nor Tel Aviv, or any other city, received a single bomb or any other attack by Egypt. Two shells were fired into Tel Aviv from the Jordan front; a single bomb was dropped in the neighborhood of Natanya by an Iraqi plane.

These allowances for the Oriental imagination were made by the sophisticated, the cynics, the optimists. To large numbers of more credulous people throughout the world it seemed certain by the second day of the war that Israel was on the brink of defeat. Thereafter the balance was restored but it was only by the end of the six days that the realization of the magnitude of the Arab defeat made its full impact.

The effect of the Arab reports was not achieved without the assistance of foreign news media which, credulously or in wishful eagerness, spread them. The Russians, whose own original contribution to the mendacities of the age had precipitated the war, (early in May they had given Nasser unfounded information that Israel had massed forces for an attack on the Syrian border) gave their own enthusiastic intonation to the news of Israeli disasters. They were themselves completely deceived, and in consequence delayed the call for a cease-fire by the Security Council lest too early a cessation might prevent the complete defeat of Israel. The British Broadcasting Corporation served as a main instrument of the Arab information services, publicly repeating even the most improbable of their reports and severely censoring the only version of events—from its reporter in Jerusalem—that corresponded to the truth. Many hours after the officer commanding the Israeli Air Force had announced the destruction of the Egyptian Air Force, British newspapers were still debating whether Britain could stand aside and see Israel destroyed.[7]

The very brevity of the war, the concentration of events, sharpened the exposure in men's minds of the magnitude of the Arab fabrications. Indeed, it awakened many thoughtful Arabs to the dangers to themselves of

[7] See Randolph S. Churchill and Winston S. Churchill, *The Six Day War* (London, 1967), Chapter 8 and Appendix 1.

their imagination. Deception was, after all, the obverse of self-deception. When President Nasser claimed that British and American planes had bombed Egyptian airfields and that Egyptian planes had bombed Israeli cities, he was misleading not only the world, but also the Arabs. He was probably misleading himself because his military chiefs were lying to him. He certainly misled King Hussein of Jordan. Hussein's decision to attack Israel—and to persist in the attack even after the Israeli Prime Minister had urged him to desist to avoid a clash—was probably based on his belief in Egyptian reports of havoc and destruction in Israel.

For it is a well-known part of the character of Arab fantasy that the inventor of a story comes to believe it himself. A charming little tale from Arab folklore tells of a man whose afternoon nap was disturbed by the noise of children playing in the courtyard below. He went out to the balcony and called, "Children, how foolish you are! While you are playing here, they are giving away figs in the marketplace." The children rushed off to collect their figs, and the man, pleased with his invention, went back to his couch. But just as he was about to drop off, a troublesome thought aroused him: "Here am I, lying around, when there are free figs to be had in the marketplace!"

Their misrepresentations of the Six Day War harmed the Arabs most of all. In the years that have followed, a far more complex web of fiction has victimized the Jewish people. The fiction of the so-called Palestine revolution or the "Palestine Liberation" movement could have results no less dangerous than those of the Cairo-Khartoum school's workings after 1918.

The Arab terrorist organizations operating without a Lawrence, adapted the tone and content of their propaganda to prevailing political currents in the world and made effective use of the modern mass media. They disseminated so plausible a statement of their motives, so lively a version of their fighting methods and achievements that the average person, with little opportunity or interest to make a study, naturally tended to accept them. Many people were thus persuaded to believe that the Arab terrorist organizations were daring bands of partisan or guerrilla fighters, springing out of the Arab population of Palestine, determined to regain a lost homeland and suffering an alien and cruel occupation. These fighters, it was maintained, sallied forth by day and by night from the underground bases provided by the sponsorship of the "Palestine nation"; they boldly engaged occupying Israeli army units, with their always superior numbers and with their tanks and their planes. Large numbers of these were thus "destroyed," and very many Israeli soldiers were "killed." No less regularly these brave guerrillas were depicted as penetrating the heart of Israel, where they attacked military installations and inflicted untold damage.

The terrorists' propagandists exploited recent history to suggest that the French maquis, the Scandinavian undergrounds, or Tito's partisans in the Second World War had come to life again in the exploits of the Fatah and its sister organizations.[8] They were pictured more specifically as the latest reincarnation of Castro's guerrillas in Cuba, as blood-brothers to Ché Guevara in the Bolivian jungle, as the tactical disciples of Mao Tse-tung, of the Algerian rebels against French rule, of the Vietcong. This is, of course, the type of story that Europeans and Americans expect to hear, attuned as they are to the taut heroic drama of liberation movements, underground or open, that have captured the public imagination during the past thirty years. The Arabs' action stories have, moreover, often been retailed and given added verisimilitude by the dispatches of eager American and European news correspondents on the spot. They were permitted to visit "secret guerrilla headquarters" and enabled to talk (and to tape-record) participants in "attacks" or "raids," both before and after; they were even permitted to take photographs. The picture thus presented of the purpose of the Arab terrorist organizations, of their origin and background, and of the nature of their activities was a sophisticated, modern fulfilment of Al-Ghazzali's permissive

---

[8] Fatah is the largest and the best known organization, but the differences are not significant in the present context. The name Fatah is therefore used to cover them all. Where required, specific reference will be made.

philosophy: it was a mixture of exaggeration and wishful thinking. It was spread abroad with great intensity by the worldwide labors of a large team of propagandists, some frankly professional, many planted as students at universities in Europe and the Americas, all maintained or subsidized by a vast budget.

In fact, the Fatah and its rival organizations have never carried out or tried to carry out an attack of any significance on any unit of Israel's Army, Air Force, or Navy. Such engagements as have occurred have been initiated by the Israeli forces. These, patrolling border areas or carrying out a search, have encountered Fatah groups, infiltrated across the Jordan river or in the mountains of Galilee at the Lebanese frontier.

Fatah operations have been directed almost exclusively against civilian targets. Except for attempts to sabotage the Israel Water Carrier—the national pipeline carrying water from the comparative abundance of the Lake of Galilee to the semiarid Negev—and mining a border road used by children on their way to school along which Israeli military patrols might be expected to travel, they have, insofar as they have succeeded in operating within Israel, tried to destroy civilian property and to kill civilians. In these operations they have confined themselves almost exclusively to two weapons: explosives with a time mechanism and hand grenades. The explosives have been planted, with becoming intrepidity, in a shopping basket in a crowded supermarket, in a package in a university students' restaurant, under an apartment house at night, and in waste baskets during the rush hours at a bus terminal.

These operations, involving penetration into Israel's population centers and in some cases a momentary mingling with the intended victims, have not been numerous. The Israeli security forces have in nearly all these cases caught the perpetrators, and the cells to which they belonged have been eliminated. By far the greater number of Fatah operations has been executed from outside Israeli territory: mainly across the Jordan River, but also to a lesser degree in the mountains of Galilee straddling the dividing line with Lebanon. Across these borders, at a safe distance, the fighters of Fatah have carried out hundreds of light-artillery attacks.

Such attacks across borders have provided the most picturesque locations for conducted visits by foreign correspondents. Here the missing ingredients of stark military confrontation and of guerrilla valor could be added at will. Journalists and television teams were, for example, taken at night to the banks of the Yabbok River in the heart of Transjordan. Facing each other across the river, two groups of Fatah fighters exchanged artillery fire with careful imprecision. The following day Scandinavian television viewers were shown the Yabbok River, now identified as the Jordan, and the battling forces, one of which was now described as the Israeli Army. The picture of the battle was accompanied by a commentary on the casualties probably inflicted on the Israeli Army and the certain destruction of specific Israeli military targets. Those news-hungry journalists, ignorant of local geography, no experts in battleground reporting, bemused by the night and the noise, unconscious of the Arab's infinite capacity for invention—what reason did they have to doubt the authenticity of the connection between what their eyes saw and what their hosts were telling them?[9]

Why should even an experienced newspaper correspondent at the always secret guerrilla headquarters, amid the noise of nearby exploding shells, speaking to warriors returning to their base, disbelieve their story of a daring crossing of the Jordan River into Israeli-held territory and the successful demolition of Israeli tanks or guns? How could he know that they had in fact merely lobbed shells over the river and then given the suitable texture of battle grime to their face and hands and uniform? Why should the reader of the illustrated newspaper in Paris or the television viewer in Cincinatti doubt the evidence provided by the picture of that begrimed Arab guerrilla and the caption composed by the reporter?

The targets of attacks from across the border were invariably the Israeli border villages—their men and women and children, their domestic animals, their little houses. As

---

[9] See Ehud Yaari, *Fatah* (Tel Aviv, 1970), p. 195.

in the days before 1967, when they were harrassed nightly by Syrian artillery fire pouring down from the Golan Heights, there are children in many villages on the Jordan who do not know what it is to sleep in their own cots; they spent their childhood nights in underground shelters. The routine may be varied by a daylight attack with Katyusha missile throwers on a school bus—described in the Fatah community as a successful attack on Israeli Army transport.

The scope and nature of the operations of the Fatah is marked by a characteristic unique in the history of liberation movements, underground or open. Hundreds of members of Fatah and other terrorist organizations—most of them described as Palestinian Arabs, the rest from the Arab states—are in Israeli detention. During the four years after the Six Day War, they were tried and convicted for taking part in or planning sabotage activities, or for organizing or recruiting for the terrorist organizations. A minority were caught during or following an operation; the rest were denounced by their comrades. As soon as they were questioned, sometimes even earlier, captured officers supplied the names of their subordinates, rank-and-file members gave away their officers. In some cases prisoners reconstructed their operations for the Israeli police, explaining the part played or due to have been played by each of the participants.

There were, of course, exceptions. Some young Arabs kept their lips sealed and showed defiance to their captors and judges. They served to provide an occasional break in the gray picture of so-called freedom fighters prepared, once caught, to jeopardize and indeed torpedo their movement and the cause they claim to be fighting for. It was not to save their lives that they were so free with the freedom of their comrades and the continuation of their struggle. The Israeli military courts do not impose the death penalty, and there is no torturing of prisoners. The advantage to be gained therefore was at most the lightening of a prison sentence.

Nor is this yet the full measure of the masquerade. Fatah and its sister organizations were not born after or as a result of the Six Day War and the Israeli occupation of Judea, Samaria, and Gaza. They came into existence some ten years earlier, when three quarters of a million Arabs in Samaria and Judea lived under Arab rule from Jordan and three hundred thousand lived in the Gaza Strip under Egyptian Arabic rule. They did not enjoy the independence which the Fatah propagandists claim to be as the breath of life to them, and they seemed quite oblivious to its absence. For those nineteen years there was no talk of independence nor any action to secure it. In those years as well Israel was the target of Fatah's activities—Israel in its cramped partition borders. Then, too, Fatah acted in the name of the "Palestinian people"—presumably the Arab-ruled Arabs of Hebron and Jenin and Nablus, as well as the Arabs of Haifa and Jaffa and Nazareth in Israel.

Yet the cardinal fact about the Fatah and its campaign against Israel is that it did not spring from the Arabs of Palestine, whom it claims to represent and for whom it claims to be living and dying. It was not welcomed in their midst or given a minimum of help and of comfort.

Fatah was not founded in Palestine. Throughout the years of non-Israeli rule in Judea and Samaria, it did not have its headquarters there and did not conduct its operations from there. It was founded in Lebanon in the late 1950s. Its first official offices were opened in 1963 in Algiers, in a building placed at its disposal by the Algerian government. Compelled to leave Algeria because of internal Algerian frictions, it established new headquarters in Beirut. In mid-1965 Fatah headquarters were moved to Damascus, where they remained until the Six Day War.

Yasser Arafat, its leader, is not uncharacteristic of the Fatah membership. His claim to have been born in the Old City of Jerusalem may well be true. It is certain that he was brought up and educated in Egypt, after his parents had emigrated there from Palestine. They were not "refugees" or exiles, they had simply moved house in the 1920s, twenty years or more before the State of Israel came into existence. Arafat is said to have served in the Egyptian forces during the invasion of Palestine in 1948. He certainly qualified in Egypt as an engineer and worked there for some time. He moved to a job in prosperous

Kuwait and there began to agitate against Israel. Henceforward his political activity dictated his mode of life. From Kuwait he went to live in Beirut, then in Algiers, then back in Beirut, and then in Damascus. Though he was a frequent traveler, in all the nineteen years of Jordanian Arab rule he did not set foot let alone try to live, still less naturalize his movement, in Judea or Samaria, not even in the city he claims as his birthplace. He gave Palestine and the people who lived there, a wide berth.[10]

Fatah operations against Israel, first launched in 1965, were planned in Syria. The fighters first crossed into Jordan or sometimes into Lebanon and from there infiltrated directly into Israel. All the attacks were hit-and-run raids on civilian targets, and seldom did they stray far from the border. For Fatah members could not expect shelter from the Palestinian Arabs, whether in Jordan-occupied Judea and Samaria or in Israel. With few exceptions the "Palestinian people" was not involved at all, nor did it offer any substantial cooperation, even passive, in these operations.

After the Arab defeat in the Six Day War and Israel's gaining of Judea and Samaria, the Fatah put its pretensions to the test. A month after the Six Day War, Yasser Arafat left his headquarters in Damascus and infiltrated into Palestine, setting up a clandestine headquarters in the market area in Nablus. Later he moved to Ramallah.

Several hundred members of the Fatah recruited in Syria, Algeria, and in European universities were infiltrated into Palestine, some of them taking advantage of the Israeli government's policy of "open bridges" across the Jordan. They succeeded in smuggling in substantial quantities of arms and military equipment.

Assuming that Israel military occupation rule would be harsh and oppressive, inspired by doctrines culled from the Algerian rebellion against French rule, and applying the tactics of the Vietcong in the South Vietnam countryside, Arafat sent agents into the Arab towns and villages of Judea and Samaria to recruit members for the organization and to establish local cells throughout the areas. He

---

[10] Yaari, p. 11.

planned gradually to build into the Arab population an armed force which would sally forth from safe billets to carry out guerrilla attacks, then fade back into the population. Into the Jewish towns and villages he would send teams of saboteurs to wreak death and destruction. His cells, moreover, were to oversee the Arab population; he would set up an underground "government" which would dominate the Arab countryside and population, at least by night. To this end leaflets were distributed clandestinely among the population calling for a boycott of Israeli economic, cultural, and judicial institutions, even of the Israeli radio and newspapers. The leaflets contained instructions for the execution of various simple acts of sabotage, such as rolling rocks down from the hills to block roads or pouring sand into the gas tanks of Israeli vehicles.

The adoption of these ideas, whatever their validity in North Africa or South Vietnam, proved only that Yasser Arafat, true to tradition, was the victim of his own fantasies. Arafat's plans did not work out, not only because the Jews in Palestine were not foreign colonists, but also because he apparently knew little about Palestinian topography, still less about "his own" people, and nothing at all of the outlook and methods of the Israelis whose "occupation" of Judea, Samaria, and Gaza is extremely liberal. (Fatah appeals dated September 1, 1967, at last "warned" the Arab population against the "soft ways" of the Israelis designed to "weaken our resistance.") When the agents Arafat sent to mobilize the Arabs in the countryside reached their destination, they told their hosts tales of their daring in making their way through the mountains and in outwitting ubiquitous Israeli army patrols. The townsmen, even the villagers, were not impressed. They listened to the stories politely. They were the kind of stories expected from heroes. They themselves knew that there were no restrictions on movement in the area in the daytime. One did not have to move in byways and mountain paths. The Israeli government early laid down and pursued a policy of letting the life and occasions of the Arab population go on with a minimum of interference. All that Arafat's agents had to do in order to travel from one town to the next was to board a bus and pay the fare.

A handful of young Arabs, understandably fired by the promise of an early expulsion of the Israelis, did join the Fatah. A few traveled into Jewish towns to carry out acts of terror. The Arab population as a whole, though certainly willing to see the Israelis disappear, turned a deaf ear to appeals for active cooperation. They refused, moreover, to provide billets for their liberators. Instead of safe bases deep in the homes of the population, the terrorists had to make their way to the hills and maintain themselves there. The season was in their favor, the Palestinian summer is well suited for living in the open. By the autumn of 1967 Fatah changed its plans. After barely three months among his "own people," a presumably sobered Arafat, narrowly escaping capture by the Israeli army, returned to Syria and briefly established his headquarters in Damascus, later moving to Transjordan. Neither Fatah nor any of the other "Palestinian" organizations made any serious renewed effort in the years that followed to establish a base within the "occupied territory."

The discrepancy between the propaganda and the reality of the "Palestinian Revolution" is most clearly demonstrated in the almost complete failure of the self-styled revolutionaries to win the physical participation of the "people" which is supposed to be yearning and fighting for its "freedom." The terrorist organizations are not, in fact, nor have they been, an arm of the allegedly homeless Palestine Arabs. Each of them has been the instrument of one or more or all of the Arab states. When the Fatah, after seven years of talk and discussion and much traveling by its founders, in 1965 finally planned a few actual sabotage operations from Syria, it was because the Syrian government had taken the organization under its wing. It remained a client of the Syrian government, which supplied money and training facilities, until after the Six Day War. The Syrian affiliation of the Fatah placed strict limits on its size: its membership was drawn exclusively from those elements among the "refugees" who had Syrian sympathies and associations. It was opposed

by other Arab leaders for reasons of their own, and therefore by their followers among the "refugees." Nasser of
Egypt, and in his wake the leaders of the other Arab
states, argued that guerrilla action was untimely.

The status of the Fatah, the powers driving it on, and
the resources at its disposal changed drastically after the
Six Day War. The Arab states, defeated and not yet able
to resume a direct attack on Israel, began to promote
"popular" terrorist activity on a large scale. They turned
to Fatah as the potential instrument of preparatory attrition, and set up additional terrorist organizations of their
own. From time to time after June 1967 a new body with
an explosive-sounding name announced its birth, but of the
thirty-odd that did so, only twelve appear to have had any
real existence. Of these, only four or five made any impact. Each of them enjoyed the all-embracing patronage
of one or more or all of the Arab states.

The largest contributions in cash came from the fabulously wealthy oil States of Kuwait, Saudi Arabia, and
Libya. Training facilities were provided by Algeria,
Egypt, Iraq, Lebanon, and Jordan. A wide range of arms
poured in from all the Arab states. Instructors were
provided by Egypt, Syria, Jordan, and Iraq. An army of
recruiting officers was set up by the Arab states and sent
out to mobilize "Palestinian refugees"—that is, young men
on the UNRWA lists who were working or studying in
one or another of the Arab states or in European Universities.

The origin, direction, and scope of cooperative action
among the Arab states in the "Palestine Revolution" are
illustrated in the story of Ahmed Arshid (known as
Sword). Classified as a refugee, he enrolled as a student of
industrial economics at Karlsruhe University in West Germany in 1960. In 1965 a Syrian agent enrolled him
nominally in Fatah, and he became its organizer among
the Arabic students of Karlsruhe.[11]

In June 1967, after the Six Day War, still a student, he

_____
[11] His story is told in Dapei Meida (Information Sheets), No. 9,
published by the Ministry of Education and Culture, Jerusalem,
1970, (pp. 11–12).

and 120 other students, were sent to a training camp at Balida in Algeria, where for three weeks they were trained in the elements of sabotage, physical fitness, fieldcraft, and marksmanship using a Chinese revolver and a French rifle, and battle practice with a Sten submachine gun and Russian and Chinese bazookas. The instructors were Algerian officers.

At the end of the course, on July 20, Arshid and thirty-eight other students were flown to Syria. In Damascus they were given more field training, this time with Czech light arms. They were also given a course in theory on the struggle against Israel and on liberation movements in the world, with special reference to China, Cuba, Yugoslavia, and Algeria.

Now qualified for action, Arshid was appointed a staff officer in the command of the Fatah in the Jenin district of Samaria. He was provided with an identity card belonging to an Arab resident of the area and taken by Syrian Army Intelligence to the village of Hama on the border with Jordan. There he transferred to an Iraqi army vehicle, which took him to Amman. He reported to a Jordanian army officer named Assad Shibli on the orders he had been given in Damascus. Shibli gave him a permit for crossing into western Palestine. He succeeded in crossing the Jordan and made contact with Fatah headquarters in the Jenin district. This was in August 1967, during the brief period when Fatah headquarters were in Palestine itself. Shortly after his arrival Arshid was arrested by Israeli security officers.

Between his recuitment in Karlsruhe and his capture in Palestine, he had been mobilized, transported, trained, indoctrinated, armed, and provided with maintenance by the war machines of four Arab states. Only the Palestinian Arabs, the alleged objects of all this activity, proved unwilling to cooperate in achieving the liberation offered them by Arshid. He shared his experience with several hundred other "guerrillas" who made their way into western Palestine that summer. His story is typical of the "Palestine Revolution" and the Palestine "Liberation Movement."

Rebuffed by all but a few of the Palestine Arabs and unable to carry on the only kind of struggle that might conceivably create a basis for the claim of a popular war, unable even to provide some grain of truth to support the stupendous tales of fiction with which the Arab propaganda crowded the communications media throughout the world, Arafat and his colleagues dismissed the episode of their rebuff and its implications. Their pan-Arab sponsors accepted the situation philosophically. They may have been disappointed at the refusal of their Palestinian brothers to make any serious effort at liberating themselves or to allow others to make the effort to liberate them from the "cruel Israeli occupation." They may have felt that Arafat, like Kaukji in 1937–1938 should have imposed his will on the population by force and intimidation. In fact, the Palestinian Arabs were not essential to the objectives.

The Arab states adapted themselves to the new circumstances, even intensifying their cooperation with Fatah. Its sabotage operations within Israel never exceeded limited proportions or rose above the simplest and most primitive techniques, such as firing into a busload of tourists or leaving a few sticks of dynamite in a paper parcel in a school playground; the main force of Fatah was now concentrated in Jordan, with a lesser force in Lebanon. Large rear bases were set up as well as a series of forward bases along the Jordan. An extensive new range of arms, especially field weapons including katyushas of 132 and 240 mm and light and heavy mortars, poured into these camps.

Thus armed—indeed, equipped like a regular army, with guidance and sometimes fire cover given them by nearby Jordan Army units, the Fatah carried out a daily artillery barrage against Israel—that is, against sitting-duck targets: the villages along the Jordan's West Bank.

Substantial damage was inflicted on the villages. Many houses were hit. Work in the fields was repeatedly interrupted. Daily life and household routine were restricted. Children could not play or run about. There was gloom in the air. Beyond this, the results were meager. Nobody ran away. There was no evacuation. No village was abandoned. From the rest of Israel, moreover, came volunteers—veterans of 1948, high-school students, new immigrants—for a stint of labor and guard duty in the harassed villages.

Again, the events themselves carved out a yardstick of confrontation between one kind of devotion to the land and another. When the Israeli Army and Air Force took retaliatory action against the Fatah bases across the Jordan, the Arab farmers in the neighborhood ran away. Though their villages, unless they actually included a base, were not attacked, the Arabs abandoned them all, leaving their houses and fields to seek shelter in the interior of the country. It was not long before the Jordan valley east of the river was emptied of its inhabitants.

Nor did the Fatah persevere in maintaining its permanent forward bases or artillery emplacements. They now continued their attacks from mobile artillery units, which were moved down to the river bank as required and withdrawn after use. The operational bases followed the civilians into the interior of Jordan.

It was precisely after the Fatah found out, and demonstrated that it had no political roots in the Arab population of Palestine that it reached the peak of its fame and its popularity. It now developed its capacity for propaganda and exploited the receptiveness of many elements in the West. The heroic image it created for itself was disseminated throughout the world. Its primary impact was, of course, in the Arab countries. Around the essential fact that operations against Israel were in fact being carried out was built a larger glittering structure of the imagination. The minor terrorist attacks were translated into an awesome campaign that instilled terror into the hearts of all Israel and inflicted such heavy losses on her armed forces that she must surely soon surrender. Operations of great boldness were reported, complete with statistics of the enemy's casualties and of his losses in guns and tanks and even planes. On occasion even accidents and mishaps in Israel were pressed into the eager service of Arab propaganda: when the Israeli Minister of Defense, General

Moshe Dayan, an amateur archaeologist, was severely injured in a fall of earth, the Fatah claimed to have wounded him in a "commando" attack, when Israeli Prime Minister Levi Eshkol died after an illness in Jerusalem, the Fatah proclaimed that he had been killed in a Fatah attack on his home in Degania on the Jordan.

Arab pride soared, and volunteers poured in. They were all absorbed: there was no lack of money or facilities in this liberation movement de luxe, financed as it was by the treasuries of some of the richest states in the world. The number of members in the terrorist organizations in the period 1968–1970 may have reached 10,000, all maintained "in the field"—as full-time soldiers, that is, with all their needs provided for.

The Fatah did in fact take on the aspect of an army on leave. Foreign correspondents in Jordan, Syria, and Lebanon at this time reported large numbers of these young members of the "liberation movement" in their picturesque green-spotted field uniforms, swaggering about in the towns, inviting the admiration of less heroic civilians for vaguely wonderful deeds of valor. There was much movement of jeeps and guns on the roads of Jordan and at Lebanon.

As for the leaders, much of their arduous underground labor resisting and outwitting the Israeli defense forces had to be performed in aircraft flying between the cities of the Middle East, in automobiles racing along highways in Syria or Egypt or Algiers, at much photographed conferences in Cairo and in the first-class hotels. They often also worked hard at being interviewed and photographed at one of their always "secret" headquarters "just before" or "just after" an operation. "Each one of us," later declared Abu Ayad—the pseudonym of Salah Halef, the Fatah leaders' second-in-command— "rode around in an automobile with three or four bodyguards. We attached undue importance to processions, to demonstrations and applause. Let us turn our backs on all this. Let us disregard the cameras. All this must come to an end."

He made this confession at a meeting in a refugee camp in Lebanon on January 3, 1971 (reported in the Tel Aviv newspaper *Haaretz* on January 5, 1971). By this time a drastic change had overtaken the fortunes of the terrorist organizations. Yet another of their bluffs had been called. The chief agent of their decline and their exposure was the Jordanian government.

The Fatah first clashed with the Jordanian government soon after its concentration in Jordan. It was proper for the Jordanian Army to help Fatah agents and saboteurs to cross the Jordan for the common purpose of harassing the Israelis and perhaps persuading the Palestine Arab population to rise in revolt. It was also proper to give intelligence support to their artillery units firing across the river. It was another matter when the Israeli artillery and Air Force retaliated and the farmers of the Jordan valley, the most fertile zone in the country, deserting their homes and their farms, deprived the people of Jordan of crops essential to their economy. No decision of the Jordan government brought this about; the area bordering on the Jordan River simply passed out of its control. Ordinary civilian life all but disappeared as it became a military enclave dominated by the Fatah. With Fatah establishing permanent bases all over the interior of the country, moreover, Israeli Army and Air Force retaliation spread far over the Jordanian countryside.

Nor was this all. The Fatah now also began to ignore the laws of the land and its authorities, arrogating to itself the rights of a regular army responsible only to its own commanders. They accepted as volunteers young citizens of Jordan who were evading enlistment in the Jordanian Army. They set up roadblocks, checking the credentials of law-abiding civilians; they imposed a tax, backed by threats and force, on businessmen; they set up courts, not only for their own members, but for trials of Arabs from western Palestine accused of spying; they set up the beginning of a state within a state.

The "liberation" movement was shifting the focus of its activities. The propaganda campaign abroad continued to mobilize considerable sympathy in the larger world. Consequently there was much less need for actual operations in Israel—especially as these became ever more difficult. Moreover, the smaller terrorist organizations discovered a way of fighting Israel with the maximum of publicity and the minimum of risk: they began to attack Jewish institutions in faraway Europe and, particularly, to hijack civilian planes, Israeli and others, bound to or from Israel. These attacks, which resulted in the murder, maiming, or detention of men, women, and children travelers, and with their overtones of sensation and drama, concentrated universal public attention. At the same time the main object of Fatah activities became the Kingdom of Jordan; and the conflict between the terrorist leaders and Hussein ripened.

From the beginning of his independent activities in Jordan and in anticipation of a clash with the government, Arafat had succeeded in mobilizing the support of substantial sections of the population. He was particularly successful with the many Arabs from Western Palestine who, as "refugees" or otherwise, had moved across the Jordan in the years between the wars. He could also depend on the backing of the other Arab governments, notably Egypt and Syria, who brought pressure to bear on Hussein to stretch the laws of the country for the "liberation" fighters. As early as November 1967 Hussein signed an agreement with the terrorist organizations which, while not giving them the degree of freedom they demanded, accorded them extralegal recognition. They issued their own identity cards, which exempted their members from carrying Jordanian cards. They were not to be allowed to arrest or question people independently, but they could do so in coordination with the government authorities. Though they were not to carry out attacks on Israel from the east bank of the Jordan, the local commanders of the Jordan Army would help them if they crossed the river to attack.

The Fatah honored the agreement more in the breach than in the observance. But the Jordanian government, while trying from time to time to put a brake on its activities within the country, succumbed to the pressures of the Fatah's Arab League sponsors and held back from a serious clash. Periods of mutual recrimination were characteristically followed by periods of demonstrative fraternity and declarations of Hussein's utter devotion to the cause of the "fedayeen." "We are all fedayeen," he once said.

The clash came in September 1970, sparked by the boldest stroke ever carried out by the smaller left-wing organization, The Popular Front for the Liberation of Palestine. In one day it hijacked four planes of different international airlines, demanding the release from prison in Europe of a number of its members sentenced or awaiting trial for previous attempts at hijacking—some of them with lethal consequences—as well as a number of prisoners in Israel. The European governments involved accepted their terms. The Israeli government was able to avoid this problem because the attempt to hijack an Israeli airliner had failed. In the worldwide agitation that accompanied the tense human drama, little attention was paid to the implications of the episode for the Jordanian government. Three of the hijacked planes had been landed near Zerka in Jordan. While the terrorists warned the world that the planes would be blown up with their passengers, the Jordanian Army stood helplessly by; Hussein and his government were powerless to interfere. This severe humiliation—which indicated that Hussein was no more than a figurehead presiding over an anarchic state— proved to be the last straw.

The Jordanian Army launched a widespread attack on the bases of Fatah and other organizations throughout Jordan. A large-scale military clash developed. After eleven days of fighting, the terrorist organizations were defeated.

Amman, the capital of Jordan, had become the center of the terrorist organizations. For eleven days both the center of the city and its suburbs—where Fatah had established bases in the refugee camps—served as a battleground. The foreign newspaper correspondents, from whose reports one might expect to be able to form a reasonably coherent picture, were immobilized in a hotel in the heart of the city.

What the world learned of these events—from the fragments the correspondents were able to piece together, from the statements of the two embattled sides, and from other Arab sources—had to be sifted and measured with very special care for grains of truth. The total number of dead, for example, was estimated by the Jordanian Army at 1,500, but the Egyptian press, drawing on terrorist sources, place it at 30,000. The Jordanian Army's figure was actually close to the truth.

The battle, in which the army made great use of tanks, was fought with the utmost ferocity. The damage to buildings was considerable, and the bodies of the killed lay in the central streets of the city, thickly intermingled with the bodies of the wounded. Many of these died in the late-summer heat, for neither side tried to arrange a truce for their evacuation.

Amman was not the only battleground. The terrorist organizations had established themselves in strength in other towns, especially in the north near the border with Syria. It seems that much of their arms and equipment came from Syria. Jarash and Irbid served at once as staging posts to Amman and as bases for artillery attacks across the northern sector of the Jordan. The Jordanian Army mounted its attack on these bases at greater leisure and continued them well beyond the signing of the truce.

The Arabian governments sponsoring the Fatah adopted an equivocal attitude, while they brought pressure to bear on the Jordanian government to stop what the terrorist organizations described as a slaughter, they did not press too hard until it was clear that the terrorists had been substantially weakened. The only sign of physical intervention came from Syria, whence, at a late stage, a force of fifty tanks arrived at Irbid. This force, grandiloquently described as a Fatah unit, aroused the expectation that the tide of battle would turn, but it turned tail and went back to Syria. (Various explanations have been advanced for the withdrawal: the threat of Israeli intervention, United States diplomacy, Egyptian disapproval.)

The battle now came to an end. The Jordanian government stopped short of an effort to crush the terrorist organizations completely. There followed a series of negotiations and agreements which, in turn, were broken by one side or the other. Reports continued to appear of mopping-up operations against the terrorists in the north and of exchanges of fire here and there. In fact, a new arrangement was reached, uneasy and marred by the bitter memory of September. It was achieved with the help of a "conciliation committee" set up by the Arab states; it reflected approximately the requirements of King Hussein and his government and the somewhat reduced demands of the terrorist organizations.

The Arab states allowed the Jordanian government to weaken the Fatah and the other organizations because they had got out of hand and needed to be disciplined. Nasser and his counterparts could tolerate the worldwide propaganda which projected the image of the terrorist organizations as the most important, the strongest, the most dynamic, and altogether the superlative, Arab factor in the world. This image had great advantages: it emphasized the Palestinians as the objects of Arab concern and struggle. But an intolerable situation was created when Arafat and his junior rivals began to believe the propaganda themselves so far as to threaten the sovereignty of an Arabian government by bringing one of the hijacked planes to Egypt and blowing it up there. By their uninhibited threats to achieve by force at least the dissolution of the State of Israel and the elimination of at least part of its Jewish population (a moderated version of earlier threats), they were further interfering with the Egyptian and Jordanian policy, developed in the latter half of 1970, of achieving that dissolution in stages, the first step being diplomatic pressure to force Israel back to the 1949 Armistice lines.

The pretensions and arrogance of the Fatah and the other organizations had, therefore, to be reduced and the Arab states welcomed Hussein's initiative. Once the organizations had been taught their place, they were expected to resume their role in conformity with the schemes laid down by Egypt and the other Arab states.

Hussein and his advisers, however, exploited their advantage to the hilt. They continued by a combination of guile and force to harass and reduce the terrorists. Progressively they eliminated them from Amman and its neighborhood. Against a remnant entrenched near the Syrian border at Jarash and Irbid, Hussein moved effectively in the spring and summer of 1971. The Fatah fought back, but its troops were routed. Many fled into Syria, some were arrested, and still others were hunted down and killed.

Now followed a most significant episode in the history of the Fatah, lighting up through the fog of propaganda the truths about their pretensions and their illusions. In their extremity they evoked sympathy and pity in all the Arab countries, as well as among the Arabs of Judea and Samaria. Between Jordan and the other Arab states a sharp crisis developed. Hussein was denounced by most of them, with Lybia in the lead, for the ferocity of his onslaught on the terrorists. Pleas for him to desist alternated with threats of boycott, sanctions, and elimination.

None of this actually helped the Fatah. Some of the terrorists now grasped the ironic reality of which they were the victims and swiftly made a choice. They set out westward to seek sanctuary among the only people whose practical compassion and reasonable humanity they could trust. Every day for a week groups of Fatah, called out from the east bank of the Jordan to Israel Army patrols and were enabled to cross the river and surrender. About a hundred succeeded. Many others were not so fortunate. Alerted Jordanian Arab Legion units intercepted them on their way to the river, and shot them down.

The debacle does not necessarily mean the end of Arab terrorist organization or of renewed attempts to harass Israel. The Arab states will no doubt have need of them again. Whatever their future, by their success in disseminating the story of a "Liberation" Movement and the hoax of the "revolution" of the "Palestinian nation," they rendered incalculable service to the Arab states. They mobilized the sympathy of many honestly ignorant people throughout the world who thus unwittingly helped the pan-Arab war effort against the restoration of the Jewish people to its homeland.

# 7

# The Cause of the Conflict

The nature of the Arab purpose in Palestine was illumined, was indeed dramatized by the clash between the terrorist organizations and the Jordanian government that began September 1970. Not an ideological confrontation nor the result of a difference of opinion on the proper fate of Israel, the clash between them was over power and authority. What the Fatah demanded was, in fact, a sharing of power and authority in Jordan. The smaller so-called left-wing organizations led by George Habash and Naif Huwatma called for a complete change of regime—that is, for Palestinian control in Jordan. In those parts of Jordan that adjoined the border with Israel, they demanded complete autonomy; throughout the rest of the country, they demanded a measure of exemption from the laws of the land for the members of their organizations. Hussein and his ministers were prepared to go—indeed, they did go—a long way to meet these demands. The conflict came over the extent of agreement. In the heat of the battle the Palestinians involuntarily abandoned the posture to which their propaganda had for years accustomed the world. Exposed suddenly was the cynical imposture of the plea of homelessness by which hearts in so many countries had been touched.

Are authority, power, autonomy—demanded as a right and, to a degree, even granted—the lineaments of "homeless people" struggling for a homeland? Do they reflect the status of a liberation movement merely enjoying the hospitality of a foreign state? The truth is—and every Arab

159

knows it—that the Fatah does not look on Jordan as a foreign state at all, but as its home, and its members feel completely at home in it. They behave "as though they owned the place"—because they feel that they do, in fact, own it.

Transjordan, the territory of the present Hashemite Kingdom of Jordan, is historically and geographically a part of Palestine. It was the nearly empty three-quarters of the territory originally entrusted to Britain expressly for the Jewish restoration; the territory had, moreover, been liberated from the Turks with the help of Jewish forces. This widely forgotten fact and the existence instead of the Arab state of Jordan underlines the myth of the Palestine Arabs as a "deprived people" driven out of their homeland. Whatever the Palestine Arabs may lack, it is not a homeland; whoever has been deprived, it is not the Arabs.

The encounter in Jordan uncovered only a small part of the not at all secret fact of the Arabs' territorial affinities. It was even more rudely exposed in the confrontation in the Lebanese republic. Though the Arabs do not claim Lebanon as a part of Palestine, in Lebanon the Fatah troops behaved exactly as they had behaved in Jordan. Throughout the country, dotted with their information and recruiting offices, they assumed the right of exemption from the ordinary civic regulations and restraints of the constituted Lebanese authority. They took over refugee camps, turned them into bases, and set up check posts on the highways. In the southern zone, bordering on Israel, they demanded and seized autonomous control. Their rule was so comprehensive that some newspaper correspondents promptly labeled the area Fatahland. It was from here that they fired their mortars across the border into Israel's northernmost villages.

For many months Lebanon, divided into two camps, was in a state of perpetual crisis which almost completely paralyzed its government. The Lebanese (even the lukewarm Christians) were prepared to, and did, go far to meet the Fatah demands. But even the fervent Moslem supporters of the Fatah declined to overstep the limits beyond which lay anarchy. In the end an uneasy compromise was worked out. In the south it was, indeed, enforced willy-nilly by the regular daily appearance of Israeli Army patrols, whom the terrorists on the whole left severely alone. Under this protection the Arab villagers who had earlier fled now came back and resumed their ordered life.

In Lebanon too it was only the exaggeration, the excessive appetite of the terrorist organizations that forced the clash. The principle was not in dispute: the Fatah had rights, the Fatah could feel at home, as Arabs, Lebanon belonged to them as well.

A glaring, and tragic illustration of the Arabs' loose territorial affinities was provided by a largely disregarded aspect of the "refugee" problem. After all has been said of the pressures that were exerted and the panic that was induced by their leaders in 1948, something uncanny remains in the picture of a community, rural as well as urban, not under any physical pressure—even, as in Haifa, asked to remain—nevertheless removing itself, men, women, and children leaving home and farm and business, leaving village and town, to go into a self-imposed exile. The ease of it, its smoothness, are remarkable.

There was no steadfast refusal to leave, as would be encountered in most of the world, certainly from farmers, from people attached to their soil. They went into exile in cold blood, before even there was any fighting. And expecting fighting, they left their fate in the hands of foreign soldiers. It was not a question of evacuating noncombatants; here everybody left, including some 95 percent of the men of military age.

A pregnant description of this phenomenon is contained in the London *Times* of June 7, 1948, in a dispatch from its correspondent in Amman. "Syria, Lebanon, Transjordan and even Iraq were filled with fugitives from Palestine, many of them young men of military age still carrying arms. . . . The cafes and hotel lobbies continued to be filled with young effendis whose idea was that though something must be done it should be done by somebody else. Some of them had spent a week or so at the front and on the strength of this they felt entitled to return to less dangerous climes."

Were they all cowards? Were they all stupid? They were neither. They did not, indeed, think long; they decided quickly. It was not difficult to decide—because they did not see the invaders from the Arab states as foreign soldiers, nor their own destination as an exile. They considered the move as being to another part of the Arab world, to another place where Arabic was spoken, to a place where they would find their own people, often their own relatives. To move from Acre to Beirut, from Akir to Nablus, was like an American's moving from Cincinnati to Detroit or from Trenton to Boston. In all fairness it must be added that not all the Arabs went into exile. Some 100,000 declined to move. Their presumed hatred of Jews and their sense of belonging to a large Arab people and territory apparently did not outweigh their love for their homes. These are the Arabs who, despite inevitable early difficulties, prospered and multiplied in Israel, numbering by 1967 (together with returnees permitted by the Israeli government) some 350,000 souls, with the highest birthrate in the world.

The phenomenon of exodus was given a new dimension in 1967. When the Six Day War was over, without any pressures or promises from any side, when there was not even the hint or rumor of a threat to the safety of life or property, some 200,000 Arabs in Judea and Samaria packed their belongings and crossed the Jordan. Day after day the caravans of trucks and buses and private cars drove down to the approaches to the river. Because the Allenby Bridge was still a collapsed mass of iron and masonry, the crossing had to be improvised. The long queues waited patiently for their turn to cross. Scores of local and foreign newspaper correspondents, photographers, and a sprinkling of unofficial visitors mingled and talked with them while they waited. Three weeks after the war I was able to visit the area. I watched the progress of the evacuees to the bridge. I asked a well-dressed young man where he came from and why he was leaving. He explained that, as an employee of the Jordanian government stationed at Bethlehem, he had been instructed to report to Amman. Once across the river, the Arabs were interviewed by foreign newspapermen. There everyone who told his story claimed to have been driven out by the Jews.

No less significantly, between 1949 and 1967, when the Jordanian Arab king ruled peacefully in Judea and Samaria, some 400,000 Arabs packed their belongings and left for other parts of the "Arab world." Today large numbers of Palestinian Arabs are living and working as ordinary citizens in Syria, Lebanon, Saudi Arabia, Egypt, Algeria, Lybia, and especially prosperous Kuwait. All these countries are home to them. There are, of course, cultural differences, even the spoken language has its local idiosyncrasies, as does the English of London, Yorkshire, or Scotland or the American in New York, Connecticut, or Texas.

The "Palestinian" movement and the "Palestinian" nation are still, in 1972, no more than a myth. The Arabs of Palestine, like all the other Arabs, have been taught to see as their territory the vast expanse between the Persian Gulf on the east and the African Atlantic coast on the west. To the north it borders on Turkey; to the south its Asian boundary is where the Arab peninsula meets the Indian Ocean, and its African frontiers are marked by a line running through the heart of the continent, beginning with the northern border of Uganda to the east and ending with the northern border of Senegal to the west. The existence of a non-Arab state in the center of "his" territory is offensive to the Arab, who has been taught to see it as incomprehensible except in terms of a rampant imperialism. That is the emotional foundation of the Arab's attitude. Israel's existence is therefore out of the question, the new state must disappear. The status and future of the Arabs living in Palestine is essentially a secondary matter, to be settled later, or fought over, among the Arabs themselves. For the time being the resources of the Arab world must be concentrated on camouflaging the reason for Israel's liquidation as a solution to a human problem—the problem of "homeless" Palestinians. The Egyptian journal *El Muswar* in December 1968 admitted frankly: "The expulsion of our brothers from their homes should not cause us any anxiety, especially as they were driven into Arab countries. . . . The masses of the Palestinian people are only the advance-guard of the Arab nation. . . . a plan for rousing world opinion in stages, as it would not be able to understand or accept a war by a hundred million Arabs against a small state."

Such is the core of the confrontation between Israel and the Arab people. It stares out, moreover, beyond the sleight-of-hand of Arab propaganda. The campaign against Israel is conducted, after all, by the whole Arab world. Every one of the Arab states is involved and makes its greater or lesser contribution. At the least, each state co-operates in the economic boycott, in the diplomatic offensive, in the propaganda campaign. What quarrel with Israel has Kuwait on the Persian Gulf, or Sudan in the heart of Africa, or Morocco on the Atlantic Coast? What quarrel, indeed, have Egypt, Syria, and Iraq?

The Arab states are, furthermore, divided among themselves on a number of important problems. The interests of the oil-bearing states conflict with those who have no oil, the rich with the poor, the puritanical Moslem states with the more permissive. Needless to say, the Arab governments, like other governments, are not altruistic. A glance at their ruling classes suggests that, in the matter of concern for others the Arabs are below rather than above average. They are model members in a world where the rule, perhaps inevitable, is for every nation to look out for itself and to pursue its own selfish interest. It is not to help the Palestine Arabs that the Arab states pursue their militant purpose toward Israel.

"If the Arabs could agree on nothing else," wrote one of their great friends, a British officer who served in the Jordanian Arab Legion, "they could at least agree that Israel as a State must be extinguished. *Israel delenda est.*"[1] Such has been the theme ever since the Arab leaders began to see the Arab empire as a tangible aim. In May

---

[1] Peter Young, *The Israeli Campaign, 1967* (London 1967), p. 32.

1946, when the Jewish state was still only a "threat," a meeting at Inshass in Egypt of leaders of the Arab States declared: "The problem of Palestine is not the problem only of the Arabs of Palestine, but of all the Arabs."

Since the Jewish state was established, Arab political and ideological literature has been filled with a mass of semantic variations on the theme.

"When Palestine is injured," said Abdel Nasser in 1953, "each one of us is injured in his feelings and in his homeland."

Eight years later, the outlook had not changed. "The Palestine problem," said Nasser in 1961, "has never been the problem of the Palestinians alone. The whole Arab nation is involved." At its conference in October 1966 the Syrian ruling Ba'ath Party went to the heart of the Arab purpose: "The existence of Israel in the heart of the Arab homeland constitutes the main base dividing the eastern part from the western part of the Arab nation."[2]

Nasser stated it more pointedly, on February 2, 1965, at the Festival of Unity: "The meaning of Arab unity is the liquidation of Israel."

The conflict, then, shorn of legend and fiction, is between the "Arab nation," which possesses eighteen states embracing an area of thirteen million square kilometers, and the Jewish people, claiming the right to its single historic homeland, whose territory even today, after the Six Day War, constitutes less than 1 percent of the territories ruled and dominated by the Arabs.

That is the moral issue in the clash between Arabs and Jews. On the one hand is the hunger of the Jewish people for national independence and physical security in its homeland, a land it has brought back to life. On the other hand is the huge, unsentimental appetite of the Arab people for the unbroken continuity of a vast empire and for the unique status of a nation which, itself dominating minority populations of millions, arrogantly and violently

---

[2] Yehoshafat Harkabi, *Arab Attitudes toward Israel* (Tel Aviv, 1972), p. 93; *Fatah in Arab Strategy* (Tel Aviv, 1969), p. 30, quoting Anabtawi, Palestinian Documents, II, p. 481.

refuses to accept that status for one small segment of its people.

The ambitions of British imperialists, aiming at their own domination of the Fertile Crescent through Arab puppet states, first aroused the idea of a reborn empire in Arab minds as a serious and practical political proposition. Their aid and patient support established the nucleus of the modern Arab empire. After they had conceived and established the Arab League in 1945, the British tended and nurtured it for years thereafter. They first envisaged Palestine as a full partner in that empire, its Jewish population being given minority status as envisaged in the British government's White Paper of 1939. No less important, the British persuaded the Arabs that this plan was feasible. They looked forward to a tangible reward for their friendship. Later, however, the strategic attractions and commercial opportunities of the Arab states drew the attention of other nations, and Britain had to content herself with only a part of the Arabs' favors.

This change flowed from a development which even the most powerful Arab imagination had not conceived. It was precisely in this period that new, unprecedentedly large discoveries of oil were made in the soil of a number of the Arab states. Their economic importance and potential increased overnight. Tremendous impact was now added to their relations in the international area, and especially with the great powers, who are the chief exploiters of the oil. The Arabs became a power in the world.

For many hundreds of years the Arab states had played no part in world affairs. (Few of them had played any part ever in the conduct of their own affairs.) Outside the sheikhdoms of Arabia itself, which pursued the slow tempo of life in the wide spaces and played out their desert rivalries, there simply were no Arab affairs. Nor was there any hunger or striving, for their revival. The Arabs warmed themselves and were contented with memories of past glory. Characteristically they tended to magnify that glory; their imagination expanded the 120 years of the purely Arab empire in the seventh and eighth centuries and fused them with the following three centuries of an empire ruled by Moslems, who spoke and wrote Arabic but, like Saladin, were not Arabs and became Arabs only in the nostalgic retrospection of later centuries. Nevertheless, the Arabs have genuine memories of glory, of military achievements that were the wonder of their age, of the wide sowing of their language and their faith over vast areas of the earth, of the glittering imperial splendor of Damascus and Baghdad, of a cultural contribution that enriched and dazzled medieval European scholarship.

For a thousand years they lived on that glory. In a prolonged and continuous stagnation they ceased, not only to rule, but also to achieve, to create, to build, to strive. Far from reviving past glories, they sank into a lethargy that brought them into the twentieth century as one of the most backward, most immobile of peoples. Students of Arabic history and culture, especially those well-disposed to the Arabs, cite the characteristics responsible for that lethargy. "The Arab is preoccupied with his past," writes the Arab sociologist, Sania Hamady. "The pleasant memories of its glory serve as a refuge from the painful reality of the present" (p. 217).

The roots of this condition are deep. As the scholars point out, lethargy and stagnation are conditioned by Islamic principles of predestination and fatalism. Nor are there reasonable prospects of a change. "It is not an exaggeration to say that after so many centuries of immobility the process of agriculture, industry, exchange and learning had become little more than automatic, and had resulted in a species of atrophy that rendered those engaged in them all but incapable of changing their methods or outlook in the slightest degree. . . . It is incapacity rather than unwillingness to learn that characterizes Arab society."[3]

The Arab leaders who themselves enjoyed a modern education may have been conscious of the stagnation and backwardness of their society. They were nevertheless not equipped, they were indeed helpless to effect any of the

---

[3] H. A. R. Gibb and H. Bowen, *Islamic Society and the West* (London, 1950), pp. 215–216.

apparently revolutionary changes that alone might raise their people to the cultural and technical levels of our age.

Yet now, suddenly, they found themselves with little effort possessed of independence, controlling states with enormous resources and vast territories important in global strategy, ruling over millions of non-Arab minorities. Now, too, they were courted by the great powers of the world. By a little effort of their imagination they saw themselves bridging the black gap of the centuries, winning the recognition of the previously supercilious Western world. Suddenly they could see themselves accepted, with no further cultural effort, as instant full partners in the complex culture of the twentieth-century world, just as they had shared in the building of its foundations during the Middle Ages.[4]

The power of the Arabs' imagination is such that they soon forgot that there had been a gap at all. They soon saw unfolding behind them one continuous stretch of centuries of glory and of Arab life dominant throughout the whole area conquered by the ancient Arabic empire in Asia and Africa. The facts of history between the eighth and the twentieth centuries ceased to exist; and the prospect they induced themselves to see was a direct continuation of what had existed 1000 years ago and more.

From the very outset of the new imperial phase, however, that prospect was scarred by one intrusion: Zionism, striving for the Jewish restoration of Palestine. The member states of the Arab League, which was formed in 1945 to supply the beginnings of coordinated modern Arabic power, were led to believe by the British that the prospect of a Jewish state in Palestine had been finally erased by the White Paper of 1939. Accordingly they announced their acceptance of the White Paper—which also recognized the rights of the Jews to minority exis-

---

[4] An amusing illustration of the full circle of Arab fantasy and sense of values is the picturesque claim of the Arab writer Mahmoud Rousan: "The Arabs invented the wheel, on which modern civilization is built and now they supply the oil which turns the wheel." *Palestine and the Internationalization of Jerusalem* (Baghdad 1965), p. 2.

tence. They were accorded an immediate earnest of British
loyalty to the compact: that same year the British, efficient-
ly and unceremoniously, finally forced the French out of
Syria. The Arabs looked forward to the equally effective
end to snuffing out of the Jewish restoration in Palestine.

The refusal of the Jews to submit to the British dictate,
their underground struggle which, to the Arabs' surprise
and dismay, resulted in the relinquishment of British power in Palestine, consequently ruled out the transfer of
sovereignty (which the British did not legally possess) to
the Arabs. Encouraged, and armed, by the British, the
Arabs rejected even the partition compromise of 1947,
rejecting Zionist pleas for cooperation. If they were to
eliminate the Zionists and to prevent the rebirth of the
Jewish state, they had now themselves to go to war, under
strikingly favorable circumstances.

Then, precisely at the beginning of the new and so
promisingly brilliant era in Arab nationalism, at the very
rebirth of the empire, the Arab states suffered one of the
greatest shocks in all Arab history.

In May 1948 they launched the war against the embry-
onic Jewish state with considerable reason for confidence.
The total Jewish population numbered no more than 650,-
000. Israel's armed force had for the most part had no
more than partisan training. She had no air force at all.[5]
She had just passed through years of strain and tension
and a bitter struggle with the British. When the invasion
by the Arab states opened, she had been under guerrilla
attack for six months by Palestinian Arabs and by advance units from the armies of Syria, Iraq, and Jordan,
aided in a hundred ways by the still ubiquitous British.
(The British civilian administration evacuated by May 14,
1948. The Army began to organize its evacuation well
after that date, completing the process on August 1.)
While the British had opened the land frontiers so that
men and arms could pour in from the neighboring Arab

---

[5] Four fighter planes were later scraped together, and they
brought about a turning point in the war by halting the Egyptian
advance at Ashdod.

countries,[6] they had refused to open a port for the Jews as recommended by the United Nations; and they maintained their blockade in the Mediterranean to prevent any reinforcements from reaching Israel. The United States had announced an embargo and enforced it strictly, so that the Jews were deprived of that source as well.

In addition to these advantages, the Arabs were given massive material support by the British government, which openly provided arms and ammunition for the war (and turned aside criticism at the United Nations that Britian was aiding aggressive invasion by the claim that the State of Israel did not legally exist and could not therefore be invaded). The Arabs further enjoyed expert British leadership; the Transjordanian Arab Legion was officered by British soldiers.

Unknown to the world at the time, the British cooperated in planning at least some phases of the war. On January 15, 1948—the day a new treaty with Iraq was signed at Portsmouth—the British Foreign Minister, Ernest Bevin, reached an agreement with the Iraqi leaders, Prime Minister Saleh Jabr, Foreign Minister Fadil el Jamali, and the elder statesman, then President of the Senate, Nuri el Said. By this agreement the British undertook to speed up the supply of weapons and ammunition ordered from the British government and to supply automatic weapons sufficient for "50,000 policemen." The purpose was to arm the Palestinian Arab fighters to enable them to participate in the liberation of Palestine.[7] A third point in the agreement was that Iraqi forces would enter every area evacuated by British troops in the whole of Palestine, so that a Jewish state would not be formed.[8]

So much for Iraq. Six weeks later, Bevin, at an interview

---

[6] The British themselves announced (in the House of Commons) at the end of February that 5,000 Arabs from the neighboring countries had entered Palestine in the preceding three months.

[7] This was a wildly optimistic estimate. The Iraqis later discovered that the total number of Palestinian Arabs taking part in the fighting was 4,000.

[8] See Kedourie, *The Chatham House Version*, 232–233, quoting Iraqi historian Abd-al-Razzaq al Hosani. The scheme, according to Jamali, was dropped when the Portsmouth Treaty was revoked.

with the Prime Minister of Transjordan attended by General Glubb (the Commander of the Arab Legion), approved the plan of Transjordan to do her share in frustrating the partition plan by invading and occupying the area allotted in the United Nations resolution to the establishment of an Arab state.[9]

Superiority in numbers, overwhelming superiority in arms and ammunition, the eager and substantial help of a major world power, a strategy based on a converging movement on three fronts against a Jewish force largely untrained, poorly armed, and defending a small but densely populated coastal strip—these were surely enough to assure victory and even the slaughter which Arab leaders openly promised.

There was a further reason for the Arabs' confidence: they were convinced of their superiority over the Jews as a fighting nation. Had not the Arabs conquered half the world? True, that had happened 1,300 years earlier, since which time they had distinguished themselves at best in minor in-fighting among rival Bedouin tribes and in the Laurentian tactic of arriving after the battle to claim the victory. They had no difficulty, however, in projecting their seventh-century martial excellence as an abiding fact in the twentieth.

Whoever reads the predictions of the Arabs in 1956, after they had suffered one defeat, and their even more bloodcurdling predictions of victory and destruction in May 1967, after they had suffered two defeats, will recognize the uninhibited, unlimited early certainty of the Arab states in May 1948 that they were about to win a stunning, historic victory and that within a few weeks, or even days, Jewish hopes would be in ruins and Palestine would be inexorably enfolded in the embrace of the reborn Arab empire.

1948 has entered Arab history as the year of the catastrophe. The Arab states were saved from complete rout by political considerations: the submission by the

---

[9] J. B. Glubb: *A Soldier with the Arabs* (London, 1957), pp. 63–66.

novitiate Israeli government to British and United States pressures. Thus Transjordan remained in possession of most of the area allotted in the United Nations resolution to the Arab states (Samaria, Judea, and eastern Jerusalem), while Egypt occupied the Gaza district. Israel, however, was not only not obliterated, she improved substantially upon the collapsible borders of the UN resolution of 1947 and emerged from the conflict with the high prestige of courage and resource in the face of overwhelming odds. Moreover, some 400,000 Arab residents of the area lost their homes.

Soon the shock and the shame gave way to the search for scapegoats and for excuses. "The Arab," notes an Arab writer, "is reluctant to assume responsibility for his personal or national misfortunes, and he is inclined to put the entire blame upon the shoulders of others. The Arab is fascinated with criticism—of the foreigner, of fellow-countrymen, of leaders, of followers, always of 'the other,' seldom of oneself."[10] There is a cultural reason for this habit. Hamadi explains: "As a result of his determinist orientation, the Arab finds a good excuse to relegate his responsibility to external forces. He attributes the ills of his society, his mistakes and failures, either to fate, to the devil or to imperialism" (p. 187).

Thus, as time went by, the material aid and the diplomatic support and military cooperation which their British allies had given the Arabs in the war of 1948 and the loaded American neutrality—which together, nearly insured the Arabs' objective of annihilation—were translated through Arabic literature into a Zionist invasion aided by British and American imperialism.

Some such far-reaching explanation of their failure was necessary to the Arabs for another important historical reason. It was unacceptable that the brave, the resourceful, the chivalrous, the lion-hearted Arabs (of the seventh century) should be defeated by, of all peoples, the Jews—the lowly, the contemptible, whom they, the Arabs, had long since condemned to death. The Arabs knew the Jews

---

[10] F. A. Sayegh, *Understanding of the Arab Mind* (Washington, 1953), p. 28.

in Palestine historically as a minority oppressed, or at least discriminated against, since the seventh century. The Jews under Moslem rule were second-class citizens. Social regulations and prohibitions singled them out. They were subject to special taxes. They were, of course, not alone—all non-Moslems were so treated. But in the eyes of the Moslems, the Jews in Palestine lived always in the image of a defeated people, in the daily shadow of their defeat in 70 and 135 C.E. The Christians, inferior though they were, had in their background a world of states, of power. The Jews had nothing, they were outcasts over large areas of the Christian world as well. Even when the Arab was himself ill treated or humiliated in Moslem non-Arab society, he saw the Jew as one grade below him. The confrontation with the Jews in British-controlled Palestine had no doubt amended this attitude, yet now to be defeated in the open battlefield, at such a historic moment and in such favorable circumstances, by the Jews—that was an overwhelming blow to Arab pride.

The State of Israel, as the instrument of the Arabs' defeat and what they described as their dishonor, thus became the focus of all their frustrations, of all their hatreds, and of a hunger for vengeance which, by force of a combination of circumstances, grew fiercer and deeper with time. Honor and pride could be restored only by the disappearance of Israel. Again, then—*Israel delenda est.*

The continuing enhancement of the Arabs' international stature only increased the frustration. This, after all, was the era of colonial disengagement. The Dutch, the Belgian, the French, and the British empires were disintegrating. Asia and Africa became a checkerboard of independent states, most of them established with little or no struggle. One Arabic-speaking country after another became independent. From seven states at the United Nations in 1948, the Arabs grew to a bloc of eighteen by 1972. The Arab states, though their average illiteracy rate is among the highest in the world, have perhaps more influence at the United Nations than any other group of nations.

The years have moreover, seen a steep increase in oil wealth. While normally a people labors for years to achieve minor improvements in the national income and the standard of living, some of the Arab states have overnight joined the richest countries in the world in terms of per capita wealth. The ease with which their wealth and influence—and in most cases their political independence —were accomplished led them all to the more to think of 1948 as an unhappy accident for which the "imperialists" were responsible. When the time came, they decided, the Israelis could be beaten and with ease "driven into the sea."

A great new force helped to bolster Arab hopes of victory and annihilation. The Soviet Union, by its steady stream of arms to Egypt, Syria, and Iraq and by unstinting political support, replaced Britian as the big brother of Arabism.

The Arabs' rejection of the Jewish state in any form was deepened and sharpened by another development. Though subjective and contrived, it held a momentous and ugly significance. As though to harden themselves and their people against any weakening of resolve, against any tendency to come to rational terms with Israel as an existing fact, the Arab intellectuals and leaders evolved a comprehensive creed, an ideology of hatred, to justify the physical destruction of the Jewish state, even the extermination of its people.

Little heed has been paid to this phenomenon outside the Arab states, even by the prospective victim herself. Just as the program outlined in Hitler's *Mein Kempf* was largely ignored and his prescription for the "solution of the Jewish problem" dismissed, as the rantings of an unbalanced mind, so presumably has the stated purpose of the Arabs been treated as too incredible to be taken seriously, despite the frequency and the unanimity with which it is expressed in speech and in writing. As much of it as has been translated has apparently been assumed to be fringe literature. Nothing could be further from the truth.

This literature consists of hundreds of books published since 1948 in Egypt, Syria, Lebanon, Jordan, and Iraq, in addition to thousands of articles. They range from the vulgar and the primitive to the sophisticated and pseudo-scholarly. Their theme is that the liquidation of Israel is not only a political necessity, but also a moral imperative; that Israel and its people—indeed, the Jewish people as a whole—are by their very nature evil; that it is thus not only desirable, but even permissible to destroy them. This doctrine has been compounded by a large measure of old-fashioned anti-Semitism. In comprehensiveness and absence of restraint the Arab demonology probably goes further even than the worst excesses by the German Nazis heralding their "final solution" of the Jewish problem.[11]

There were cases after 1948 where Arabs with a Western education were compelled to admit that, if Egypt was governing Gaza—which was certainly not part of Egypt—and if the government of Transjordan was governing Eastern Jerusalem—which was not part of Transjordan—it did indeed seem to be the Arab states which had invaded Western Palestine. Yet the Arab attack, they claimed, was an act of self-defense. For the establishment of the Jewish state was *as such* an act of aggression against the Arab people. Israel was established in order to destroy Arab nationalism. This was a constant theme with Abdel

---

[11] The catalogue of anti-Israel and anti-Jewish attack is a very long one. So far only one scholar has ventured on the task of examining in detail this horrifying aspect of the Arab war on Israel. Yehoshafat Harkabi has made a study at once comprehensive and penetrating of the major part of this literature. What began as a doctoral thesis before 1967 developed into several major works. They are all presented with scholarly restraint and almost line-by-line documentation from thousands of publications and speeches, mainly after 1948. The people of Israel, and liberal-minded people everywhere, owe Dr. Harkabi (formerly a general on the Israel Defence Force General Staff) a debt of gratitude for the painstaking and tireless research which may arouse an awareness of the monstrous ideology of hatred that has been injected into the public mind in the Arab countries and beyond. The material in the following pages is based largely on Dr. Harkabi's central work, now available in English: *Arab Attitudes toward Israel*, (Tel Aviv, 1972).

Nasser. "We all know," he said, for example, on May 14, 1956, the eighth anniversary of the birth of Israel, "why Israel was established. Not only to set up a National Home, but to be one of the factors in liquidating Arab nationalism."

Any Arab attack on Israel was therefore an act of self-defense, any act by Israel to defend herself against attack was a new act of Zionist aggression. Consequently, when Israel retaliated for Arab sabotage and murder across the Armistice lines, it was Israel that had committed a breach of the Armistice Agreement. Moreover, every achievement by Israel which strengthens her or improves living conditions in the state is considered an act of aggression against the Arab people—the opening of the new Knesset building in 1966 was such an act of aggression. Any act of friendship toward Israel by any state or individual is a hostile act toward the Arab people.

The charge of aggression by existence, however, was only the opening of the Arabs' black charter. The next phase was the charge of further aggression by expansion. A considerable literature thus developed on Israel's plans to expand at the expense of the Arab states. A Syrian Ba'ath Party Conference resolution in October 1966 declared that Israel "serves as a solid base for attack, to secure the interests both of imperialism in the zone and of the reactionary regimes . . . threatening constantly to swallow other portions of the Arab homeland and to destroy their Arab qualities."[12]

> The forces at the disposal of Zionism throughout the world are capable, once they strike roots in Palestine, of threatening all the Arab countries and to be a frightening and constant danger to their lives. The means employed by the Zionist forces for growing and expanding will put the Arab world at their mercy, paralyze its vitality and prevent its progress and improvement in the scale of civilization—if the Arab is allowed to continue to exist at all.[13]

---

[12] Harkabi, *Fatah*, p. 30, quoting Anabtawi, Palestinian Documents, II, p. 481.

[13] Constantine Zurayk, *The Meaning of Disaster* (Beirut 1956), p. 69.

It is thus an accepted belief throughout the Arab world that there is a map on the wall of the Knesset in Israel delineating the borders of Isreal in accordance with the divine promise in the Bible: from the Euphrates to the river of Egypt.

The charge of expansionism was, however, not in itself enough. It was elaborated to read that it is not the desire for expansion that motivates Israel, but sheer hatred of the Arab people. Israel seeks to destroy their unity, she is the enemy of their liberation, their independence, their progress. "Israel has an abiding hatred of all that we do for our advancement," wrote one Arab author "because our advancement spells death to Israel."

Distributed throughout Arabic literature is a substantial list of activities pursued by Israel to this end. Israel is said to have interfered in various international negotiations to prevent the grant of loans and other forms of aid to Arab countries, in order to keep them backward. Again, Israel has been fighting Arab culture. In order to minimize and distort Arab achievements and capacities, Israel executed a comprehensive plan for installing Israeli lecturers in American universities to teach the Arabic language and culture. This was done in such a way as to bring the Arabs into contempt. In Africa—so the Africans are told —Israel has distributed falsified copies of the Koran and of various Christian writings.

Inevitably considerable competition reigned among Arab writers and politicians in the composition of frightening descriptions of the state of the Arab minority living in Israel. Israel was depicted as enforcing a brutal oppressive rule over the Arabs, depriving them of all civil rights, even preventing them from making a living. Arabs in Israel, the story continues, had no recourse to civil courts, being tried only by military courts. Their lands and their water for irrigation were taken from them. There was not a single Arab among the 35,000 civil servants. They were prevented from opening their own schools, where their children could be taught Arabic. They were prevented from celebrating their holidays. Special taxes were imposed on them. As for religion, they were simply prevented from going to their mosques. Moslem (and

Christian) holy places were constantly under "attack" by the Israeli authorities.

Now the onslaught deepened. It was not only in relation to the Arabs that Israel was portrayed pejoratively. The people of Israel were said to be inherently evil. They were frustrated by failure, and as a form of compensation, they let the army rule them. They were cowards, quaking even during times of quiet at every sign of progress in the Arab countries. In battle they ran away at the very sight of the brave Arab fighter. Their victories in war were won for them by the imperialists.

The Israelis were corrupt. The government, the army, and the police, all cooperated with smugglers, thieves, drug peddlers, and white slave traffickers. In fact, there was no government in Israel to speak of; the country was headed by a number of criminal gangs who had become a ruling class.

Yet the vilification of Israel and of its people was only a part, perhaps the smaller part, of the incredible demonic structure built around its image. The Arabs made a comprehensive effort to create around the Jewish people as a whole an atmosphere of hatred and contempt intended to smooth the path, when it becomes physically possible, to their extirpation.

At first the Arabs applied practical anti-Jewish measures: they extended their economic boycott of Israel to Jews as such everywhere. In the Arab states, trade with, for example, American companies is conditional on their owners, managers and employees sent to serve in the Arab country not being Jews. In at least one case, under pressure from the Lybian government, an oil company stopped using on its ships Swedish safety matches carrying a trademark similar to the Star of David.

The leaders of Arab thought gathered up all the well-worn and some long-forgotten themes of Western Christian horror stories about the Jews and added whatever was available in the Koran and other Moslem writings as well as pearls of their own wisdom and presented the finished brew as "well-known" facts. Throughout all these writings runs the common theme that all Jews are the lowest, most contemptible people in creation. They are arrogant, domineering, and cunning; they are treacherous and cowardly; they are mercenary and wanton; they are liars and swindlers. They used to destroy states from within by Communist subversion; though now, since the Arab alliance with Soviet Russia, they destroy them as capitalists and colonialists, by lending money to governments at exorbitant interest. They hate each other and everybody else. They are parasites who hate hard work, which is why there are no Jewish farmers. They think of themselves as the Chosen People and interpret this as the right to commit any crime with impunity.

Their Bible is an immoral book, being an emanation of the Jewish spirit, which is intrinsically evil. The Talmud is no less immoral. By it the Jew, who is forbidden to steal, is yet permitted to steal from non-Jews; forbidden to commit adultery, he is permitted to take his neighbor's wife if the neighbor is not Jewish; forbidden to kill, he may yet kill a non-Jew.

This demonology gone berserk was further provided with frequent supporting quotations from Western anti-Semitic sources, such as Hitler or Rosenberg in Germany, Leese or Jordan in England; from ancient Moslem sources; sometimes, in imitation of the sophisticated Western anti-Semites, even from Jewish sources.

On the foundations thus laid the Arabs proceeded, exactly as had the Nazis, to level the accusations of specific contemporary evil against the Jewish people which, in Europe, led logically to the "final solution" of the gas chambers. Thus (borrowing from the Nazis) they charged the Jews specifically with having corrupted the pure Moslem and Christian society in Palestine by bringing prostitution to the country. They borrowed from old Moslem literature to charge them with practicing witchcraft to achieve their ends. Borrowing once again from Western sources, they held the Jews, the eternal enemies of humanity, responsible also for two world wars.

The list is long, nothing is omitted. The Arabs do not hesitate to draw on the lowest depths of twentieth-century anti-Semitic incitement. They became the revivers of the blood libel. The accusation that the Jews use the blood of non-Jewish children for religious purposes, usually on the Passover, is disseminated as historic truth over a substantial range of Arabic literature since 1948. Everything that was ever written by European haters of the Jews in order to provoke pogroms, and by the Christian anti-Semites who, to the same end, introduced the blood libel into the Ottoman Empire in the nineteenth century, is now reproduced by the Arabs. A book designed to indoctrinate the blood libel was published under the authority of the Egyptian government in 1962.

Further, the Arabs having committed themselves to the purpose of annihilation, exploited the most notorious of all the Christian anti-Semitic fabrications: the Protocols of the Elders of Zion, which has long been a central pillar of the vast edifice of anti-Semitic indoctrination. More than any other book in the first half of the twentieth century, the Protocols provided the ideological justification for the physical destruction of the Jewish people. It was employed in Tsarist Russian anti-Semitism, it was one of the textbooks of German Nazism, and it has been called the "father of the Holocaust."[14] The Protocols were taken up by the Arab leaders of thought as a major weapon in their campaign to prepare the ground once again for the extermination of the Jewish people. No fewer than seven Arabic translations of the full text were published between 1949 and 1967. Harkabi lists five additional books containing précis of the Protocols and thirty-three in which the Protocols are quoted with approval.

Imperceptibly, as though it were self-understood, even this most comprehensive of anti-Semitic libels has been woven into the official "doctrine" of the Arab governments. The prime minister of Iraq, in an official letter sent on his behalf by the head of his secretariat, expressed his appreciation to the translator of one of the Arabic editions of the Protocols in 1967. More significantly, Abdel Nasser

---

[14] By Norman Cohn, *Warrant for Genocide: The Myth of the Jewish World Conspiracy and the Protocols of Zion* (London, 1967).

called the Protocols to the attention of a visiting Indian writer, assuring him that it "proved beyond any shadow of doubt that three hundred Zionists control the destinies of Europe."[15]

To insure total and most fruitful insemination of their doctrine, the Arab leaders then compiled a curriculum of hatred for use by their children. The anti-Israel and anti-Jewish catalog became a basic element in the study of history in the schools, which began with teaching "ancient Jewish history" to ten-year-olds in the fourth grade. It was also injected, more subtly and insidiously, into subjects completely unrelated to political or national affairs. Geography, grammar, literary readings, arithmetic, both in the classroom and in hundreds of textbooks, inculcated the theme of the Zionist or the Jew as the embodiment of evil, the ultimate bogeyman, the proper object for "killing" or "destroying."

Arab children are taught the blood libel. In 1962 the Egyptian government produced for use in the schools a reprint of an old text on the blood libel, *Talmudic Human Sacrifices*. The new edition contains an up-to-date foreword by Abdel Qati Jalal, which states: "The Talmud believes that the Jews are made of different material from the rest of mankind, those who do not share the beliefs of the Jews being animals devoid of sense or they are servants and chattels of the Jews. ... Their wise men laid it down that there is no law but their own desire, and no doctrine but their own lust. They commanded their people to bring harm to the other peoples, to kill their children, suck their blood, and take away their wealth." This book, like others on the same theme, recounts the story of a number of the blood libels in history and presents them to the children of Egypt as proven truth. Nor did the education authorities overlook the Protocols of the Elders of Zion. This is taught to Arab teenagers as a factual work, a Jewish admission of the conspiracy to dominate the world.

Under the auspices of the state, the new generation of Arabs is brought up to hate, despise, and fear the Jews;

---

[15] R. K. Karanjia, *The Arab Dawn* (Bombay, 1958), p. 330.

to believe not only that it is right and proper for every good and self-respecting Arab to fight the Jewish state, but that it is just and desirable and even vital to destroy it; that it is necessary not only to destroy Israel, but also to treat its inhabitants like an evil growth that must be extirpated.

The annihilation of Israel and of its people is thus not merely a convenient political objective. It has become a self-understood purpose demanded by the Arab future no less than by Arab history, by Arab honor and pride no less than by Arab pragmatic interest. It has become basic to all Arab thinking, and it is not kept secret. No Arab politician and—with the exception of one or two notable exiles[16]—no Arab intellectual has expressed contradictory opinions.

---

[16] The Algerian writer in exile Abdel Razek Kader has boldly championed Israel's cause. See his reasoned article, "Real Enemy of the Palestinian People" in the *Jerusalem Post*, January 8, 1969.

# 8

# Israel's Function in the
# Modern World

Only once throughout the eighteen years of the Armistice Agreement did any Arab leader challenge the thesis that war alone would bring about the elimination of Israel. There were continual and often acrimonious discussions on the timing of the predestined onslaught on the Jewish state. The optimists—led usually by the Syrians and, in later years, by the Fatah—called for immediate military action. The realists—first among them President Nasser—explained repeatedly that war on Israel required careful and long preparation and insisted on the prior fulfillment of three conditions: Arab military superiority, Arab unity and the diplomatic isolation of Israel. One superrealist appeared to challenged the thesis itself. This was Habib Bourguiba, the President of Tunisia, then at loggerheads with Nasser. Bourguiba believed that the problem could be tackled piecemeal, first of all by subtle diplomacy and propaganda. The Arabs, he urged, should announce their acceptance of the United Nations partition proposal of 1947. They should thus recognize Israel, provided she withdrew from the Armistice borders of 1949 to the "borders of 1947." If Israel refused this offer, the world would understand and view sympathetically a combined military attack on her by the Arab states. Should Israel accept the offer, however, it would be simple to crush her then in the narrow, disjointed, incredibly vulnerable frontiers proposed in 1947.

183

This proposal of destruction by stages was seen as so revolutionary and moderate that all the walls of Arabdom outside Tunisia shook with the denunciation of its author. Bourguiba was hard put to recall to his critics that he differed from them only in method. On the common aim the ruler of modern Carthage was as steadfast as they: *Israel delenda est*.

Tunisia was a minor and somewhat passive participant in the confrontation with Israel, and Bourguiba's influence was minimal. Nasser, however, hastened to remove all doubt or misunderstanding about both purpose and method. "The liquidation of Israel," he said on March 8, 1965, "will be liquidation through violence. We shall enter a Palestine not covered with sand, but soaked in blood."

He was to pursue for two years more his policy of cautious build-up. The irrational assumption in May 1967 that his three conditions had materialized and that victory was assured led to the Six Day War. Thus, in the three weeks before the war broke out, the full meaning of Arab intentions was made clear to the world.

Never in history could an aggressor have made his purpose known in advance so clearly and so widely. Certain of victory, both the Arab leaders and their peoples threw off all restraint. Between the middle of May and the fifth of June, worldwide newspapers, radio and, most incisively, television brought home to millions of people the threat of politicide bandied about with relish by the leaders of these modern states. Even more blatant was the exhilaration which the Arabic peoples displayed at the prospect of executing genocide on the people of Israel. To Jews everywhere the contents of the speeches and the crowd scenes from Egypt and the other Arab states conjured up, by voluntary association, memories of Auschwitz. In those three weeks of mounting tension people throughout the world watched and waited in growing anxiety—or, in some cases, in hopeful expectation—for the overwhelming forces of at least Egypt, Syria, Jordan, and Iraq to bear down from three sides to crush tiny Israel and slaughter her people.

Israel's victory in the Six Day War has been described in superlative terms. It has been the subject of a vast literature. What effect did their defeat have on the Arabs? Did it alter their purpose? Were they now capable of making a more sober summing up of the factors operating on each side? Now that Israel was for the first time established within truly defensible borders, and with the evaporation of their last hope of wiping her off the face of the earth in one lightning battle—did the Arabs begin to think of possible coexistence?

The Arab states, having recovered from the shock of the defeat they had brought on themselves, deliberately demonstrated a sharpened intransigence. Such a posture was, from their special imperialist point of view, even more logical than before. Israel, whose existence in any proportions they would not tolerate, had in fact expanded. If before June 1967 the Arabs had seen Israel established as a wedge between Asian and African Arabdom, they now saw her as a barrier. Her elimination, an objective now more complicated than before, was all the more a historic necessity.

The Arab states moved to adjust their policy to the new circumstances. All their efforts had now to be concentrated on an essential first step: to get the Israelis back to the old Armistice lines. Those lines, notwithstanding the defeat, still held out a theoretical hope of victory. Once she had withdrawn to those lines, Israel would be subjected anew to all the former diplomatic, economic, and paramilitary pressures and, if necessary, to military action. This policy had to be made clear without delay to the Arabic people. Two months after the Six Day War the leaders of the Arab states met in Khartoum. There they laid down three negative, unequivocal principles: no recognition of Israel, no negotiations with Israel, no peace with Israel.

They had no difficulty, moreover, in producing their justification for this, in the circumstances, bizarre pretension. Quite simply, Israel had been the aggressor. Without turning a hair both the Egyptian leader and King Hussein (to whom the Israeli Prime Minister had addressed an appeal to desist even after the Jordan attack had been launched in Jerusalem), and with them the whole apparatus of Arab propaganda, transmuted their own frustrated attempt on the life of Israel into an act of Israeli aggression—which must be reversed. For greater effect, "Israeli aggression" was now presented as proof of Israel's expansionist purpose, which must be thwarted.

But now the Arabs chose their words carefully. They had been reprimanded by their friends for offending civilized susceptibilities before the Six Day War by crude proclamations on "driving the Jews into the sea" and by premature gloating over the wholesale shedding of Jewish blood that would accompany their victory. Consequently they evolved a number of semantic variations of the formula. Henceforth they promised, or demanded, the "erasure of the consequences of Israeli aggression" and the withdrawal of Israel from all "Arab territory" or Arab "lands." This restoration of the status quo of June 4, 1967, would, of course, they hastened to add, be only the necessary prelude to the "restoration of the rights of the Palestinian people" or the "return of the refugees to their homes."

Anwar Saadat, who became President of Egypt on the death of Abdel Nasser in September 1970 and who was more responsive to advice than his predecessor, was persuaded that the text evolved by Nasser would be more palatable to Western nations if the words "peace with Israel" could be inserted. A suitable clause was therefore insinuated into the overall formula. Since then Saadat's complete formula, used in whole or in part, as required, runs roughly as follows:

1. He is prepared for peace with Israel.

2. There can be no peace with Israel, or even negotiations with Israel, until she has withdrawn to the lines of June 4, 1967 (thereby erasing the consequences of her aggression).

3. When that withdrawal is completed, there will remain the problem of the Palestinian people, who will receive the support of the Arab states in fighting for the

"restoration of their rights"—in the Israel of the Armistice lines.[1]

With all the West's knowledge of the Arab's mental processes, their capacity for self-delusion, and their unchanging purpose to liquidate Israel, this Arab attitude has nevertheless been sustained since 1967 by more than sheer wishful thinking or mental inertia. It has been made possible by the support, in varying measure, of the leading states of the world.

The principle that Israel, in May the anticipated victim of successful attack, having in June turned the tables on her would-be destroyers, should now restore to them the bases of their aggression, was accepted almost without question not only by the Arabs' Soviet allies, their French friends, and their original British mentors, but also by the United States. The principle was even given formal sanction in a decision of the United Nations Security Council (November 22, 1967), which established in its preamble "the inadmissibility of the acquisition of territory by war." The text of the resolution was sufficiently ambiguous to leave scope for negotiation and disagreement on the precise degree of rectification of frontiers. But even the United States government in interpreting the principle, gradually evolved the formula that Israel should "restore" to the Arab states all the territory she conquered in 1967 "with insubstantial modifications."

The principle that the victim of aggression should restore the means of aggression to the aggressor does not only sound preposterous, it *is* preposterous. There was, of course, no public precedent for such an immoral principle. In our own time there have been two famous cases of unprovoked aggression that failed: The German campaign of piecemeal aggression against nearly the whole of the rest of Europe, and the Japanese onslaught in the Far East. When the Germans were defeated, the map of Europe was redrawn. Large tracts of territory wrested from the aggressor were retained by his victims—the Soviet

---

[1] This jolly tongue-in-cheek double talk is well brought out (if involuntarily) in an interview with Saadat published in the Paris newspaper *Figaro*, March 24, 1971.

Union, Poland, Czechoslovakia. These included territories historically part of the German Reich. The Soviet Union also annexed territories in Finland and Romania which had collaborated with Germany in the attack on Russia (see Map No. 8). The Soviet Union found incorporation of these large border areas essential to its security. Similarly, with the defeat of the Japanese in the Far East, the Soviet Union annexed the Kurile Islands and part of the island of Sakhalin—to insure its security against renewed attack. The United States also decided to retain control of a Japanese island—Okinawa—as a security measure. This, described as a temporary occupation which ended in 1972, lasted twenty-six years. Even after termination the United States intends to retain military bases on the island—which, it should be added, is situated 5,000 miles from the American mainland.

These arrangements express a principle which governs international relations: if an aggressor is successful, the victim goes to the wall. This was, in fact, the grim experience of all the countries in Europe which were overrun by Nazi Germany and all the countries in Asia overrun by the Japanese, until the tables were turned in 1945. If the victim, however, succeeds in repelling the aggressor, he holds the territory he has conquered or regained, at least until he is ready to make a peace treaty; and only the peace treaty will determine the fate of those territories. Such is surely also the only possible morality. Otherwise the aggressor inevitably has nothing to lose from his aggression, and everything to gain.

It is the victim, moreover, who decides his security needs. It was the Soviet Union who, having paid a gruesome price in deaths and ruin before it succeeded in repelling the German onslaught, decided what territory it required to make itself secure against future attack.

Characteristic of the accepted ethical attitude toward such decision was the reaction of British Prime Minister Winston Churchill to the annexation by the Soviet Union of areas equivalent to one-third of Poland immediately after the Red Army had conquered them (and long before the end of the war). He said in the House of Commons:

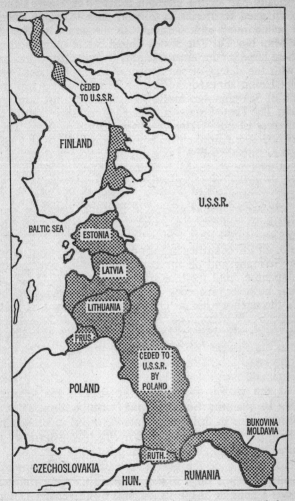

MAP No. 8: Border changes in Europe in favor of the
Soviet Union after the Second World War

Twice in our lifetime Russia has been violently assaulted by Germany. Many millions of Russians have been slain and vast tracts of Russian soil devastated as a result of repeated German aggression. Russia has the right of reassurance against future attacks from the West, and we are going all the way with her to see that she gets it.[2]

A generation after the end of the Second World War, it may be difficult to discern a proximate or even remote danger from a Germany divided in two, apparently cured of militarism, seemingly weaned from the dream of domination. There is no apparent sign that the security of the titanic Soviet Union or any other European country is threatened in any way by the Germans. Yet no international statesman, however opposed to the USSR, seriously suggests that Eastern Prussia or Silesia be restored to Germany. Nor is there any serious historian who is prepared to prophesy that if East Prussia and Silesia were returned to her, and Germany were reunited, her old dream of domination would not repeat itself.

The assessments of the Soviet Union were, in fact, recognized by her Allies without question at the end of the Second World War. For twenty-five years the new territorial arrangement was the accepted irreversible status quo. Then the beaten aggressor himself, finally resigned to the claim of his victims, accepted the situation. On August 12, 1970 the Soviet Union and West Germany signed a Nonaggression Treaty. In its third article, the parties declare that they

are agreed in their recognition that peace in Europe can only be maintained when no one infringes the present frontiers.
They declare they have no territorial demands against anyone, nor will they have such in the future.
They regard the frontiers of all states in Europe today and in the future as inviolable as they stand on the day of the signing of this treaty, including the Oder-Neisse line which forms the western frontier of Poland.[3]

---

[2] *Hansard*, Vol. 397 (February 22, 1944), Col. 698. Poland was later compensated by territory taken from Germany.
[3] *International Herald Tribune*, August 12, 1970.

A similar clause was included in the treaty concluded between Poland and West Germany on December 7, 1970.

As for the United States, it decided, as of right, that even after the end of her military occupation of the Japanese aggressor's mainland the island of Okinawa was essential to its security; and it insisted, as a condition of relinquishing administrative control, on military domination of the island.

The central European areas, and the island of Sakhalin, are doubtless important to the security of the Soviet Union, as is the island of Okinawa to the security of the United States, when seen in the light of bitter historic experience with Germany and Japan and remembering the responsibility of governments for the safety and integrity of their countries and peoples.

Yet their importance pales into insignificance, almost into irrelevance, compared with the problem of security against aggression with which Israel has to contend. For the Soviet Union and the United States, the territorial safeguards they have established provide an additional buffer, a tenth or twentieth coat of armor, a cozy standby. For Israel, the territorial cordon created as a result of the Six Day War is the first defensive covering of the bare bones of her existence.

If the Soviet Union were to give up the areas it incorporated after 1945 and withdraw to its 1941 frontiers, and were then attacked on her soil, its army could conceivably lose a hundred battles, retreat many hundreds of miles, and yet win the war. That is what it achieved in the Second World War. Nor was this achievement unique in history. It expressed the universal minimum formula of defensible borders. No territory is hermetically impregnable. To be defensible, it requires the resilience of depth. Soviet Russia, with her experience of the invasions of Napoleon and of Hitler, is only one example, though an extreme one, of that axiom.

Israel in her pre-1967 borders could not afford to fight a single battle on her own soil. One battle lost in the ten-mile-wide coastal strip of what was Israel on June 5,

1967, would cut the national territory in two. Sir Basil Liddell Hart, the British military scholar, calculated that "an armoured force striking by surprise from the Jordan frontier might reach the coast in half an hour." Then, with a pincer movement operating from south and north, even a mediocre enemy general staff would be capable of destroying the state piecemeal.

That is why Israel's strictly defensive strategy over all the years before 1967 had to be based on what has been described as interceptive self-defense,[4] the technical firing of the first shot. That alone, however, could not normally prevent serious damage and casualties by air attack. Were it not for the combination of a stroke of genius by the Israeli Air Force and an incredible display of inefficiency by the Egyptians, whereby the Egyptian Air Force was destroyed on the ground on June 5, 1967, victory would certainly have been accompanied by a higher rate of casualties on the battlefield; by a considerable loss of civilian life, property, and installations; and by disruption of Israel's civic fabric.

The temerity of the suggestion that precisely Israel should restore bases of aggression to her enemies is emphasized by the fact that all this has happened before. When Israel's birth was threatened by Arab invasion in 1948 and she repelled the Egyptians, she was browbeaten into withdrawing from Sinai, then cajoled into leaving the Gaza area in Egyptian hands.[5] In return, she secured an Armistice Agreement which turned out to be worthless, a worldwide Arab boycott, and a heavy toll of life from endemic Arab forays across the Armistice lines. In 1956–1957 the pattern was repeated. Forced for the first time to take preemptive action against the immediate threat of attack, and having then driven the Egyptians from Sinai and the Gaza area, Israel was persuaded by Western guarantees and finally lulled by a United Nations

---

[4] Y. Dinstein, "Legal Issues of 'Para-War' and Peace in the Middle East," St. John's Law Review, 44 (1969–1970).

[5] The story of United States pressure is told, inter alia by the then American Ambassador to Israel, James G. Macdonald, in *My Mission in Israel, 1948–51* (London, 1951).

military presence into handing Sinai and the Gaza Strip to Egypt once more.

The threat of the Arab onslaught resounding throughout the world in the spring of 1967, and the Egyptians' closure of the Straits of Iran were followed by an incredible international response. The United Nations force in Sinai and Gaza—established as an international "guarantee" for Israel in 1957—was immediately withdrawn at a word of command from Cairo. The American President could not find in the state archives the record of promises made ten years earlier to insure Israel's freedom of navigation. The President and the British Prime Minister together were unable to get the United Nations Security Council (including the members who had joined in that promise) to consider the Egyptians' demonstrative flouting of that freedom. Overnight the gossamer safeguards by which Israel had been deluded, were blown away. At that moment it would have seemed unbelievable that should Israel once more by her own effort escape annihilation, the powers would subsequently once again press for and bully her into renewed renunciation of the minimum conditions of national security. Yet that is what happened. The governments of the great nations of the world have proved capable and willing to join in a campaign of pressure which reeks at every pore of historic injustice, of a callous illogic, which countenances and promotes a monstrous historic fraud. which views calmly the elements of the planned ruin of the Jewish people for the second time in a generation; and which then, moreover, insists that Israel aquiesce and cooperate in its consummation.

Yet there is a rational explanation for the behavior of these statesmen and politicians. They are not judges, moral arbiters, or teachers of righteousness. Each is engaged in pursuing the interests of his country as he sees it. If sentiment happens to accord with that interest, well and good. If not, sentiment must be overridden. If morality or justice happen to harmonize with a nation's interest, excellent. If not, it is sad, but in politics, certainly in international relations, morality is expendable. All that is required are the appropriate words to cloak pragmatic policy with a semblance of respectability or, if a government is fortunate in its diplomatic draftsmen, even with a halo of sanctity.

The salient surface facts (shown in Map No. 4) make the policy of the great powers understandable. It appears that, faced with alternatives, their choice can be frighteningly simple. On the one hand are the Arab states, fifteen of them already in the United Nations Assembly, usually voting as a bloc, their combined population totaling some 100 million (potential consumers of goods), their industries in their infancy, and owning the richest oil-bearing area in the world, in which the western powers, first of all America, have made huge investments and on which the countries of Western Europe are largely dependent for their oil supplies. On the other hand is Israel, with one vote at the United Nations, with a consumer population, after the Six Day War, of no more than four million; Israel which has no oil to sell or withhold, where none of the nations has a substantial economic stake. In a conflict of interests, it is clear whose favors the pragmatic statesman will seek and whom he will be inclined to sacrifice.

There is nevertheless important and fascinating variety in the attitudes of the western powers, and there is a gulf between them and the purposes of the Soviet Union.

The simplistic attitude has been most pronounced in the policy of France.[6] During the period of the British Administration, successive French governments, while formally endorsing the Zionist purpose of the Mandate, remained cool to Zionism. Catholic influences, powerful in France, were one element at work; but the French also chose to regard Zionism as a British puppet, which had been exploited ever since 1916 in Britain's effort to eliminate French influence in the Levant. In 1920 France successfully pressed on Britain the crippling exclusion from Palestine of the part of upper Galilee containing the country's vital water sources (disregarding the outraged protests, among others, of President Wilson of the United

---

[6] It is no accident that a similar principle has governed France's relations within NATO. Parallel with her abandonment of Israel, she has also shaken off her responsibilities in the joint defense of Europe.

States). These were included, and remained unexploited, in southern Lebanon.

These circumstances changed after 1945. Weakened by the agony of the Second World War, "biffed" out of Syria and Lebanon by the British, France was now faced with a growing movement of revolt in her largely Arab North African colonies. Precisely at this stage, at the other end of the Mediterranean, the Jewish resistance movement brought about Britain's relinquishment of the Mandate in Palestine. Britain was, however, actively trying to stage a partial comeback behind the hopefully victorious Arab armies in 1948. The first Arab attack on the nascent State of Israel, if successful, would have established British-Arab domination clear through from the Persian Gulf almost to the borders of the French dependencies in the Maghreb.

The French government therefore was more receptive to Jewish approaches for assistance and, from 1948, gave Israel an increasing measure of diplomatic aid and sold her most of the arms she required. This arrangement reached a climax when France collaborated with Israel in the Sinai Campaign. Her policy of aid and cooperation (Israel was able to reciprocate in many fields) continued in substantial proportions until the Six Day War. A change of tone had, however, begun to appear soon after the French grant of independence to Algeria in 1959.

Having abandoned any form of overlordship in the Maghreb and having granted Arab demands, France now followed the pragmatic logic of circumstances and tried to establish the best possible relations with them and with all the Arab states. In the hope especially of gaining economic advantages in the Arab states, President de Gaulle gradually loosened the ties of friendship with Israel. The Six Day War presented him with the opportunity for a spectacular about-face. With magniloquent cynicism he called Israel the aggressor because she had fired "the first shot." (He unblushingly ignored the fact that even from that narrow technical viewpoint, Egypt had committed a flagrant act of war by blockading the Straits of Tiran—whose freedom France had, incidentally, joined in guaranteeing in 1957.) De Gaulle's contrived moral censure was so severe that fifty aircraft purchased by Israel, and paid for, were impounded and never delivered.

The French government's subsequent efforts to secure material benefits from the Arab states were only partially successful. In Iraq an attempt to obtain oil concessions failed, and by the spring of 1971 French relations with Algeria over the terms of oil supplies had become considerably strained. In other spheres, particularly the sale of arms, she had greater success. Thus Lybia bought 110 Mirage 3 aircraft from France, even though the country had only a handful of pilots. The balance of advantage remained in favor of a thoroughgoing pro-Arab policy.

As M. Schumann, the French Foreign Minister pointed out in July 1971, this policy paid off precisely during the crisis with Algeria, when France was able to obtain oil from other Arab sources. There was thus no diminution in French diplomatic activity against Israel, nor in the promotion of every fantasy of Arab propaganda.[7]

The attitude of the British was more complex. While France was engaged in establishing a new commercial foothold in the Arab states and to secure wherever possible the status of protector, Britain had not yet completed the process of formal disengagement from them. The fabulously wealthy oil principalities on the Persian Gulf still maintain a formal connection with Britain, though this is slated to end in 1972. Her direct oil interests there and in Iraq were especially substantial. These material considerations may explain why Britain, despite many rebuffs and disappointments at the hands of the Arabs, always finds herself able, in all cordiality, to urge Israel to act against her own best interests. Britain's attitude, however, appears to be influenced also by historic "ideology." Those responsible for British policy have not yet forgiven the lowly Jews for having forced them to relinquish Palestine; and by some strange logic, the doctrine governing policy toward Palestine has not changed since the days when Whitehall

---

[7] While this book was in preparation, the Israeli government agreed to relinquish her rights to the impounded planes and accepted return of the money paid for them.

planned and shaped events from the Persian Gulf to the borders of Libya.

This was clear from the sometimes ludicrously anti-Israeli attitudes that continued to be struck by the ideological mentor of the Foreign Office, the Royal Institute of International Affairs, and its faithful handmaiden, the BBC. It was given startling and authoritative definition in 1970 by the Minister of State in the outgoing Labour Government, Alun, Lord Chalfont. Reviewing his six years of service at the Foreign Office and illustrating the conservatism of that establishment, he spelled out a list of the "fiercely protected . . . sacred symbols of the immutable aims" of British foreign policy. Among them, in the reasonable modern company of such subjects as "NATO" and "Anglo-American relations," he includes what many even knowledgeable people probably thought long dead: Laurentian Arabism."[8]

Considered from any possible angle, Laurentian Arabism has only one possible significance as a live issue in the context of today's reality. With Arab sovereignty established throughout the area envisaged by the Laurentians except for one corner, the only possible remaining reason for the survival of "Laurentian Arabism" in the world of practical politics, and the thrust of its application, is the consummation of the pan-Arab dream in that remaining area. It means, in short, identification—perhaps unwitting, perhaps oblique, but unavoidable—with the pan-Arab theme of Israel's destruction.

And what was the calculation that made it possible for the United States to endorse the Arab demands almost in their entirety? The so-called Rogers Plan of 1969 called for a withdrawal by Israel to the Armistice lines of 1949 with "insubstantial modifications." Subsequent American statements in effect accepted the thesis that even after such a withdrawal Israel would not be entitled to formal peace. In strict accordance with the Arab doctrine for the annihilation of Israel, "the rights of the refugees would have to be restored."

---

[8] Alun Chalfont, "The Praying Mantis of Whitehall," *New Statesman and Nation,* November 6, 1970.

The calculation dictating this policy was purely pragmatic—though that was undoubtedly not the only consideration in United States policy, which has always been characterized by a system of checks and balances. At every critical phase in the conflict between Arabs and Israel, the pragmatic considerations have predominated. There is a heavy American economic stake in the oil of the Arab states. Already in 1948 it was described as the United States' "greatest potential investment in a foreign country." The spokesmen of the oil interests—warning of a nonexisting Arab threat to cut off oil supplies—were largely influential in 1948 both in the American government's formal withdrawal of support for the 1947 partition plan and in the United States' subsequent pressure on the Zionist leaders to "postpone" the declaration of the Jewish state. It was those interests which, together with the British government (which supplied the Arabs with arms), achieved the imposition of an American embargo calculated to operate only against Israel.[9] It is a matter of simple arithmetic that if in 1948 Israel's birth and her survival had depended on the help of the United States, the country would not have come into existence at all. The declared Arab plan for a campaign of destruction of Jewish life in Palestine to rival those of the Mongol hordes and the Crusaders—that is, genocide—would then have gone into operation.

It was only when Israel, with the help of the Soviet Union and France, and at heavy cost of life, had survived—had become, that is, an accomplished fact—that American policy once more turned a friendly eye and accorded substantial economic aid. The political bias favoring the Arabs, however, remained predominant. It is now common knowledge that agents of the United States played a significant part in the consolidation of the Nasser regime in Egypt. At that time American policy-makers aimed at

---

[9] For the facts of the oil companies' activities and the realities of Arab oil policy, see report of the Saudi-Arabian correspondent of the New York *Herald Tribune*, February 27, 1948; St. John Philby, *Arabian Jubilee* (London, 1952), p. 218; Benjamin Shwadran, *Middle East Oil and the Great Powers* (New York, 1955).

the elimination of British influence in Egypt, which accorded with Nasser's purpose. They decided at the same time that Nasser was the predestined leader of the "Arab world," that the shortest way to a special relationship with the Arabs in general was thus through Cairo.

When Nasser received from Czechoslovakia the first shipment of arms resulting from his deal with the Soviet Union in 1955, it was American CIA agents who advised him how to conceal from the British ambassador the fact that the agreement had been made with the USSR. They drafted Nasser's communique that he had made the agreement with Czechoslovakia and gave Nasser's reason for the deal as an act of self-defense.[10] When the ships carrying the tanks, guns, jet planes, and submarines arrived at Alexandria, Cairo Radio proclaimed: "Israel's end is approaching. There will be no peace on the border. We demand revenge, and revenge means death to Israel." Those were the arms Nasser poured into Sinai the following year for his projected offensive against Israel.

The same American agents whitewashed Nasser's policies toward the other Arab states, including his campaigns of subversion and assassination. One of them has publicly likened his activities against leaders of other Arab States to the crushing of scabs by a trade-union leader (Copeland, p. 172). Even the imperialist-style Egyptian aggression against the Yemeni Arab people did not alienate them from Nasser.[11] Indeed the doctrinaire pragmatism of United States policy was no more vividly demonstrated than by its complaisance toward the Egyptian invasion of Yemen.[12]

In 1957 the United States government played the central role in saving the Egyptians from the consequences of their defeat in the Sinai campaign, persuading Israel to

---

[10] Miles Copeland, *The Game of Nations* (London, 1969), pp. 133–135.

[11] Copeland, who was one of the CIA agents in Egypt, writes: "Nasser's view of Yemen, in itself, was similar to our own—to wit, the human race would not be seriously inconvenienced if the whole country were to slide quietly into the Indian Ocean" (p. 226).

[12] A vivid, factual, largely eye-witness account is given in Dana Adams Schmidt, *Yemen: The Unknown War* (New York, 1968).

leave Sinai and Gaza for a second time and retreat into her indefensible 1949 Armistice borders.

It would be absurd to suggest that any American administration as such, or even a doctrinaire State Department, actively sought the destruction of Israel. On the contrary, the United States would be very saddened should any serious harm come to Israel or to its population, for whom there is undoubtedly much genuine affection in the country. The United States government after 1948 gave concrete evidence of its belief that the existence of Israel was in the American interest. Considerable economic aid was given to Israel. It played a significant part in helping her battle with the unexampled problems of absorbing large numbers of refugees and other immigrants. After 1967 the United States took the place of France as the main source of Israel's arms purchases. Throughout, the United States appeared to the world as Israel's friend, incurring considerable antagonism from the Arabs for not denying Israel the minimal means of self-defense.

Ambivalence is at least as common a function of international relations as it is of ordinary human intercourse. It is the common formula for satisfying conflicting interests. The United States policy on the conflict between Israel and the Arabs has often reflected the differences between the stiffly pro-Arab oil-oriented State Department establishment and a usually more widely ranging, more sensitive, outlook in the White House. Hence, too, the sometimes surprising fluctuations in American foreign policy (as in the tug-of-war between President Truman and his State Department in 1948).

The intrinsic merits of a pro-Arab policy have always been open to serious doubt on a longer view even of the pragmatic and political considerations—certainly in the case of Britain and the United States. But the politicians and bureaucrats who pursued it could always make out a case to themselves and their colleagues. That case since the Six Day War, become increasingly irrelevant to the interests of the Western nations. The Western statesmen have appeared to be unaware of the vast geopolitical change taking place—a change that in fact reduces to insignificance their commercial and political bookkeeping. Clinging to the formula of giving back to the Arabs their domineering territorial status preceding the Six Day War, believing facilely that at most only Israel will be merely crippled thereby, they have in fact weakened the structure of Western defense, bringing into doubt the future of democracy and Western culture over large parts of the globe. They have ignored, or pretended to be unaware of the connection between the metamorphosis already in progress in the Mediterranean and in the Middle East, and the far-ranging historic purpose of the intense activity by the Soviet Union over the oceans and continents.

The intervention of the Soviet Union was the most momentous, most far-reaching happening in the development of Arab intransigence after 1948. Russian interest went far beyond the material considerations of trade benefits. The purpose of the Soviet Union and of its consequent activity was on the order of the historic adventures which brought about the vast colonial empires between the sixteenth and nineteenth centuries. Planning in the context of the later twentieth century, employing its scientific and technical resources, applying the methods perfected in two generations of its own efforts at subversion, the Soviet Union is in the midst of one of the great imperialist leaps forward that have marked Russian policy for two hundred years.

In the nineteenth century Russian expansionism, thrusting toward the Middle East and directed specifically against Turkey, created the so-called Eastern Question. It was halted by energetic British initiative at the Congress of Berlin in 1878. Other Tsarist essays in expansionism in the Far East and in Europe followed. Some proved successful; others were frustrated. The Communist regime set out on its own expansion after the Second World War. Its objectives were by then not secret—they had been made clear in the published documents of the Nazi regime. In Molotov's Berlin dialogue with his Nazi allies in November 1940, on parceling out the British Empire after its projected dissolution by the Germans, it was the Persian

Gulf zone that the Soviet Foreign Minister demanded as the Soviet Union's share of the spoils.

After the defeat of Germany and after the Soviets had established their dominion over the satellite states in Eastern and Central Europe, they turned once more to the Middle East. They directed their attentions and their pressures first to Turkey and Iran. Checked there by American steadfastness, they undertook a major effort to achieve domination of the rest of the zone. Success here would not only give them control of the Arab oil-bearing areas, but would also in fact enable them to outflank Turkey and Iran from the south.

The political strategy of the USSR in the Middle East after the Second World War presents a picture of pragmatism in action. For nearly thirty years the Soviet regime had outlawed Zionism and persecuted its supporters as "agents of British imperialism." When they discovered that the success of the underground struggle for Jewish independence would mean the end of British rule in Palestine, they made gestures of sympathy. This was followed by strong and consistent diplomatic support for the proposal to establish a Jewish state. The USSR was the only power, apart from France, which supplied arms (through Czechoslovakia) to help the embattled state ward off the Arab invaders and prevent a British comeback in 1948.

The brief collaboration with Zionism having achieved its object, it was terminated abruptly. With the end of the British presence in Egypt, came the injection of direct Soviet influence. No genius in Moscow was required to realize that in the Middle East spheres of influence, bases, staging posts, and jumping-off grounds toward consummation of Mother Russia's historic destiny could be acquired only through friendly relations with the Arab states. By the mid-1950s the Soviet Union appeared in the arena as the champion of the Arabs against "Zionism and imperialism."

Through identification with the Arab purpose and supplying arms and aid in unprecedented quantities and on most generous terms, in the decade that followed the Soviet Union won increasing influence in the Arab states. Egypt and Syria were the main recipients, but help was also accorded to Iraq, Algeria, the Yemeni Republic, and Southern Yemen. By the middle of 1971 the Soviet Union had invested civil and military aid to the value of nearly five billion dollars in the Arab states[13], more than half of which went to Egypt.

In constant dynamic thrust, the Soviets developed and extended their objectives southward. They sought to widen their foothold of influence on the East African littoral down to the gates of South Africa and to establish a substantial presence in the Indian Ocean. Soviet activity in East Africa derived greater impulse from the need to compete with the growing influence of China.

Soviet penetration was comprehensive. Precisely like the classic "capitalist" imperialists of earlier centuries, the Russians established economic footholds, fostered military dependence, vigorously inseminated and propagated their ideology. "It is not difficult," one perceptive historical writer of our times has written, "to envisage—given the necessary acquiescence—a great Soviet empire of the future in which the Soviet Union, with perhaps some territory still to be annexed to it, would form the 'united provinces,' while the rest is left to be indirectly administered through native princes and tributary chiefs, no doubt suitably emblazoned with the left-wing equivalents of imperial style and titulature."[14]

It is an ironic fact that it was the Soviet Union itself that played a major part in forcing on Israel the role of barring its imperial progress. Moscow provoked the Arab leaders into opening the war of June 1967, by proclaiming the imminence of an Israeli attack on Syria. Nasser confirmed this circumstance in his broadcast of June 9, 1967. Levi Eshkol, the Israeli Prime Minister, immediately invited the Soviet ambassador to accompany him to the Syrian border to see for himself that no Israeli troops were concentrated there: but the ambassador refused (UN Document A/PV/1526, p. 37). The Soviet Union presumably helped the Arabs believe that the conditions laid

---

[13] This figure is according to official American estimates.
[14] Bernard Lewis, "Russia in the Middle East," *The Round Table,* July 1970.

down for victory already existed. The USSR may have believed that the Arab states could crush Israel quickly while the United Nations were still engaged in discussion. The Soviet delegate to the United Nations delayed the speedy adoption of a cease-fire resolution which might force to a halt the destruction of Israel that was being described in the official Arab communiqués and news reports. He realized too late that he was the victim of a fantasy. By the time a cease-fire was achieved the Israeli Army stood along the Suez Canal and the Jordan and was established on the Golan Heights in depth.

The presence of Israeli forces on the banks of the Jordan and on the Golan Heights was of no immediate concern to the Soviet Union. Their presence on the Suez Canal, however, brought in its train a severe blow to Russia's operational schedule and long-range plans for expansion. The Egyptian dictator closed the Canal, he would not countenance its being reopened while Israel controlled its east bank. By this entirely unexpected outcome of the war, the Soviet supply train to North Vietnam was disrupted and the vast Russian move across the world was brought into disarray.

During the 1960s the Soviet Union quietly established its power throughout the Mediterranean area. It acquired bases covering the complete length of the sea. Its vessels put in not only at Port Said, Alexandria, and Matrûh in Egypt, but also at Latakia in Syria in the east and at Mers-el-Kebir in Algeria in the west. Without much noise Algeria has become the central base of Soviet power in the western Mediterranean. Algeria—threatened, after all, by nobody—was supplied with 150 Mig aircraft, 3,000 Soviet advisers were installed in the country, Soviet Tupolev planes fly in and out of bases at Laghouat and Ouargla; and a missile base has come into being at La Calle. All these face Western Europe. A force of between forty and sixty warships of various kinds has become a standard feature of the Mediterranean scene.

The Mediterranean Sea is indeed bursting at the seams with Soviet activity. For the Soviet Union intends it to be more than a base, it is also to be a corridor. Part of the concentration of power in the Mediterranean was designed for application in the vast area south and east of Suez where traditional Russian ambitions were now merging with new modern horizons. Southward and eastward in the Red Sea and the Indian Ocean there are clear signs of the beginnings of Soviet penetration. At Aden in the South Yemen republic, Soviet vessels can enjoy the facilities once possessed by the British Royal Navy. At Socotra, an island also belonging to that republic, the Russians planned the establishment of a base. In the southern Indian Ocean they concluded an agreement for facilities on Mauritius. In the eastern Indian Ocean they were negotiating for base facilities at Trincomalee in Ceylon. Their actual use of facilities, however, has remained sparse— because the short passage of the Suez Canal is barred. Soviet vessels can reach the Indian Ocean and any point on earth by the roundabout route across the Pacific Ocean or by way of the Mediterranean to the Atlantic Ocean, then along the West African seaboard and around the Cape of Good Hope. Communications are also maintained by other than naval means. But these possibilities provide only a comparative trickle. For the Soviet grand design, for the strong swinging flow of ships and goods and guns, for sheer ubiquitous Soviet presence whenever and wherever required south and east of Suez, the Canal is still irreplaceable. The most intensive pressure has been exerted on Israel to withdraw from the Canal. In this effort the Soviet Union and Egypt have been given consistent public support by the United States, against whom the Soviet strategy is primarily directed.

There is indeed a startling similarity between the psychology of the United States policy toward the Soviet Union in the Middle East in 1971 and the British appeasement of Germany in the 1930s which led to the Munich Pact, the piecemeal subjugation of Czechoslovakia, and the Second World War.

The consequences of a withdrawal by Israel in Sinai can be foreseen as clearly as were the obvious consequences of the surrender to Hitler of the Sudetenland with its formidable fortifications. Israeli withdrawal from Sinai would almost certainly be followed within days by an Egyptian armed occupation of Sinai, the Egyptian force being accompanied by part of the 20,000 Soviet advisers now in Egypt and by Soviet missiles. The base for a new offensive against an attenuated Israel could thus be built up. Or such an offensive might merely be threatened and the concentration of force used to impose a permanent state of siege on Israel, confined behind a long, vulnerable land line. The maintenance of permanent large-scale mobilization would have disastrous consequences for Israel's economy and her very way of life. The Soviet Union might, it is true, oppose the Arab plan for the complete physical destruction of Israel, finding it more useful to reserve a place in her imperial system for a small, dependent Israel.

The Soviet presence would be free to move on the large objectives when conditions would permit establishing hegemony over Saudi Arabia. While Soviet warships maintained a westerly warning presence in the Red Sea along the southern shore of the Arabian Peninsula and in the Persian Gulf on the east, and while a demonstrative base in Sinai warded off any interference across the land border, it would probably need no more than an Egyptian political offensive against Saudi Arabia to bring about the establishment of a republican "progressive" government to take over from the Wahabite king. If forces were required, Egypt's resources would be adequate for this purpose.

To Turkey and Iran—whose northern borders march with the Soviet's—the full arrival of Soviet power in their strategic rear in an encircling posture, with a now fading Israel their only buffer on the south, would be the irrebuttable proof of Soviet supremacy and of the valuelessness of America and of NATO plans and undertakings. There would then be no sense in their resisting the Soviet embrace.

The Soviet Union, moving forward in full confidence and with the heightened purpose of a triumphant imperialism, would in that case not need decades to establish itself. Both in the Middle East and in Africa there would be no lack of local leaders to extend the appropriate invitations and to open the required doors for speeding the process. The outflanking of southern Europe would then assume its full dramatic significance. At that point, the only way for the West to try to halt the Soviet advances would be by war.

Such a prospect, or the alternative of a bloodless Soviet victory, is certainly not inevitable. For the Suez Canal is Russia's Rubicon. Of all the lessons to be learned from the recent history of the Soviet Union's expansionism, not the least important is its refusal to risk war for objectives outside Europe. It has gained much by the comparatively peaceful means of shows of force against European satellites, such as Hungary or Czechoslovakia, or by purchasing advantage, as in some Arabic and some black African states. The USSR certainly does not contemplate a major war.

The United States itself has had first-hand experience of the Soviet Union's backing down, even risking loss of face, when confronted by a resistant attitude. In Turkey, in Iranian Azerbaijan, and most incisively in Cuba, the pattern of retreat was unequivocal. The Soviet Union has been likened by the United States senator Henry Jackson to a burglar going down a hotel corridor trying the doors and going in only when he finds one unlocked.

This had indeed been the pattern in Egypt itself. Direct Soviet penetration has been gradual and cautious, each step forward taken unobtrusively, to be consolidated only when it became certain that there would be no resistance, not even on the diplomatic level, by the United States. The Soviet settling in in Egypt has even been eased by substantial American collaboration. At every secret Soviet step forward, warning signals from Israel were immediately met in Washington by reproachful denials—ostensibly based on United States intelligence reports—and amplified by inspired press charges of Israeli "invention" or "exaggeration." Washington next found itself "unable to confirm" the Israeli reports. Finally came admission of the by then accomplished facts, accompanied by minimizing of their importance or impact. The most encouraging example of this behavior for the Soviets was Washington's reaction to the breach of the cease-fire and standstill agreement between Egypt and Israel of August 1970. The ink on the agreement had hardly dried when the Egyptians and the

Russians moved forward their SA3 missiles to the Canal Zone.

That move reduced the confrontation at the Canal to its base elements. Not for the first time in history, a single thin line marks a crucial turning point. The loss of a single mountain pass, the opening of a single breach in the wall has changed the direction of world events. Such, in our day, was the Munich surrender "only" of Sudetenland— which followed resigned acceptance by Britain and France during the previous two years of the Nazis' reoccupation of the Rhineland, of their intervention in Spain, and of their invasion and annexation of Austria. Such, after the complaisant American acceptance of an advance of Soviet men and weapons along the length of Egypt, is the danger on the Suez Canal.

Not by choice—certainly not by Israel's choice—the Canal has become the essential front line of defense for Israel's own basic security; and Israel has become the irreplaceable guardian of a crucial front line of Western defense. The line can be held by Israel alone—if she is adequately armed and equipped. The Soviet Union cannot and will not cross the Suez Canal by force, the price in men and material which would have to be brought—and lost—would be too high. Nor is the water line the only barrier. Both the Soviet's own inexperience in waging and sustaining remote wars across the seas and the lesson of the United States in Vietnam will hold them firmly back. They are consequently trying to achieve their objective by political finesse. They are trying to persuade the Americans to believe that it is perfectly safe to hand them the keys to their imperial ambitions on a platter.[15]

---

[15] This was written many months before the dramatic development of July, 1972, when the Egyptian President Anwar Sadat announced that he had asked the Soviet Government to withdraw their "advisers" from Egypt. The reason, he said, was that they had refused his requests for more sophisticated weapons with which he could attack Israel. The Soviet Government consequently recalled most of their military personnel to the U.S.S.R.

Thus was revealed officially the intense frustrations that had built up on the Egyptian side of the Suez Canal as a result of Israeli firmness in not withdrawing from its east bank. The claim of Egyptian and Soviet propagandists, supported in some Western

The vilification of Israel has, of course, been an essential part of the campaign against her. The Soviet dissenting liberal, Andrei Amalrik, wrote a book published in the West under the title *Will the Soviet Union Survive Until 1984?* Amalrik himself would no doubt agree that in important respects the Soviet Union has long ago reached 1984, has survived, and is indeed flourishing. The Soviet Union has transmuted absolutely the concept of truth. Truth, if it does not serve the immediate Soviet interest, enjoys the status of a crime, a hindrance, at best an irrelevance. Amalrik himself was sentenced to three years' imprisonment for writing his book and publishing it abroad. According to reports in the summer of 1971, he was sent to one of the labor camps in the far north. At any given moment Moscow will be found to be supplying the world with information especially composed to suit the purpose the country is at that moment pursuing. Inanities, nonsense of all degrees, and most particularly, denunciation of her victims or its opponents for actions and policies of which she is guilty, are repeated and reiterated and disseminated through many channels, until at least some people begin to believe some of them.

One of the leading experts in the West on the policy and methods of the Soviet Union has described Soviet propaganda as "an amalgam of truth and falsehood."

---

quarters, that Soviet arms and military presence in Egypt were invited and intended only for purposes of defence against potential Israeli attack, was unblushingly discarded. The Soviet Union, once more meeting determined resistance, had once more drawn back. She refrained stubbornly from the fateful step of encouraging Egyptians calculations of victory-through-better-weapons which, in the almost certain case of Egyptian defeat, might well involve her directly in military intervention against Israel across the Canal.

The alacrity with which the Soviet leaders acceded to Saadat's demand suggests moreover that they were not altogether displeased at being able to cut their losses and to withdraw from what had become an impasse. Such services as they require for their own specific purposes in the Mediterranean area (especially for their naval vessels) Egypt will continue to give them. Nor will there be any diminution in their political collaboration with Egypt in trying to achieve by diplomatic action (especially pressure on the West European States) the objective so far withheld from them by Israeli non-withdrawal.

"There is a great deal of whispering campaigning," he notes, "and a great deal of untrue information as well as exploitation of things that are true."[16]

Propaganda campaigns of this kind are directed with special energy and persistence against those who obstruct the Soviet Union in its expansionism. Such victims, for example, were the Yugoslavian government during Stalin's day, the more liberal Czech leaders in 1948 and again in 1968, the Western powers over the years because of their defense of Western Europe—especially the United States which, for all its weaknesses and errors, has tried to counter Soviet expansion in various parts of the world. What evil, what crime, was not attributed to each of them?

Zionism has been a principal target for most of the Soviet era. Inevitably Israel, the ordained "puppet of Western imperialism" and in her own right an "aggressor" and "expansionist," has been the object of one of the more comprehensive campaigns of Soviet denunciation. In this the Soviets are ideally mated with the Arab fantasists.

A study of the Western press during the past twenty-five years would reveal astonishing if spasmodic, support for various Soviet themes designed to lull Russia's victims or undermine her opponent. Widespread ignorance in the West of the character of the Soviet regime has helped its brainwashing campaign achieve notable successes in camouflaging its own ambitions and even its short-range purposes. This is notably true of the campaign of the Soviets, in partnership with the Arabs, against Israel. Because of their desire to support or at least not to anger the Arabs, Western governments have countenanced, if only by silence, and organs of opinion have helped to disseminate wildly mendacious propaganda against Israel. A major example is that none of the Western governments has said a single word to refute the Soviet-Arab "axiom" that Israel was the aggressor in 1967. Again, the most fantastic versions of the events accompanying the birth of the Arab

---

[16] Professor Leonard Schapiro, in *Hearings Before the Sub-Committee of the U.S. Senate On National Security and International Operations,* April 16, 1970 (Washington, 1970).

refugee problem in 1948 are published as established fact in Western newspapers, which do not even bother to check their own back files and the reports of their own correspondents at the time.

Predictably, this propaganda has been welcomed and supported by all the traditional enemies of the Jews. A motley collection of bedfellows has in fact collaborated since 1967 in berating and besmirching Israel. Russian, Chinese, and Yugoslav Communists, feudal and republican Arabs, American capitalist oil companies and nihilist New Left patrons of mythical underdogs, British Laurentian and post-Laurentian pan-Arabists, French exponents of calculating Gaullism—all are to be found rubbing shoulders in the same gallery. They have been joined by old-style anti-Semites: the so-called philo-Semitic period that followed the revelations of the Nazi holocaust and awakened a flickering of conscience in the Christian world has gradually evaporated, and from many parts of the world—including Germany—come warning signals of renewed anti-Semitic activity and respectability. Where anti-Semites have not dared to undertake organized action against local Jewish communities, long-suppressed anti-Jewish feelings have found an outlet in the dissemination of every possible libel on the State of Israel and its people. In the unfolding story of our time the restored Jewish state, for all the strength and self-confidence it has injected into the still dispersed Jewish people—and maybe because of them—has become the focus, the ready-to-hand target of the anti-Semites.

The Catholic Church, which played a leading role over the centuries in the persecution of the Jews and in the indoctrination of contempt and hatred for Jews in generation after generation, and which in our time active in trying to prevent the Jewish restoration, has indeed in recent years (notably at the instance of the saintly Pope John XXIII and his school) relaxed its harsh attitude toward the Jewish people and many are the ardent forward-looking Catholics who would seek a fuller rapprochement. A hard core of influential makers of policy in the Church, however, continues to cherish and to foster the doctrine that the very revival of the Jewish state is intolerable. By sheer logic they hope for the reversal of the Jewish restoration. As long as the State of Israel was excluded from the Old City of Jerusalem—which is the historic Holy City—the existence of a Jewish state in Palestine could, no doubt, still be rationalized as not being a real "restoration." (And the Arabs' vandalistic destruction of Jewish synagogues and desecration of Jewish graves in the City could perhaps be accepted as further evidence of God's will.) But now that Israel governs the whole City, what happens to the doctrine that the Jews could not and must not be restored and must be eternally punished because of their rejection of Christ?

The very benevolence of Israeli rule, the relaxed liberalism for the first time in history operating since 1967, under which all the religious sects in the City have had equally free and unconditioned access to their Holy Places, only emphasizes a Jewish sovereignty which requires no bans on other religions for its self-assertion or destruction of their property for its self-assurance.

Strangely enough, despite many centuries of the Church's expertise in the dissemination of ideas, its spokesmen have not found any better public means of combating Israel than the Soviet and Arab method. Thus, as an example, a reputable Vatican journal published in the summer of 1971 an article by a Vatican official, Professor Federico Alessandrini, alleging Israeli desecration of Christian cemeteries in Jerusalem. The account he gave was an uncritical repetition of a story disseminated for years by the Arab propaganda machine in Beirut.[17]

The interests of the variegated front of warriors waging the propaganda and psychological warfare against Israel are themselves varied and often conflicting. Uniformity is,

---

[17] *Osservatore della Domenica*, July 14, 1971. There is a basis for the story, precisely contrary to the Alessandrini's account. The cemeteries in question, one belonging to the Armenian and one to the Greek Orthodox Church, were both damaged, presumably by cross fire, between 1948 and 1967, when they were not in Israeli hands. When they came under Israeli control, the Israeli government helped both Churches to repair and restore them. Three years before Alessandrini wrote his attack, the Patriarchs of both Churches had expressed their appreciation to the Israeli government for this help. See *Jerusalem Post*, July 20, 1971.

however, easily achieved by invoking in their support such semantic euphonies as justice, humanity, and even peace, all of which their activities are most calculated to undermine and destroy.

To maintain a correct perspective, it must be said that while Israel—and indeed the Jewish people at large—have been an outstanding target of pragmatism and cynicism, they are not alone in this role. In our own time we have been and still are witnesses to severe, and even gruesome, examples of smaller, weaker peoples being crushed politically and even physically. A special tragic fate has been borne by Czechoslovakia, which has been subjugated three times in a generation. In 1938, collaboration existed between her would-be destroyers and the leaders of Western democracy, of which she herself was an honest and justly admired exponent. At that time most blatantly, Western democratic organs of opinion (notably the London *Times*), depicted Czechoslovakia as the obstinate villain frustrating the search for justice by a peace-loving and reasonable Adolf Hitler. A second time, in 1948, barely three years after the restoration of her independence, she was forced by a combination of subversion and brutality into the Soviet orbit. The Western democracies remained neutral. Twenty years later, when the Czech leaders tried to free themselves even partially from the Soviet straitjacket and to humanize the Communist way of life, the Western powers tacitly acquiesced in the Soviet invasion and in the brutal crushing of the Czech leaders and of the liberalizing reforms they had begun to introduce.

Other small peoples have had to suffer the interlocking effects of imperialist brutality and the pragmatic complaisance of the world's democratic powers. For five years, from 1962 to 1967, the Western nations looked on and gave aid and comfort to the Egyptians who, in pursuit of their imperialist purpose (primarily, to gain control of Saudi Arabia and its fabulous oil wealth), carried out an aggressive invasion of Yemen. The invasion was spearheaded by air attacks, with liberal use of napalm bombs, against the rural civilian population. Even sympathy for the certainly innocent Yemeni villagers was minimal. Not only governments bear that guilt. The combined front of self-declared humanist intellectuals, liberals, and Socialists, looked the other way or gave their propaganda support to the "progressive" invaders.

Acquiescence also accompanied the killing of vast numbers of Ibo people in Biafra by the forces of the Nigerian government in their effort to put an end to the striving for Ibo autonomy. Here there was international and even indeed interbloc collaboration. There was no remonstrance against the active intervention of Egypt and the Soviet Union, who carried out low-flying air attacks on defenseless Ibo villages. The Nigerian forces were armed by Britain. The United States looked on. Probably a million people were killed or died of hunger in the two years between 1967 and the collapse of the Biafran struggle.

For several years, quietly, a campaign of large-scale extermination was in progress against the Nilotic Negro people of southern Sudan. A community of pagans and Christians, they dislike and resent the oppressive and discriminating rule of the northern Arab Moslems. When they raised the banner of autonomy, the Sudanese Army launched a merciless slaughter of the population, combatant and noncombatant alike. According to the findings of visiting journalists, at least half a million people were exterminated. This operation, too, enjoyed the active support in arms and material, and even some personnel, of Egypt and the Soviet Union. It proceeded with the silent acquiescence of the Western states, none of which lifted a finger to help the hard-pressed southerners or even to admonish the Khartoum government. No voice was raised in protest. In this conflict, too, the United Nations found that it had no role to play. Appeals to the Secretary General by spokesmen for the Nilotic Negroes remained unanswered.

The grim series has been supplemented—one dare not say completed—by the unbelievable tragedy that overtook the people of East Pakistan in the spring and summer of 1971. In this conflict, the principles on which Western democracy prides itself were trampled underfoot, every human value was crushed. On this tragedy there was indeed no silence. Despite the efforts of the Pakistani gov-

ISRAEL'S FUNCTION IN THE MODERN WORLD          215

ernment to prevent the spread of information, journalists succeeded in conveying the truth of the events in East Pakistan.[18]

In March 1971 the ruling party in Pakistan was defeated in a general election by East Bengali autonomists. Instead of handing over the reins of office, the defeated government sent the army to crush the autonomist movement. The army set about systematically liquidating intellectuals and other leaders, an action which developed into an operation of mass extermination. Harrowing eyewitness reports of deliberate slaughter of men, women, and children, of dead bodies littering the streets or being carried down the river, sketched out the quality and the scope of the massacre. People began to flee into neighboring India. By the end of October ten million refugees were estimated to have crowded into the poverty-stricken, already overcrowded Indian province of West Bengal. Extreme squalor, hunger, and disease reigned among this stricken mass of people. Many countries sent food and medical supplies. All together they could achieve but slight amelioration.

Finally, a meaningful military offensive against Pakistan by India, bringing about the secession of East Bengal, made possible the return of the refugees to their often devastated houses. The behavior of West Pakistan did not alter her status: she remained an honored member of the world community. No government so much as recalled an Ambassador in protest either at the crushing of democracy or at the mass murder. The United States continued to supply the Pakistan government with arms. Nor was this concentrated agony of a whole people a matter of concern to the United Nations. The people of East Bengal, too, now discovered that that organization, which sponsored the Declaration of Human Rights, was the last source from which they could expect succor. That is the way of

---

[18] One journalist, Anthony Mascarenhas, himself a Pakistani, went into voluntary exile in order to publish what he had seen in Sunday *Times*, London, June 13, 1971. A first-hand account was also given in *Time* magazine, August 2, 1971.

the world; and the United Nations is no more than a faithful sounding board of its constituents. The powerful and the influential use it at will, or ignore it at will, or silence it at will, for their purpose. It could not, it seems, be otherwise.

It is saddening to see the savagers of Czechoslovakia and those of Yemen, the Iraqi oppressors of the Kurds, the murderers of the South Sudanese, the destroyers of East Bengal conferring in the halls of the United Nations, in amity and parliamentary decorum with the reformed imperialists and unreformed commercial moguls of the West, wrestling over a formula somehow to break for their diverse selfish purposes the resistance and the spirit of Israel; while all aver that their only objects are peace and justice. As long as this collaboration continues, there can be neither peace nor justice in Palestine; but at best a cease-fire with possibly recurring efforts at attrition.

Peace will not come as long as the powers abet Arab visions of a paradise on earth, encourage them in their hopes of destroying and inheriting Israel and equip them with the instruments for the undertaking. The prospect of peace will appear on the horizon when the Arab leaders realize that they cannot change the present geopolitical reality by force and that no one else will change it for them.

Then the Arabs will begin to look inward. They will discover that what they lack is not more territory—certainly not the territory of the single Jewish homeland, set geographically in the vast mosaic of their eighteen states. They will discover that their urgent need is to break with the backwardness and stagnation of their society, to free themselves from the deadening hold of their military rulers, to launch a great reform for the education of their peoples so that they may master the scientific and technological realities of the twentieth century, and to exploit those realities for their social and economic betterment. This road to peace between Israel and the Arabs seems to be long and difficult. It is the only road.

Every student of Arab society, every honest Arabist, knows that this is the truth. All who are not merely looking selfishly to exploit the Arabs' weakness for their own ends, or to use them as a whip with which to beat the Jews, should not be afraid to publish the truth abroad and sow its seed among the Arab peoples themselves.

# 9

# Guarantees of Peace

If the borders of Israel are established securely and in reasonable tranquillity on the Suez Canal, the Jordan River, and the Golan Heights, Israel will be able for the first time to face freely and directly the question of the relations between the Jewish majority and the Arab minority. (See Map No. 9.)

Coexistence between ethnic groups in one political unit is not the happiest state in creation. Mankind has not, however, yet discovered the formula that will make self-government possible for every group of people. Destiny has so far seen to it that 10 per cent of the world's people live as minorities. For a group to live as a minority does not in itself involve special hardship. Life for a minority becomes hard and even tragic only when it is discriminated against, when it is ill-treated, and when it lives only as a minority, with nowhere a national territory of its own. Such an example, in varying degrees of severity, is the state of the Basques in Spain, of the Kurds in Iraq and Syria, of the Ibo in Nigeria. Such was the case, before 1948, of the Jews throughout the world.

On the other hand, there is hardly a large people of which a part does not live in some other people's state. Even for a minority concentrated just across a border, the joy of life may be only comparative. Its members, however, have the alternative of leaving, of going to their own state.

The Arabs are in this respect an extraordinarily favored people. No other people in the world harbors so many

218

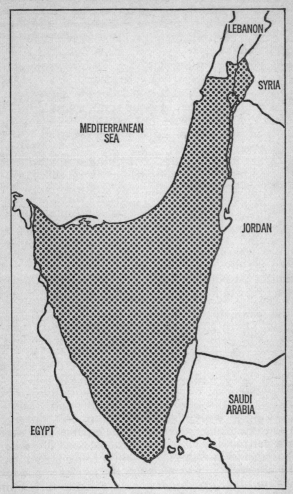

MAP No. 9: Israel in the cease-fire lines since 1967

clear-cut ethnic and religious minorities, making up probably more than one-quarter of the population of all the Arab states together. Among them are the Kurds, the Nilotic Negroes, the Berbers of the Maghreb (Algeria, Morocco, and Tunisia), each speaking a non-Arabic language; the non-Moslem Arabic-speaking Druze in Syria, the Christian Copts in Egypt, and the Maronites in Lebanon, who claim descent from the ancient Phoenicians (they make up nearly half the population and share power constitutionally with the Moslems). Indeed, nearly all these minority populations—just like the Jews of Iraq, North Africa, and Yemen—lived in their countries before the Arabs came.

The Arabs in their states have accommodated themselves enthusiastically to this universally sanctified phenomenon. Some seventy million Arabs live as majorities and rule over their minorities, sometimes discriminating against them moderately, sometimes exercising brutal repression, everywhere without embarrassment. It would be absurd, even grotesque, to suggest that there is something wrong, unjust, or immoral in the remaining million's living as a minority.

The inevitability of this ultimate and normal relationship was clear from the outset of the modern Zionist enterprise. It was given noteworthy formulation in measured terms by Herbert (later Lord) Samuel in a speech in the London Opera House on November 2, 1919:

> No responsible Zionist leader has suggested the immediate establishment of a complete and purely Jewish State in Palestine. . . . The policy propounded before the Peace Conference, to which the Zionist leaders unshakeably adhere is the promotion of Jewish immigration and of Jewish land settlement . . . in order that the country might become in time a fully self governing Commonwealth under the auspices of an established Jewish majority.

Nevertheless the Arab leaders' antagonism, inspired, organized, and financed by the British authority, drove the harassed Zionist leaders (though they knew how contrived was the character and how unrealistic were the pretensions

of the Arab national movement) to make concessions in
the hope of appeasing them. This policy caused the great
dispute between the Zionist schools of Weizmann and
Jabotinsky. Weizmann's ideas prevailed.

One concession after another was proposed to the Arabs. In the early 1930s the Zionists finally offered them a
measure of political recognition which, had it been accepted, would have jeopardized the very foundations of
Jewish independence. The offer consisted of parity—
constitutional equality regardless of majority and minority. In case of disagreement, the decisive vote was to be
cast by the British government, which the Zionist leaders
continued to trust. No reasoned reply was ever made to
this offer; it died in the flames of the pan-Arab attack of
1936.

Later, in 1937, the Zionist leaders agreed, again for the
sake of peace, to share out the country, dividing what
remained of the original mandated territory of Palestine
after eastern Palestine had been given to the Arabs by the
British. They accepted as a basis the partition scheme
proposed by the British Royal Commission (see Map No.
10). The proposed Jewish miniature state would have
been highly indefensible. The Arab leaders rejected the
plan out of hand, and the British government buried it.

A third major effort at accommodation was made in
1947. The Jewish underground having compelled the British to relinquish their hold on Palestine, the Zionist leaders once again announced their willingness to accept a
scheme of partition as a means of putting an end to the
conflict. The Zionist leaders accepted the United Nations'
partition proposal, which included a ludicrously vulnerable Jewish state (see Map No. 2). They persuaded themselves once more that a heavy sacrifice would win the
heart of the Arabs.

That continuing illusion was drowned, and Jewish acceptance of the compromise was nullified in the bloodshed and destruction let loose in reply by the Arabs of
Palestine and then by the Arab League invaders. The
Zionist leaders, now governing the infant state, still refrained from driving home the military advantage gained
during the latter phase of the fighting. Though they might

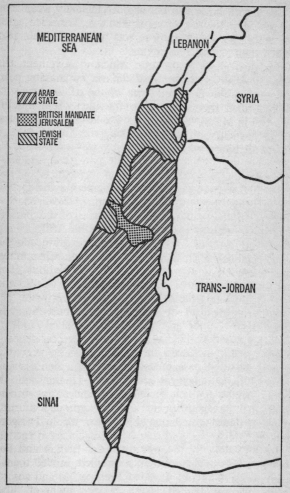

MAP No. 10: Partition proposal of the Royal Commission (1937)

have restored the whole of western Palestine, they again accepted a compromise which left Palestine partitioned and Israel with improved but still strategically weak frontiers (see Map No. 1). Israel signed the Armistice agreements with the Arab governments who over the years breached their clauses one by one.

Never throughout those years did any movement arise among the Arabs of Judea and Samaria for making peace with Israel in the cramped lines of the 1949 Armistice. They identified themselves with the idea of eliminating Israel; and in May 1967 there were among them outbursts of joyful participation in the general pan-Arab festival of belligerent exhilaration.

At that time too, as throughout their short modern history, the Arabs of western Palestine were following a lead given them by others. The concept of these Arabs as a national entity capable of independence, of independent thought and action, has remained baseless. It is no accident nor the result of any overwhelming pressure that they did not establish a state of their own even when it was offered them on a platter by the United Nations. They passed over the opportunity a second time in 1949, when the war against Israel was over, the Armistice was signed, and the Arab army of Transjordan was occupying Judea and Samaria.

Nor did they express any desire for independence or take any action to achieve it in the nineteen years that followed. They made no move when Abdallah formally announced the annexation of Judea and Samaria to his kingdom, which he now renamed Jordan. They became "Jordanians" or even "West Bankers" without a murmur, even when they learned that the annexation had angered the other Arab states and that it had been given recognition, in the whole world, only by Great Britian and Pakistan. The same spirit, or absence of spirit, moved them in refusing to serve as a base and to provide aid and comfort for what was proclaimed as "their" movement of "liberation from the Israeli occupation." The swift success of the Israeli authorities in thwarting the Fatah's attempt to establish a base in Samaria and then in Judea was not due only to Israeli brainwork and efficiency. Indeed, if relations between the Jews and the "conquered" Arab population are reasonably relaxed, this is due in no small measure to the absence of any militant, or indeed any warm, local "Palestine" nationalist fervor.

The fiction simply refuses to become a fact. The Arabs of Palestine are not a nation. There is no "Palestine Arab" nation. They were and have remained a fragment of the large Arab people. They lack the inner desire, the spiritual cement, and the concentrated passion of a nation. Though their number has grown in the past half-century, they have not developed a specific national character. Their constant merging in the plots and sallies of the pan-Arab policy-drivers has exhausted their ardors. Their personal attachment, moreover, is not to the country but to a family, to a clan, to a village or a city. In this they do not differ from 1918, when T.E. Lawrence discovered the situation for himself.

There is truth in the repeated observation that the modern history of the Arabs of Palestine is a tragedy. They have consistently been used as pawns in the power game. Originally the British sponsored and created the pan-Arab movement, which battened on the Palestine question as its only source of life. Latterly pan-Arabs, Russians, French, British, all have incited the Palestine Arabs to reach out for the unreasonable and unattainable.[1] If, by some mischance, the objective of the Arab states and the Soviet Union were achieved and Israel were forced back to the Armistice lines of 1949, the tragedy of the Arabs in Judea and Samaria would be perpetuated and, under the new circumstances, multiplied.

The certain outcome of an Israeli withdrawal and surrender of territory is not that the Arabs of Judea and Samaria would become an independent political unit. They would be subjected at once to a violent power struggle of such groups as the Fatah, sponsored by one or the other Arab governments, against an invading Jordanian army, with the neighboring Arab states' sending in "aid," as Nasser did in Yemen. Then Judea and Samaria

---

[1] See Kedourie, *The Chatham House Version*, Chapter 4.

would become the base and the battleground once more in the next "final" war for Israel's annihilation.

On the other hand, even those Israelis who, pliant to international pressures or chary of a large Arab minority, speak of a physical Israeli withdrawal will not agree to an Arab military presence on the west side of Jordan. Even the most forgiving, the most forgetful, and the most short-sighted among them insist that the security of Israel can be insured only by an Israeli military presence on the Jordan itself or on the heights overlooking the Jordan Valley.

Only when they grasp these realities will the Arabs of Palestine be able to see an end to their anomalous condition. They will then realize that the restoration of the unity of Palestine under Israeli auspices, at once a development of historic justice and a vital necessity for Israel's security—indeed, for her existence—holds out for them also the only hope of achieving political as well as cultural self-expression. Their political status will be that of a national minority, but they will live in civic equality and in free communication with the major centers of Arabic life and culture. And in peace.

That this is a sober assessment will be evident from the history and character of Zionism. It is, after all, the values of Zionism that have been poured into the bloodstream of Israel. Three-quarters of a century after its foundation, it is possible to see in perspective the weight and depth of purpose of the modern Zionist Movement for the Jewish people and its effect on the Arabs now living in Palestine.

The twentieth century has seen no movement more revolutionary than Zionism, none more progressive or more humane. Its mistakes in performance have often been grave, and the Jewish people has itself paid the full price. The success of Zionism has been partial and late. The six million Jews of Europe whom Zionism did not save from annihilation are the everlasting witnesses to failure. Yet the tragedy of the Holocaust itself emphasizes the magnitude of the upheaval that Zionism has wrought in the Jewish people and of its impact on the world.

Zionism was one of the impossible movements. At every stage of its progress struggling for Jewish independence it faced what seemed impossible odds, and it was regularly written off by a chorus of respectable realists and established intellectuals. After he published *A Jewish State* in 1895, Theodor Herzl is said to have called on Dr. Max Nordau to determine whether in fact, as Herzl's whole personal milieu insisted, he was clinically insane. Twenty years earlier, at the height of the tension over the Eastern Question, when political thinkers in Britain and in Europe were receptive to the idea of Jewish restoration in Palestine and all were sharply conscious of the desolation and the emptiness of the country, neither Disraeli nor Bismarck would have thought Herzl insane. Indeed, an energetic Zionist political initiative at that time might have brought the idea to germination in the deliberations of the Congress of Berlin.

No Herzl, however, materialized in 1878. When he did, the international political circumstances, as well as the cultural climate, were radically different. In the circumstances of the tail end of the century, Herzl's idea was rationally and fashionably disposed of as utopia.

With the means at its disposal and in the settled order of the world, the revolution the Zionist Organization sought to achieve must indeed have seemed incredible. It aimed, after all, at more than a change in the status of an almost derelict piece of territory in the Ottoman Empire. It even envisaged the solution of a problem which had plagued and become embedded in world society for many hundreds of years—the transformation of a people dispersed throughout the nations, everywhere treated with contempt, everywhere subjected to a hatred which, imbibed by children with their very mother's milk, could not be eradicated. The vast majority of Jews lived in poverty and in a misery lightened only by their own spiritual resources, their intense belief in God and in the ultimate return to Zion. The victims of sharp economic discrimination, they were at best protected like serfs by their overlords. Driven off the land by the ban of centuries, barred from particular professions in various countries, some of them at best found a place in the nebulous middle-world between producer and consumer.

Generation after generation in Europe had its own experience of violence against Jews, of organized sudden slaughter and rape and destruction. The Jews in many countries became history's most famous scapegoat for the failings of governments, an outlet and a target for the anger and frustrations of their peoples. "Beat the Jews and save Russia" was a wondrously effective formula for relieving public grievance, and it was paraphrased and adapted in many other countries. One Russian two-syllabled word illustrated the status and the condition of the Jews in Exile: *pogrom* means a mass attack on Jews sponsored or permitted by the authorities. Throughout the nations Jewish life became a cheap commodity—not only for those who killed, but also in the eyes of those who merely watched; even, sometimes, in twisted reflex, in the souls of the victims themselves.

From pity as the highest emotion through bare tolerance, through unadorned intolerance and discrimination to pogrom—that was the natural range of the climate in which most of our grandfathers lived, as did many of our parents and some of our own generation. From that almost universal order there was neither relief nor appeal. Herzl was a Western Jew. It was not in barbaric feudalistic Russia, with its Pale of Settlement which determined where a Jew might live and where he might not, that he became sharply conscious of the Jewish plight. It was in democratic, revolutionary France, where Jews could reside wherever they pleased, yet where each of them, because he was a Jew, could be treated like Dreyfus.

The Zionist Organization thus set out to reverse what had been for centuries a fixed feature of the human scene—the existence of a helpless, vulnerable minority—and to restore the human right of the Jews, not only to live, but even to live as equal citizens of the world. The only way this rescue could be achieved was by restoring the Jews' national independence.

That was only Zionism's first task. It set out to revive the mutual flow of vitality between the people and its native soil, to restructure completely its abnormal, lopsided social pyramid; and it envisaged the Jew's achieving self-expression as himself, not as an emaciated, or exaggerated, imitation of the people among whom he lived and not merely in twisted reaction to their contempt.

The Zionist solution would in the result free the peoples of the world of a source of the degeneration and self-abasement which discrimination brings about in those that discriminate and which persecution breeds in those that persecute. Anti-Semitism could be and was often lethal for its intended victim; it was certainly dangerous to the peoples that practiced it.

The world did not rush to help the Zionist reformers. Most anti-Semites were not exhilarated by the prospect of their own unemployment. The Zionist revolution was achieved by the Jewish people alone. With minor exceptions, it was not until after the "utopia" had become a fact, and the Jews had a state, that the Zionist undertaking, as a "developing" country, qualified for material aid from other than Jewish sources.

By the time the Jewish state was established, and when the political revolution signaled fifty-three years earlier by Herzl had been thus consummated, the Zionist Movement had essentially effected its social revolution as well. In spite of a variety of social and political backgrounds (and severe internal political differences), and in spite of foreign rule, the Jews of Palestine lived a full national life, as ordered, comprehensive, and effervescent as any democratic people in the world. Its economic structure, built up on a progressive agriculture and a developing industry, belonged entirely to the twentieth century, even to its difficulties and imperfections.

Now Zionism took on a new social dimension. In the circumstances of the birth of the Jewish state, its immediate function was that of a refuge. Into it flowed primarily the remnant of the Jews of Europe—the survivors of the Nazi extermination camps—and the majority of the Jews fleeing from the Arab states.

The country of Palestine is very poor in natural resources. By the end of 1951, the 650,000 Jews who had made up the population of Israel at its birth in 1948 had absorbed 690,000 Jewish immigrants.[2] Little housing was available; there was not enough food or clothing; the existing services, for years retarded by a hostile British administration, were inadequate even to the earlier population. The overwhelming majority of the newcomers, whether from the Nazi camps or the Arab countries, were penniless; many of them were ill. Most of them were unskilled, large numbers were untaught in any modern sense and therefore for years could add very little to the productive capacity of the economy. The Jews of the world provided generous financial help and lightened the burden. Yet given the gigantic pressure of numbers in so short a time, every two Jews in Israel certainly had to carry one newcomer.[3] These statistics have come to be mentioned as a commonplace, or drowned in the noise of Arab fantasies of the Arab "refugee problem." Their significance may be made clear by imagining that the United States, wealthy and abundant, with its population of about 200 million, were to absorb seventy million penniless newcomers a year for three or four years.

That was only the beginning. For hundreds of thousands of newcomers from the Arab states—some medieval, all backward—the State of Israel has been a school, very often the first school. It provided these newcomers with the rudiments of a formal education which the country of their birth denied them. It provided many of them with their first awareness of public hygiene, of sanitation, of civic pride and responsibility, of democracy. A vast investment of money and energy and love has been and continues to be made in a backbreaking effort to overcome the yawning cultural gap between them and their fellow citizens, average products of Western education.

The undertaking is far from consummated. The ills of centuries will be eradicated only slowly. The final closing of the gap may not come about for a whole generation

---

[2] The estimated non-Jewish population of 120,000 in 1948 had also increased by 50 per cent in that period. Data from Central Bureau of Statistics, reproduced in *Facts About Israel, 1970* (Jerusalem, 1970).

[3] The total number of new Jewish *immigrants* to the end of 1970 was approximately 1,350,000.

or even two. Errors in judgment and planning, blunders in execution are not lacking. The unsolved areas of social inequality and sheer economic deprivation are painfully visible. The human stresses and strains and frictions are in constant evidence in Israel. Yet even today, in its state of becoming, Israel compares reasonably well in the world's social and economic scale with the most progressive of the nations.

Some revolutions of our time have achieved political status for peoples, others have improved the economic lot of the individual. Which of them can compare with the profound and varied achievements of Zionism? It brought independence to a uniquely dispersed, downtrodden, decimated people; it rebuilt its social structure from the foundations; it changed the life and the lot of the individual, freeing him from discrimination and contempt, often from hunger and the threat of death, endemic or immediate. In the process of building its society, and in spite of a constant state of either war or siege, it has protected the democratic freedoms. A lively parliamentary democracy (with an abundance of political parties) and a free and critical press preside over the process.

What revolution of our time can compare with Zionism? The Soviet revolt, whose price of revolution was the murder of millions and the exile of millions more to suffer near-death in "correctional" labor camps in the freezing Arctic north? Russia, where—after fifty years and more of the revolution to establish egalitarianism—material inequalities, especially between rulers and ruled, between professionals and workers, between preachers and the preached-at are accepted as facts of life? Where favorites of the regime may buy even imported luxuries in declared exclusive shops, while the mass of the people spend hours every day in long queues for the bare necessities of food? Where totalitarian regimentation, protected by a ubiquitous secret police, has remained the self-understood and unchanging character of society? Where every newspaper is a government product and every line in it, like every radio or television broadcast, tells the people only what the government has decided is good for them to know?

Where dissenters are jailed as felons or locked up as lunatics?

Where then? In the countries of Eastern Europe, which were forced to follow willy-nilly in the footsteps of the Soviet Union, chaining their economies and their social order to Moscow's chariot? Or perhaps the Arab states, where every bloody military putsch is labeled "revolution" to justify the unchanging totalitarianism of the "revolutionaries" and to obscure the unalleviated poverty and the political powerlessness of the mass of their people?

Zionism, existing to solve the uniquely complex problem of one people, could not by definition, and did not, aim at a universal revolution. Yet its ultimate success can bring many benefits to the whole vast area and the many peoples surrounding the Jewish homeland. It has been a truly humanist revolution, unequaled in our time. Though its humanist principle may sometimes be too sentimental, it has been a large factor in the Zionist attitude and in the policies it has tried to pursue toward the non-Jewish inhabitants of Palestine.

The physical reacquisition of land from the handful of existing inhabitants presented no moral problem of choice for the Zionists. It was one of the great myths of Arab propaganda elements in the period of the Mandate that the Arab farmers of Palestine had been dispossessed or rendered landless. In fact, every square inch of land acquired from the Arabs was paid for. The British government, largely ignoring its obligation under the Mandate to place state lands at the disposal of the Zionists, enabled the Arabs to establish a virtual sales monopoly. Britain actually gave away large tracts of land to the Arabs, including absentee landlords in Egypt and Syria. These Arabs then sold to the Zionists. Of all the lands acquired by the Zionists, only 9 percent were by concession from the government. The sellers exploited to the full the heaven-sent conjunction of an eager buyer and a closed market. The prices rose consistently and finally reached exorbitant dimensions. In 1944 Jews were paying Arab sellers $1100 an acre for arid or semiarid land that had lain fallow for centuries. At the same time rich black soil in

the State of Iowa in the United States was selling for
one-tenth of that price.[4]

Altogether 27 percent of the land purchased by the
Jews came from fellahin-owners themselves. The remainder, usually unworked land, was bought from absentee
landlords in Syria or Lebanon or in Palestine itself, whose
families had bought it from the Turkish Sultan for a song.
When in response to Arab propaganda—disseminated or
financed in most cases by the very landlords who had
made fortunes selling the land—the British called for
individual claims of dispossession, they discovered that
even the handful whose claims they validated (as having
been "sold" by the Arab landlord) were given and accepted other land or, at their own preference, financial
compensation. When the State of Israel was established,
70 percent of all her land was not in private ownership
but was a part of precisely the land which the British were
to have made available to the Zionists. The Mandate
government had, of course, inherited it from the Ottoman
regime.[5]

Jewish immigration and development brought no harm
to the individual Arab resident. Further, the new settlers
rapidly became famous for their tremendous beneficial
impact on the social and economic life of the Arab community. Moreover, they reversed the trend of Arab migra-
tion. Instead of the traditional exodus of Arabs, Zionism
brought about a large Arab immigration. Arabs within
the country also moved into the areas which, previously
swamp or desert, the Zionists had transformed into
blooming farms, or into the flourishing cities which the
Zionists had made out of nondescript villages.[6] As a
result of modern health and sanitation methods introduced
by the Jews, the Arab death rate dropped steeply; Jewish
methods in agriculture adopted by the Arabs increased
their yield out of all recognition. The standard of living of

[4] For details and statistics, see Moshe Aumann, *Land Ownership
in Palestine* (Jerusalem), pp. 6–10.

[5] Government of Palestine, *Survey of Palestine* (Jerusalem,
1946), p. 257.

[6] Yaakov Shimeoni, *Arviyei Eretz Yisrael* (Tel Aviv, 1947),
pp. 422–423.

the Arabs soared beyond anything known in the Middle East.

The Zionist revolution thus had the effect of improving considerably the lot also of the non-Jewish population of Palestine, and large numbers of incoming Arabs who had no connection with Palestine at all.[7]

With Israel's victory in the Six Day War, the Arab population of Judea and Samaria came under her control. The Arabs' notions about the Zionist had been fed for nearly twenty years by their own educational system and propaganda, embellished by a famously vivid imagination. Their views on the natural behavior of a conqueror were shaped by their knowledge of Arab practice in such cases— even against fellow Arabs—and by the fate they themselves had in mind for the Jews of a defeated Israel.

There were some with a particularly guilty conscience. The Arabs of Hebron had in 1929 carried out a house-to-house slaughter of the Jewish community of completely defenseless and unsuspecting Talmud students and their families. Altogether they knew perfectly well the reckoning of blood and tears that had accumulated from their repeated aggressions before and since 1948. Moreover, half of Israel's population, half her armed forces, originated in the Arab countries—in families, therefore, who had been persecuted, hounded, and finally robbed of their possessions before being driven out to find refuge in Israel. They had a special reckoning of their own which they might be expected to settle.

Viewed thus, the Arabs of Judea and Samaria, by their own standards, had reason to fear the arrival of the Israeli Army in their towns and villages. This was no doubt the reason for the apparently inexplicable flight of some 200,-000 Arabs in the first days and weeks after the end of the Six Day War.

These notions also explain and provide the raw material for the fantastic tales of oppression, murder, rape

---

[7] The literature on the subject is considerable. A useful summary of the facts and statistics are in the *Palestine Royal Commission Report* (1937).

and destruction which Arab propaganda has disseminated lavishly and indiscriminately against Israel since the Six Day War. They represent a reasonable picture of what the Arabs would have done if they had won. In fact, nothing happened. The Israeli soldiers, when they arrived, apart from insuring security arrangements, left the population alone.

There has probably been no more benevolent occupation than the Israeli government of the Arab population of Judea and Samaria and Gaza. There have inevitably been punitive measures to put a stop to disturbances of the peace and to acts of violence. In four years of Israeli rule there has not been one execution. A handful of Arabs have been kept in administrative detention. In some cases, where an Arab has preached violence against Israel, he has been banished across the Jordan, where he is of course free to continue to preach and even to practice violence. The most serious punishment meted out to those who have given shelter to terrorists has been the destruction of their houses after due warning.

That sums up the measures taken by the Israeli government to preserve law and order in the areas she governs. Where in the history of our times has there been such another occupation over a frankly hostile conquered population?

That is not all. The Israeli government has also gone to great lengths, probably unprecedented in the history of military occupations, both to create an easy and relaxed relationship with the people and to improve their lot. From the beginning it established the principle of not interfering with the tenor and manner of life of the Arab population, with only two exceptions. First, it insisted on the correction or replacement of school texts containing political propaganda—that is, the anti-Israel and anti-Semitic demonology and crude justifications of genocide with which the textbooks abounded. The second exception consisted in a considerable expenditure of money and effort and expertise to improve the economic condition of the population. Special teams were sent to instruct Arabic farmers in modern methods and the use of modern equipment in agriculture. Loans were granted for the erection of new industrial plants and the extension and improvement of existing plants.

Israel has opened vocational training centers to raise as many young Arabs as possible out of the rut of unskilled work. Moreover, she opened the gates to Arab workers from Judea, Samaria, and Gaza. By 1972 forty thousand workers from their towns and villages traveled to work every morning to Israeli building sites and factories. In addition to buying a part of their agricultural crop herself, Israel, in spite of the hostile activities against her beyond the Jordan, allows the Arabs in western Palestine to send their products for sale across the river.

The result has been the elimination of unemployment, both among the "regular" population and among the refugees still living in camps—most of the latter in the Gaza area, where they had been kept deliberately in squalor and idleness by the Egyptians. A sharp rise in the standard of living has followed and a widening of the economic horizons of the whole Arabic community in western Palestine.

The Israeli government has been at special pains to insure the maintenance of the cultural and even the social links of the Arabs of Palestine with other parts of the Arab nation. In spite of the Arabs' failure to honour the cease-fire, of terrorist infiltration and attempts at infiltration, of the campaign of incitement, Israel kept open the bridges across the Jordan. She permits Arabs to cross those bridges and visit their relatives and friends across the Jordan. She allows Arabic students to go abroad to study at Cairo and other Arab universities. Every year, at the summer holiday season, thousands of people from the Arab states cross the Jordan to visit their relatives in Judea and Samaria.

Gradually, too, the Israeli Government extended the travel facilities of these visitors. In the summer of 1971 and of 1972 large numbers of Arabs from various Arab states at war with Israel, as well as from Samaria and Judea could be found enjoying themselves on the holiday beaches of Israel. An Arab writer Atallah Mansour has drily described this summer influx as "taking a vacation in the Zionist hell." (Haaretz, July 30, 1971).

The Arabs of Judea and Samaria and the Gaza district have been able, in the years since the Six Day War, to discover also how life has been for the Arabs who were citizens of Israel in the years between 1949 and the Six Day War.

The people of Israel in 1949 owed the Arab community nothing. Except for a minority, they had identified themselves with the forces aiming at Israel's destruction. They had withdrawn from Israel in order to clear the field for the convenience of the invaders from the Arab states. Nevertheless, a comparatively large number were allowed to return in the years after 1949 to reunite families or for other compassionate reasons. They were, of course, treated with some suspicion. The dangers of a fifth column were ever present. Groups or nuclei of groups of active enemies of Israel were indeed uncovered from time to time. The areas with concentrated Arab populations in the northern part of the country continued to be governed by a military administration, and Arab citizens had to obtain permits to travel out of those areas.

Though the Arab states continued to prepare for Israel's destruction and her Arab citizens were subjected to the daily incitement of a dozen radio stations, these security restrictions were gradually relaxed. It was discovered that the dangers had become minimal. An increasingly alert Jewish public opinion persuaded the government in 1964 to abolish the military regime.

The relations between the Jewish state and its minority of Arabs reached a turning point in May and June 1967. One of the most striking phenomena of the days before and during the Six Day War was the behavior of those Arabs. Exposed to the confident exhilaration of leaders in Cairo, in Baghdad, in Amman, in Beirut, and in Damascus, conveyed to them day after day for three weeks on radio and on television, promising early and swift fulfillment of the dream of the destruction of Israel, they did not lift a finger to help in its consummation. There was not one subversive move, not one act of sabotage. Some undoubtedly hoped that Nasser's bellicosity would be vindicated. The majority was clearly not at all sure it wanted to see Israel defeated. Certainly hostility to Israel was not strong enough to move any Arab to bold action.

For the truth is that, though slow, their integration into Israel's society was and is proceeding. Problems remain that cannot be solved in the span of half a generation and while the Arab states as such persist in their war against Israel. Absolute equality is still ruled out. The young Arab of seventeen, unlike his Jewish and Druze fellow citizens, is not called to serve in the Israeli Army—though in this, too, there have been some exceptions. The Arabs' share in the public services is growing. As the beneficent effects of Israel's education system spread, the Arabs' share in higher education grows. They enjoy, moreover, an unexampled economic prosperity. Their birthrate, aided by the state's health and welfare services, is among the highest in the world, 50 percent higher than that in Judea and Samaria (in 1970, 4.6 per 1000, as compared to 3.1).

There is, however, a much more significant truth that the Arabs in Israel have been able to learn from close contact with the Jews. Notwithstanding bitter, or sour, Jewish memories going back to 1948 and 1936 and 1929 and 1920, in spite even of Jewish attitudes of present caution toward them, as part of the Arab people still at war with Israel, there is no semblance of a climate of hatred toward them. There never has been. Zionism, with its intense fervor and programmatic intent, has preached a positive Jewish patriotism, it has fostered love—love of the Jewish people, love of the country, it has never preached hatred. The student of the vast Zionist literature of the past fifty years will be hard put to find any such teaching even in the days of greatest crisis. Zionism has consistently inculcated a striving for relaxed relations with the Arabs.

How to achieve such relations has indeed been the subject of historic disagreement and continuing debate. Conflicting political attitudes toward the Arabs ever since 1920 have not affected an almost universal liberalism on the proper status of the individual Arab citizen. Zeev Jabotinsky, who opposed the efforts of the official Zionist leaders to appease the Arabs by making far-reaching concessions of rights or territory and who insisted that the first essential step to understanding with the Arabs was to make absolutely clear the Zionist purpose of full independence in the whole of the homeland, urged at every opportunity the fullness of civic rights for the Arab citizens. He foretold a happy and prosperous coexistence of Jews and Christians and Moslems in the Jewish state he dreamed of. It was he who proposed that in the future Jewish State the deputy prime minister should be an Arab.

He saw this outcome as feasible in a Jewish state living in peace. In the Jewish state as it emerged, plagued by war or by the threat of war throughout its existence, the Arab minority has yet from the outset easily exercised its full civic rights; there have been Arab members in every Knesset, and now, since 1971, an Arab deputy minister sits in the government.

All this the Arab of Judea and Samaria, even of Gaza, has by now been able to hear and see. His own briefer experience of the application of Zionist values does not contradict the experience of his fellow Arabs in Israel. While the air of the world resounded with the uncontrolled fabrications of Arab, Soviet, and other simply anti-Semitic propagandists, describing in detail the alleged ills of the Arabs of Judea and Samaria, those Arabs themselves have been shedding many of the prejudices induced by their anti-Israel education.

As each of them goes to his familiar work in the morning—now often to a Jewish place of employment across the old Armistice lines—and as he goes back to his home in the evening, and ponders on the changes actually wrought in his life since rule from Amman was replaced with rule from Jerusalem (or more directly by the local military governor), he can find only tangible material improvement and a broadening of horizons for himself and for his children. At first, no doubt unbelieving, he has gradually begun to grasp that such improvement and broadening, and indeed his welfare, have in fact become a function of the Zionist state.

Zionism was not born to further the welfare of anybody but the Jewish people, still largely dispersed. It carries a burden unequaled in this troubled world—from absorbing, year after year, large numbers of penniless new-comers from the various corners of the exile, to completing the social and economic transformation within the home-land. It cannot, and will not give up its historic heritage, nor can it surrender the territorial conditions of its securi-ty. But, whatever the Arab sins and ills of the past, the existence of a large Arab community in the country is a reality, no less than the right and reality of the Jewish people's control of its only homeland. The innate human-ism of Zionism, and its still powerful revolutionary drive, can take this reality in its stride.

Given free play, it will create a pattern of coexistence and peaceful cooperation between Jews and Arabs which, even within a generation, can make the tragic conflict a closed episode in the history of the past.

# APPENDICES

# APPENDIX A

## Agreement Between Emir Feisal and Dr. Weizmann, January 3, 1919

His Royal Highness the Emir Feisal, representing and acting on behalf of the Arab Kingdom of Hedjaz, and Dr. Chaim Weizmann, representing and acting on behalf of the Zionist Organisation, mindful of the racial kinship and ancient bonds existing between the Arabs and the Jewish people, and realising that the surest means of working out the consummation of their national aspirations is through the closest possible collaboration in the development of the Arab State and Palestine, and being desirous further of confirming the good understanding which exists between them, have agreed upon the following Articles:

### Article I

The Arab State and Palestine in all their relations and undertakings shall be controlled by the most cordial goodwill and understanding, and to this end Arab and Jewish duly accredited agents shall be established and maintained in the respective territories.

### Article II

Immediately following the completion of the deliberations of the Peace Conference, the definite boundaries between the Arab State and Palestine shall be determined by a Commission to be agreed upon by the parties hereto.

### Article III

In the establishment of the Constitution and Administration of Palestine all such measures shall be adopted as will afford the fullest guarantees for carrying into effect the British Government's Declaration of the 2d of November, 1917.

## ARTICLE IV

All necessary measures shall be taken to encourage and stimulate immigration of Jews into Palestine on a large scale, and as quickly as possible to settle Jewish immigrants upon the land through closer settlement and intensive cultivation of the soil. In taking such measures the Arab peasant and tenant farmers shall be protected in their rights, and shall be assisted in forwarding their economic development.

## ARTICLE V

No regulation nor law shall be made prohibiting or interfering in any way with the free exercise of religion; and further the free exercise and enjoyment of religious profession and worship without discrimination or preference shall forever be allowed. No religious test shall ever be required for the exercise of civil or political rights.

## ARTICLE VI

The Mohammedan Holy Places shall be under Mohammedan control.

## ARTICLE VII

The Zionist Organisation proposes to send to Palestine a Commission of experts to make a survey of the economic possibilities of the country, and to report upon the best means for its development. The Zionist Organisation will place the aforementioned Commission at the disposal of the Arab State for the purpose of a survey of the economic possibilities of the Arab State and to report upon the best means for its development. The Zionist Organisation will use its best efforts to assist the Arab State in providing the means for developing the natural resources and economic possibilities thereof.

## ARTICLE VIII

The parties hereto agree to act in complete accord and harmony on all matters embraced herein before the Peace Congress.

## ARTICLE IX

Any matters of dispute which may arise between the contracting parties shall be referred to the British Government for arbitration.

Given under our hand at London, England, the third day of January, one thousand nine hundred and nineteen.

*Chaim Weizmann.*
*Feisal ibn-Hussein.*

### RESERVATION BY THE EMIR FEISAL

If the Arabs are established as I have asked in my manifesto of January 4th addressed to the British Secretary of State for Foreign Affairs, I will carry out what is written in this agreement. If changes are made, I cannot be answerable for failing to carry out this agreement.

*Feisal ibn-Hussein.*

# APPENDIX B

## From the Proposals Presented by the Zionist Organization to the Paris Peace Conference, 1919

The Zionist Organisation respectfully submits the following draft resolutions for the consideration of the Peace Conference:—

1. The High Contracting Parties recognise the historic title of the Jewish people to Palestine and the right of the Jews to reconstitute in Palestine their National Home.
2. The boundaries of Palestine shall be as declared in the Schedule annexed hereto.
3. The sovereign possession of Palestine shall be vested in the League of Nations and the Government entrusted to Great Britain as Mandatory of the League.
4. (Provision to be inserted relating to the application in Palestine of such of the general conditions attached to mandates as are suitable to the case.)
5. The mandate shall be subject also to the following special conditions:—
    (I.) Palestine shall be placed under such political, administrative and economic conditions as will se-

cure the establishment there of the Jewish National Home, and ultimately render possible the creation of an autonomous Commonwealth, it being clearly understood that nothing shall be done which may prejudice the civil and religious rights of existing non-Jewish communities in Palestine or the rights and political status enjoyed by Jews in any other country.

(II.) To this end the Mandatory Power shall *inter alia*:

    (*a*) Promote Jewish immigration and close settlement on the land, the established rights of the present non-Jewish population being equitably safeguarded.

    (*b*) Accept the co-operation in such measures of a Council representative of the Jews in Palestine and of the world that may be established for the development of the Jewish National Home in Palestine and entrust the organisation of Jewish education to such Council.

    (*c*) On being satisfied that the constitution of such Council precludes the making of private profit, offer to the Council in priority any concession for public works or for the development of natural resources which it may be found desirable to grant.

(III.) The Mandatory Power shall encourage the widest measure of self-government for localities practicable in the conditions of the country.

(IV.) There shall be for ever the fullest freedom of religious worship for all creeds in Palestine. There shall be no discrimination among the inhabitants with regard to citizenship and civil rights, on the grounds of religion, or of race.

(V.) (Provision to be inserted relating to the control of the Holy Places.)

### The Boundaries of Palestine.
### Schedule.

The boundaries of Palestine shall follow the general lines set out below:—

Starting on the North at a point on the Mediterranean Sea in the vicinity south of Sidon and following the watersheds of the foothills of the Lebanon as far as JISR EL KARAON, thence to EL BIRE, following the dividing line between the two basins of the WADI EL KORN and the WADI ET TEIM, thence in a southerly direction following the dividing line between the Eastern and Western slopes of the HERMON, to the vicinity west of BEIT JENN, thence eastward following the northern watersheds of the NAHR MUGHANIYE close to and west of the Hedjaz Railway.

In the east a line close to and west of Hedjaz Railway terminating in the Gulf of Akaba.

In the south a frontier to be agreed upon with the Egyptian Government.

In the west the Mediterranean Sea.

The details of the delimitations, or any necessary adjustments of detail, shall be settled by a Special Commission on which there shall be Jewish representation.

### Great Britain as Mandatory of the League of Nations.

We ask that Great Britain shall act as Mandatory of the League of Nations for Palestine. The selection of Great Britain as Mandatory is urged on the ground that this is the wish of the Jews of the world, and the League of Nations in selecting a Mandatory will follow as far as possible the popular wish of the people concerned.

The preference on the part of the Jews for a British Trusteeship is unquestionably the result of the peculiar relationship of England to the Jewish Palestinian problem. The return of the Jews to Zion has not only been a remarkable feature in English literature, but in the domain of statecraft it has played its part, beginning with the readmission of the Jews under Cromwell. It manifested itself particularly in the nineteenth century in the instructions given to British Consular representatives in the Orient after the Damascus incident; in the various Jewish Palestinian projects suggested by English non-Jews prior to 1881; in the letters of endorsement and support given by members of the Royal Family and Officers of the Government to Lawrence Oliphant; and, finally, in the three consecutive acts which definitely associated Great Britain with Zionism in the minds of the Jews, viz.: the El Arish offer in 1901; the East African offer in 1903, and, lastly, the British Declaration in favour of a Jewish National Home in Palestine in 1917. Moreover, the Jews who have gained political experience in many lands under a great variety of governmental systems, whole-heartedly appreciate the advanced and liberal policies adopted by Great Britain in her modern colonial administration.

It may be stated without doubt that all of these things account for the attitude taken by the Jews with reference to the Trusteeship, as evidenced by the following:—

On December 16th, 1918, the American Jewish Congress composed of delegates representing 3,000,000 American Jews adopted the following resolution:

"The American Jewish Congress instruct their delegation to Europe to co-operate with representatives of other Jewish Organisations and specifically with the World Zionist Organisation, to the end that the Peace Conference may recognise the aspirations and historic claims of the Jewish people with regard to Palestine, and declare that, in accordance with the British Government's Declaration of November 2nd, 1917, endorsed by the Allied Governments and the President of the United States, there shall be established such political administrative and economic conditions in Palestine, as will assure under the trusteeship of Great Britain, acting on behalf of such League of Nations as may be formed, the development of Palestine into a Jewish Commonwealth; it being clearly understood that nothing shall be done which shall prejudice the civil and religious rights of existing non-Jewish communities in Palestine, or the rights and political status enjoyed by Jews in other countries."

Similar action was taken in Jaffa in the month of December, 1918, by a conference of representatives of the Jewish population in Palestine, and on January 4th, 1919, by Jewish Congresses representing about two million Jews of the reconstituted States of Austria-Hungary and of Poland.

## Boundaries.

The boundaries outlined are what we consider essential for the necessary economic foundation of the country. Palestine must have its natural outlets to the seas and the control of its rivers and their headwaters. The boundaries are sketched with the general economic needs and historic traditions of the country in mind, factors which necessarily must also be considered by the Special Commission in fixing the definite boundary lines. This Commission will bear in mind that it is highly desirable, in the interests of economical administration, that the geographical area of Palestine should be as large as possible, so that it may eventually contain a large and thriving population which could more easily bear the burdens of modern civilised government than a small country with a necessary limitation of inhabitants.

The economic life of Palestine, like that of every other semi-arid country, depends on the available water supply. It is, therefore, of vital importance not only to secure all water resources already feeding the country, but also to be able to conserve and control them at their sources.

The Hermon is Palestine's real "Father of Waters," and cannot be severed from it without striking at the very root of its economic life. The Hermon not only needs re-afforestation but also other works before it can again adequately serve as the water reservoir of the country. It must, therefore, be wholly under the control of those who will most willingly as well as most adequately restore it to its maximum utility. Some international arrangement must be made whereby the riparian rights of the people dwelling south of the Litani River may be fully protected. Properly cared for, these headwaters can be made to serve in the development of the Lebanon as well as of Palestine.

The fertile plains east of the Jordan, since the earliest Biblical times, have been linked economically and politically with the land west of the Jordan. The country which is now very sparsely populated, in Roman times supported a great population. It could now serve admirably for colonisation on a large scale. A just regard for the economic needs of Palestine and Arabia demands that free access to the Hedjaz Railway throughout its length be accorded both Governments.

An intensive development of the agriculture and other opportunities of Trans-Jordania make it imperative that Palestine shall have access to the Red Sea and an opportunity of developing good harbours on the Gulf of Akaba. Akaba, it will be recalled, was the terminus of an important trade route of Palestine from the days of Solomon onwards. The ports developed in the Gulf of Akaba should be free ports through which the commerce of the Hinterland may pass on the same principle which guides us in suggesting that free access be given to the Hedjaz Railway.

## Conclusion.

In every part of the world on the Day of Atonement the Jews pray that "all nations may be united by a common bond, so that the will of God may reign supreme throughout the world." In the fulfilment of this prayer, the Jews hope that they will be able to take an honorable place in the new community of nations. It is their purpose to establish in Palestine a government dedicated to social and national justice; a government that shall be guided, like the community of old, by that justice and equality which is expressed in the great precept of our Lawgiver: "There shall be but one law for you and the stranger in the land."

All of which is respectfully submitted.

ROTHSCHILD (LORD WALTER ROTHSCHILD).

On behalf of the Zionist Organisation,
NAHUM SOKOLOW.
CHAIM WEIZMANN.

On behalf of Zionist Organisation of America,
JULIAN W. MACK.
STEPHEN S. WISE.
HARRY FRIEDENWALD.
JACOB DE HAAS.
MARY FELS.
LOUIS ROBISON.
BERNARD FLEXNER.

On behalf of the Russian Zionist Organisation,
ISRAEL ROSOFF.

On behalf of the Jewish Population of Palestine in accordance with Mandate received,
NAHUM SOKOLOW.
CHAIM WEIZMANN.

# APPENDIX C

## Feisal-Frankfurter Correspondence

DELEGATION HEDJAZIENNE, *Paris, March 3, 1919.*

DEAR MR. FRANKFURTER: I want to take this opportunity of my first contact with American Zionists to tell you what I have often been able to say to Dr. Weizmann in Arabia and Europe.

We feel that the Arabs and Jews are cousins in race, having suffered similar oppressions at the hands of powers stronger than themselves, and by a happy coincidence have been able to take the first step towards the attainment of their national ideals together.

We Arabs, especially the educated among us, look with the deepest sympathy on the Zionist movement. Our deputation here in Paris is fully acquainted with the proposals submitted yesterday by the Zionist Organization to the Peace Conference, and we regard them as moderate and proper. We will do our best, in so far as we are concerned, to help them through: we will wish the Jews a most hearty welcome home.

With the chiefs of your movement, especially with Dr. Weizmann, we have had and continue to have the closest relations. He has been a great helper of our cause, and I hope the Arabs may soon be in a position to make the Jews some return for their kindness. We are working together for a reformed and revived Near East, and our two movements complete one another. The Jewish movement is national and not imperialist. Our movement is national and not imperialist, and there is room in Syria for us both. Indeed I think that neither can be a real success without the other.

People less informed and less responsible than our leaders and yours, ignoring the need for cooperation of the Arabs and Zionists have been trying to exploit the local difficulties that must necessarily arise in Palestine in the early stages of our movements. Some of them have, I am afraid, misrepresented your aims to the Arab peasantry, and our aims to the Jewish peasantry, with the result that interested parties have been able to make capital out of what they call our differences.

I wish to give you my firm conviction that these differences are not on questions of principle, but on matters of detail such as must inevitably occur in every contact of neighbouring peoples, and as are easily adjusted by mutual good will. Indeed nearly all of them will disappear with fuller knowledge.

I look forward, and my people with me look forward, to a future in which we will help you and you will help us, so that the countries in which we are mutually interested may once again take their places in the community of civilised peoples of the world.

Believe me,
  Yours sincerely,

(*Sgd.*) *Feisal*.
5TH MARCH, 1919.

ROYAL HIGHNESS:
  Allow me, on behalf of the Zionist Organisation, to acknowledge your recent letter with deep appreciation.

Those of us who come from the United States have already
been gratified by the friendly relations and the active
cooperation maintained between you and the Zionist leaders,
particularly Dr. Weizmann. We knew it could not be otherwise; we knew that the aspirations of the Arab and the Jewish
peoples were parallel, that each aspired to reestablish its
nationality in its own homeland, each making its own
distinctive contribution to civilisation, each seeking its own
peaceful mode of life.

The Zionist leaders and the Jewish people for whom they
speak have watched with satisfaction the spiritual vigour of
the Arab movement. Themselves seeking justice, they are
anxious that the just national aims of the Arab people be
confirmed and safeguarded by the Peace Conference.

We knew from your acts and your past utterances that the
Zionist movement—in other words the national aims of the
Jewish people—had your support and the support of the Arab
people for whom you speak. These aims are now before
the Peace Conference as definite proposals by the Zionist
Organisation. We are happy indeed that you consider these
proposals "moderate and proper," and that we have in you a
staunch supporter for their realisation. For both the Arab and
the Jewish peoples there are difficulties ahead—difficulties that
challenge the united statesmanship of Arab and Jewish leaders.
For it is no easy task to rebuild two great civilisations that
have been suffering oppression and misrule for centuries. We
each have our difficulties we shall work out as friends,
friends who are animated by similar purposes, seeking a free
and full development for the two neighbouring peoples. The
Arabs and Jews are neighbours in territory; we cannot but
live side by side as friends.

Very respectfully,

(Sgd.) *Felix Frankfurter.*

His Royal Highness Prince Feisal.

# APPENDIX D

## Outline of Tentative Report and Recommendations of the Intelligence Section of the American Delegation to the Peace Conference, in accordance with instructions, for the President and the Plenipotentiaries, January 21, 1919*

### 26. Palestine.

It is recommended:

1) That there be established a separate state of Palestine.

2) That this state be placed under Great Britain as a mandatory of the League of Nations.

3) That the Jews be invited to return to Palestine and settle there being assured by the Conference of all proper assistance in so doing that may be consistent with the protection of the personal (especially the religious) and the property rights of the non-Jewish population, and being further assured that it will be the policy of the League of Nations to recognize Palestine as a Jewish state as soon as it is a Jewish state in fact.

4) That the holy places and religious rights of all creeds in Palestine be placed under the protection of the League of Nations and its mandatory.

### Discussion.

1) It is recommended that there be established a separate state of Palestine.

The separation of the Palestinian area from Syria finds justification in the religious experience of mankind. The Jewish and Christian churches were born in Palestine, and Jerusalem was for long years, at different periods, the capital of each. And while the relation of the Mohammedans to Palestine is not so intimate, from the beginning they have regarded Jerusalem as a holy place. Only

---

* Quoted in David Hunter Miller, *My Diary at the Conference of Paris*, Vol. *iv*, pp. 263–264.

by establishing Palestine as a separate state can justice be
done to these great facts.

As drawn upon the map, the new state would control
its own source of water power and irrigation, on Mount
Hermon in the east to the Jordan; a feature of great
importance since the success of the new state would depend upon the possibilities of agricultural development.

2) It is recommended that this state be placed under Great
Britain as a mandatory of the League of Nations.

Palestine would obviously need wise and firm guidance. Its population is without political experience, is
racially composite, and could easily become distracted
by fanaticism and bitter religious differences.

The success of Great Britain in dealing with similar
situations, her relation to Egypt, and her administrative
achievements since General Allenby freed Palestine from
the Turk, all indicate her as the logical mandatory.

3) It is recommended that the Jews be invited to return to
Palestine and settle there, being assured by the Conference of
all proper assistance in so doing that may be consistent with
the protection of the personal (especially the religious) and
the property rights of the non-Jewish population, and being
further assured that it will be the policy of the League of
Nations to recognize Palestine as a Jewish state as soon as it is
a Jewish state in fact.

It is right that Palestine should become a Jewish state,
if the Jews, being given the full opportunity, make it
such. It was the cradle and home of their vital race, which
has made large spiritual contributions to mankind, and
is the only land in which they can hope to find a home
of their own; they being in this last respect unique among
significant peoples.

At present, however, the Jews form barely a sixth of
the total population of 700,000 in Palestine, and whether
they are to form a majority, or even a plurality, of the
population in the future state remains uncertain. Palestine, in short, is far from being a Jewish country now.
England, as mandatory, can be relied on to give the
Jews the privileged position they should have without
sacrificing the rights of non-Jews.

4) It is recommended that the holy places and religious rights of all creeds in Palestine be placed under the protection of the League of Nations and its mandatory.

The basis for this recommendation is self-evident.

# APPENDIX E

## Preamble to the League of Nations

### Mandate for Palestine, 1922.

The Council of the League of Nations:

Whereas the Principal Allied Powers have agreed, for the purpose of giving effect to the provisions of Article 22 of the Covenant of the League of Nations, to entrust to a Mandatory selected by the said Powers the administration of the territory of Palestine, which formerly belonged to the Turkish Empire, within such boundaries as may be fixed by them; and

Whereas the Principal Allied Powers have also agreed that the Mandatory should be responsible for putting into effect the declaration originally made on November 2nd, 1917, by the Government of His Britannic Majesty, and adopted by the said Powers, in favour of the establishment in Palestine of a national home for the Jewish people, it being clearly understood that nothing should be done which might prejudice the civil and religious rights of existing non-Jewish communities in Palestine, or the rights and political status enjoyed by Jews in any other country; and

Whereas recognition has thereby been given to the historical connection of the Jewish people with Palestine and to the grounds for reconstituting their national home in that country; and

Whereas the Principal Allied Powers have selected His Britannic Majesty as the Mandatory for Palestine; and

Whereas the mandate in respect of Palestine has been formulated in the following terms and submitted to the Council of the League for approval; and

Whereas His Britannic Majesty has accepted the mandate in respect of Palestine and undertaken to exercise it on behalf of the League of Nations in conformity with the following provisions; and

Whereas by the afore-mentioned Article 22 (paragraph 8), it is provided that the degree of authority, control or administration to be exercised by the Mandatory, not having been previously agreed upon by the Members of the League, shall be explicitly defined by the Council of the League of Nations.

# BIBLIOGRAPHY

WORKS IN ENGLISH AND FRENCH

Aldington, Richard. *Lawrence of Arabia, A Biographical Enquiry.* 2nd ed. London: Collins, 1969.

AlRoy, Gil Carl, ed. *Attitudes Toward Jewish Statehood in the Arab World.* New York: American Academic Assn. for Peace in the Middle East, 1971.

Antonius, George. *The Arab Awakening.* London: Hamish Hamilton, 1938.

Atiyah, Edward. *The Arabs.* London: Penguin Books, 1955.

Aumann, Moshe. *Land Ownership in Palestine.* Jerusalem: Israel Academic Committee on the Middle East.

Balfour, Lord Arthur James. *Speeches on Zionism.* London: J. W. Arrowsmith, 1928.

Benas, Bertram B. *Zionism: The Jewish National Movement.* Liverpool: D. Marples, 1919.

Bilby, Kenneth. *New Star in the Near East.* New York: Doubleday, 1950.

Bremond, General Edouard. *Le Hedjaz dans la Guerre Mondiale.* Paris: Payot, 1931.

Churchill, Randolph S., and Churchill, Winston S. *The Six Day War.* London: Heinemann, 1967.

Cohn, Norman. *Warrant for Genocide: The Myth of the Jewish World Conspiracy and the Protocols of Zion.* London: Eyre & Spottiswoode, 1967.

Copeland, Miles. *The Game of Nations.* London: Weidenfeld & Nicholson, 1969.

Crawford, Alexander William Crawford Lindsay, Lord Lindsay. *Letters on Egypt, Edom and the Holy Land.* London: H. Colburn, 1847.

Curtis, Michael, ed. *People and Politics in the Middle East.* New Brunswick, New Jersey: Transaction Books, 1971.

257

Dawson, John William. *Modern Science in Bible Lands*. New York: Harper, 1889.

De Haas, Jacob. *History of Palestine, the Last Two Thousand Years*. New York: Macmillan, 1934.

Djemal, Ahmed. *Memories of a Turkish Statesman 1913-1919* New York: Doran, 1922.

Engle, Anita. *The Nili Spies*. London: Hogarth Press, 1959.

Finn, James. *Stirring Times*. London: Paul & Co., 1878.

Gawler, George. *Tranquillisation of Syria & the East*. London: T. & W. Boone, 1845.

Gibb, H. A. R., and Bowen, H. *Islamic Society and the West*. London: Oxford University Press, 1950.

Glubb, J. B. *A Soldier with the Arabs*. London: Hodder & Stoughton, 1957.

Hamady, Sania. *Character and Temperament of the Arabs*. New York: Twayne, 1960.

Harkabi, Yehoshafat. *Fedayeen Action and Arab Strategy*. London: Institute for Strategic Studies, 1968.

————. *Arab Attitudes to Israel*. Jerusalem: Israel Universities Press, 1972.

Hitti, Philip K. *History of the Arabs*. 9th ed. New York: Macmillan, 1967.

Hollingsworth, A. G. H. *Remarks Upon the Present Condition and Future Prospect of the Jews in Palestine*. London: Seeleys, 1752.

Jabotinsky, Vladimir. *Story of the Jewish Legion*. New York: Bernard Ackerman, 1945.

————. *The War and the Jew*. New York: Dial, 1942.

Jarvis, C. S. *Three Deserts*. New York: Dutton, 1936.

Joseph, Bernard. *British Rule in Palestine*. Washington, D. C.: Public Affairs Press, 1948.

Karanjia, R. K. *The Arab Dawn*. Bombay: Blitz Publications, 1958.

Katz, Samuel. *Days of Fire*. London: W. H. Allen, 1968.

Kedourie, Elie. *The Chatham House Version and Other Middle Eastern Studies*. London: Weidenfeld & Nicholson, 1970.

————. *England and the Middle East: The Destruction of the Ottoman Empire, 1914-1921*. London: Bowes & Bowes, 1956.

Keith, Alexander. *The Land of Israel*. Edinburgh: W. Whyte, 1844.

Lamartine, Alphonse. *Recollections of the East*. 2 vols. London: G. Virtue, 1845.

Laqueur, Walter. *The Road to War*. London: Pelican Books, 1969.

Lawrence, T. E. *Letters*. Ed. by David Garnett. London: Jonathan Cape, 1938.

————. *Secret Despatches from Arabia*. London: Golden Cockerel Press, 1939.

————. *Seven Pillars of Wisdom*. London: Jonathan Cape, 1935.

Leroy-Beaulieu, Anatole. *Israel Among the Nations*. Trans. by F. Hellman. London, 1895.

Le Strange, Guy. *Palestine Under the Moslems*. London: A. P. Watt, 1890.

Lewis, Bernard. *Notes and Documents from the Turkish Archives*. Jerusalem: Israel Oriental Society, 1952.

Lloyd George, David. *The Truth About the Peace Treaties*. London: Gollancz, 1936.

Lowenthal, Marvin. *Henrietta Szold: Life and Letters*. New York: 1942.

Macdonald, James G. *My Mission in Israel*. London: Gollancz, 1951.

Malek, Yusuf. *The British Betrayal of the Assyrians*. Chicago: Assyrian National Federation and Assyrian National League of America, 1935.

Massey, William Thomas. *Allenby's Final Triumph*. London: Constable, 1920.

Meinertzhagen, Richard. *Middle East Diary 1917-1956*. London: The Cresset Press, 1959.

Merrill, Selah. *East of the Jordan*. New York: Scribner's, 1881.

Nicholson, R. A. *A Literary History of the Arabs*. London: Cambridge University Press, 1930.

Oliphant, Laurence. *The Land of Gilead, With Excursions in the Lebanon*. Edinburgh: W. Blackwood, 1880.

Parkes, James. *Whose Land? A History of the Peoples of Palestine*. London: Pelican Books, 1970.

Patterson, J. H. *With the Judeans in the Palestine Campaign*. New York: Macmillan, 1922.

Philby, St. John. *Arabian Jubilee*. London: Robert Hale, 1952.

Pinner, Dr. Walter. *How Many Refugees?* London: McGibbon & Kee, 1959.

————. *The Legend of the Arab Refugees*. Tel Aviv: Economic and Social Research Institute, 1967.

Rousan, Mahmoud. *Palestine and the Internationalization of*

*Jerusalem.* Baghdad: Ministry of Culture and Guidance, 1965.

Samuel, Horace B. *Beneath the Whitewash: A Critical Analysis of the Report of the Commission on the Palestine Disturbances of August 1929.* London: Hogarth Press, 1930.

————. *Revolt by Leave.* London: New Zionist Press, 1937.

————. *Unholy Memories of the Holy Land.* London: L. & V. Woolf, 1930.

Sayegh, F. A. *Understanding of the Arab Mind.* Washington, D.C.; Organization of Arab Students in the United States, 1953.

Schmidt, Dana Adams. *Yemen: The Unknown War.* New York: Holt, 1968.

Shamir, Moshe. *My Life with Ishmael.* London: Vallentine Mitchell, 1970.

Shaw, Thomas. *Travels & Observations Relating to Several Parts of Barbary & the Levant.* Second Edition. London: Millar & Sandy, 1767.

Shechtman, J. B. *European Population Transfers 1939-1945.* New York: Oxford University Press, 1946.

————. *Jordan—A State That Never Was.* New York: Cultural Publishing Co. 1968.

————. *The Refugees in the World.* New York: Barnes, 1963.

Shwadran, Benjamin. *Middle East Oil and the Great Powers.* New York: Praeger, 1955.

Sidebotham, Herbert. *British Policy and the Palestine Mandate.* London: Benn, 1929.

————. *England and Palestine.* London, 1918.

Sokolow, Nahum. *History of Zionism: 1600-1918.* London: Longmans, 1919 (2 vols).

Stafford, Lt. Col. A. S. *The Tragedy of the Assyrians.* London: Allen & Unwin, 1935.

Temperley, H. W. V. *History of the Peace Conference.* London: British Institute of International Affairs, 1920-1924.

Treves, Sir Frederick. *Land That is Desolate.* New York: Dutton, 1912.

Trisham, H. B. *The Land of Israel: A Journal of Travels in Palestine.* London, 1865.

Twain, Mark (Samuel L. Clemens). *The Innocents Abroad.* New American Library. New York, 1966.

Volney, Constantine Francois Chasseboeuf, Conte de. *Travels*

*Through Syria & Egypt in the Years 1783, 1784 & 1785.*
London: G. G. J. & J. Robinson, 1787.

Weizmann, Chaim. *Trial and Error.* London: Hamish Hamilton, 1949.

Wiskemann, Elizabeth. *Germany's Eastern Neighbours.*
London: Oxford University Press, 1957.

Young, Brigadeer Peter. *The Israeli Campaign, 1967.* London:
Kimber, 1967.

Ziff, William B. *The Rape of Palestine.* New York: Longmans, 1938.

Zurayk, Constantine. *The Meaning of Disaster.* Beirut:
Khayat, 1956.

WORKS IN HEBREW

Aaronson, Aaron. *Yoman 1916-1919* [Diary 1916-1919]. Tel
Aviv, Karni 1970.

Assaf, Michael. *Toledot Ha'aravim Be'eretz Yisrael* [History
of the Arabs in Palestine]. 3 vols.

Ben-Sasson, H. H. *Toledot Hayehudim Bi'mei Habeinayim*
[History of the Jews in the Middle Ages]. Tel Aviv: Dvir,
1969.

Ben-Zwi, Yitshak. *Shear Yashuv* [A Remnant Will Return].
Jerusalem: Yad Ben-Zwi, 1966.

————. *Fatah Ba'istrategya Ha'aravit* [*Fedayeen Action and
Arab Strategy*] Tel Aviv: Ministry of Defense, 1969.

Harkabi, Yehoshafat. *Bein Yisrael Le'arav* [Between Israel
and the Arabs]. Tel Aviv: Maarakhot, 1968.

Horon, A. G. *Eretz Hakedem* [The East Land]. Tel Aviv:
Hermon, 1970.

Ish-Shalom, Michael. *Masaei Notzrim Be'eretz Yisrael* [Christian Travels in the Holy Land]. Tel Aviv: Am Oved-Dvir,
1965.

Livneh, Eliezer. *Aaron Aaronson Ha'ish Uzemano* [Aaron
Aaaronson, The Man and His Times]. Jerusalem: Mosad
Bialik, 1969.

Livneh, Nedava y, and Efrāti y: *Nili: Toledoteha Shel Heazah
Medinit (Nili: The Story of a Daring Political Venture).*
Tel Aviv: Shocken, 1961.

Malmat, A.; Tadmor, H.; Stern, M.; Safrai, S. *Toledot Am
Yisrael Bimei Kedem* [*History of the Jewish People in
Ancient Times*]. Tel Aviv: Dvir, 1969.

Porat, Yehoshua. *Tsemihat Hatenua Haaravit Hapalestinait
1918-1929* [The Growth of the Palestinian Arab Movement 1918-1929]. Tel Aviv: Hamachon Lelimudei Asia
Veafrika, 1971.

Shamir, Shimon. *Toledot Ha'aravim Bamizrah Hatichon Bazeman Hehadash* [History of the Arabs in the Middle East in Modern Times].

Shimeoni, Yaakov. *Arviyei Eretz Yisrael* [The Arabs of Palestine]. Tel Aviv: Am Oved, 1947.

Yaari, Avraham. *Igrot Eretz Yisrael* [Palestine Letters]. Tel Aviv: Gazit, 1943.

Yaari, Ehud. *Fatah*. Tel Aviv: Levin-Epstein, 1970.

STATISTICAL SOURCES

*Behind the Curtain* (Hebrew). Tel Aviv: Maarakhot (Publishing House of the Ministry of Defence), 1954.

*Facts About Israel*, 1970. Jerusalem: Keter, 1970.

Government of Palestine. *Survey of Palestine*. Jerusalem: Government Printer, 1946.

Israel Information Office. *Israel's Struggle for Peace*. New York: Israel Information Office, 1960.

*Palestine Royal Commission Report*. London: HMSO, Cmd. 5479 (1937).

# Index

*Don't wait until tomorrow!*

# SEND FOR YOUR FREE BANTAM BESTSELLERS CATALOG TODAY!

It lists hundreds of money-saving bestsellers originally priced from $3.75 to $15.00—bestsellers that are yours now for as little as 60¢ to $2.25.

The catalog gives you a great opportunity to get the books you missed, while it also helps you build your own private library at huge savings.

So don't delay any longer—send for your catalog TODAY! It's absolutely FREE!